THE BIG
POLICEMAN

Also by J. North Conway

Nonfiction

King of Heists: The Sensational Bank Robbery of 1878
That Shocked America

American Literacy: Fifty Books that Define
Our Culture and Ourselves

The Cape Cod Canal: Breaking Through
the Bared and Bended Arm

Shipwrecks of New England

New England Women of Substance

New England Visionaries

From Coup to Nuts: A Revolutionary Cookbook

Fiction

The Road to Ruin

Zig Zag Man

Poetry

Life Sentences

My Picnic With Lolita and Other Poems

THE BIG POLICEMAN

The Rise and Fall of America's First,
Most Ruthless,
and Greatest Detective

J. NORTH CONWAY

LYONS PRESS
Guilford, Connecticut
An imprint of Globe Pequot Press

Lyons Press is an imprint of Globe Pequot Press.

Text design: Sheryl Kober
Layout artist: Kevin Mak
Project editor: Kristen Mellitt

Library of Congress Cataloging-in-Publication Data is available on file.

ISBN 978-1-59921-965-3

Printed in the United States of America

10 9 8 7 6 5 4 3 2 1

This book is dedicated to my Block Island family and friends—Julia, Nate, Andrew, Kelly, Leah, Aria, Ella, Benjamin, Little Nate, Molly, Chrissy, Carl, Bobby, Lisa, Ava, Tara, Colby, Ronna, John, Lois, Bart, Murdoch, and Elizabeth. Also to my friends at Starbucks in Taunton, Massachusetts, Winnie and Nolan. And to my good friends Connie and Penny.

TABLE OF CONTENTS

Introduction

THE LIFE AND TIMES OF
THE GREAT AMERICAN
DETECTIVE

Accounts of true crime have always been enormously popular among readers. The subgenre would seem to appeal to the highly educated as well as the barely educated, to women and men equally.

—JOYCE CAROL OATES

W hy would anyone want to read about the exploits of New York City police detective Thomas Byrnes? Aside from being credited as the father of modern detective work, Byrnes was instrumental in solving some of the most sensational cases in the city during the latter part of the nineteenth century (1863–1894).

He tracked down and captured New York City's "Jack the Ripper"; pursued the ghoulish grave robbers who reportedly stole the body of one of New York's wealthiest merchants and held it for ransom; and solved the infamous Manhattan Savings Institution case, the largest bank heist in American history.

Thomas Byrnes ". . . shaped not just New York's Detective Bureau but the template for detective work as it would come to be organized and practiced in every modern American metropolis," according to noted social reformer and newspaper reporter Jacob A. Riis. Larger than life, Byrnes was a renowned investigator—a giant in the history of criminal justice. The press coverage of his often brutal methods of interrogation popularized the term *the third degree*. Some writers reported that Byrnes coined the phrase himself. The third degree as practiced by Byrnes included a combination of physical and psychological torture and led to the capture of some of New York City's most heinous criminals.

After serving as a Union soldier during the Battle of Bull Run, Byrnes (1842–1910) began his career as a New York City police officer in 1863. He immediately distinguished himself that summer as a heroic law enforcement officer during the New York City draft riots, when an angry mob caused nearly $3 million of property damage, killed four police officers, and lynched a dozen African Americans in the streets. Byrnes rose quickly through the ranks and served as the head of the New York City Detective Bureau from 1880 to 1892. In 1892, he became the superintendent of the city's police force.

Byrnes's force of will and strength of character forever changed the detective bureau. According to Riis, Byrnes was the ". . . personification of the police department." Riis, who covered most of Byrnes's cases over the years, wrote that Byrnes was ". . . a czar, with all the autocrat's irresponsible powers, and he exercised them as he saw fit. But he made the detective service great."

Byrnes was instrumental in the Detective Bureau's incorporation of intelligence gathering as a vital part of police work. He ordered detectives to keep and submit detailed notes of all their undercover activities and initiated the practice of photographing criminals when they were arrested. He was the first in American law enforcement to catalog criminal histories of felons in a central data bank, including photo albums of known criminals. Byrnes instituted the first "Rogues' Gallery," a photographic lineup of suspected criminals. He made sure that his detectives, nicknamed *the immortals* by the New York City press, kept up-to-date records on all known and suspected criminals, and he introduced pioneering forensic techniques into the detective department's operations. A master self-publicist, Byrnes published *Professional Criminals of America*, which became a must-read for most police departments throughout the country.

Over his many years of service, Byrnes was able to gain wealthy and influential political support that allowed him to wield enormous and often unchecked power within the police force. His detectives were depicted in the press as all-knowing, all-seeing public avengers who lurked behind every corner. He was considered a master psychologist who knew just the right approach with each criminal brought before him for interrogation. Backed by his uncanny detection abilities, his all-encompassing files, and his shadowy detective force, Byrnes always seemed to get his man.

The truth of this fell far short. Byrnes did in fact modernize New York's Detective Bureau, making it the model for every other big-city police department, but the aura of an omnipotent detective force was an illusion that Byrnes carefully crafted. The conclusions of the city's "Jack the Ripper" case and the body-snatching case of A. T. Stewart would tarnish Byrnes's gilded reputation.

Despite his many flaws and self-aggrandizement, Byrnes flourished as New York City's premier police detective, endearing himself to law-and-order-minded citizens, especially wealthy bankers, merchants, and industrialists, whose money and valuables he pledged to protect—at a price. Byrnes was the first to open a police station on Wall Street in order to demonstrate his commitment to protect the fortunes of the city's rich and well-to-do. Byrnes also dedicated himself to the cause of capitalism by breaking up union and socialist organizations. He was responsible for tracking down and arresting noted anarchist Emma Goldman in Philadelphia in 1893 on a violence-incitement charge arising from a speech she had made in New York.

But Byrnes's rise to power and wealth didn't go unnoticed by many of New York City's reform-minded citizens. On a meager police superintendent's salary of $5,000 a year, Byrnes amassed a personal fortune estimated at between $300,000 and $350,000. That money, how it was earned, and the reaction of New York City police commissioner Theodore Roosevelt are just as relevant as Byrnes's innovations in crowning him "Father of the Modern Detective."

The life and times of Thomas Byrnes is the compelling story of the rise and fall of the man who epitomized law and order a century before there was *Law & Order.*

———

There is clearly a fine distinction between historians who write and writers who write history. It may be a fine line of distinction but it is a clear one. The aim of every writer, whether a historian who writes or a writer who writes history, is to enlighten and entertain the reader. Good for them. The difference between a historian who writes and a writer who writes history is that the historian usually enlightens and entertains the reader, while the writer who writes history entertains and then enlightens. Clearly, for me, as a writer who writes history, the litmus test is this: If you were to take away all the dates, times, and places—all the historical minutiae necessary in writing history— if you were to take all that away from a book written by a writer who writes history, the book would still stand because of the *story*. The story is at the heart of every book. At least that's what E. M. Forster once said, and I believe him. Forster was no slouch when it came to storytelling. Writers write stories. That's what we do. If we're lucky, we can also fill in good stuff like dates, times, places, and historical minutiae. I'd like to think that this book passes that litmus test. I'd like to think that first and foremost, it is a good story. I hope you do too. I also hope it enlightens you.

Author's Note: Newspaper headlines and articles are authentic reprints of the originals, including all capitalization and spelling; errors have not been corrected.

Our liberties are interfered with and curtailed in so many ways, that it is useless to attempt an enumeration. We are robbed and swindled right and left—by the wealthy corporation, which seizes upon our property with impunity and without remuneration, down, through all the various grades, to the thief with political influence who "snatches" your watch; while human life, as I have previously observed, can be taken with safety by the great millionaire or party leader.

—GEORGE WASHINGTON WALLING,
RECOLLECTIONS OF A NEW YORK CHIEF OF POLICE, 1887

1

THE CASE OF
JACK THE RIPPER

In which Chief Inspector Thomas Byrnes solves the case of the brutal slaying of the aging prostitute Carrie Brown, whose mutilated body was found in the seedy East River Hotel. The murder prompts authorities and the press to speculate that London's Jack the Ripper has struck in New York City.

FRIDAY, APRIL 24, 1891

James Jennings made his way up the narrow staircase to the fifth floor of the seedy East River Hotel on New York City's dangerous waterfront. When he reached the landing, he saw the trail of blood leading from room 31. The blood-splattered floor was not an unusual sight for Jennings, who owned the run-down place, since the hotel was frequented by an assortment of riverfront thugs, sailors, and prostitutes. There were always drunken fights and stabbings, but this was different. There was too much blood, and it was everywhere—on the floor, carpet, even spread on the door to the room. Jennings didn't bother to knock. He let himself in with a spare key. Jennings, who thought he had seen it all, there, along the waterfront, was not the kind of man who was easily horror-struck. What he discovered inside the room horrified and sickened him.

Lying on the bed was the body of a woman well past her prime. She was lying on her side with her right arm stretched awkwardly beneath her. Her left arm lay across her chest, and her legs were drawn up into a fetal position. Her blouse was pulled up around her neck. The rest of her body was naked. Something had been knotted around her throat, and there was blood everywhere. She had been disemboweled, her intestines spread across the bed and the floor. The killer had carved an X on her left thigh. Jennings did all he could do to keep from vomiting.

Choked, Then Mutilated
A Murder Like One Of Jack
The Ripper's Deeds

White Chapel's Horrors Repeated
In An East Side Lodging House
—An Aged Woman The Victim—
Several Arrests On Suspicion

A murder which in many of its details recalls the crimes with which "Jack the Ripper" horrified London was committed late Thursday night or early yesterday morning in a small room in the squalid lodging house known as the East River Hotel, on the southeast corner of Catharine and Water Streets. The victim was an old, gray haired, and wrinkled woman, who had for years past haunted the neighborhood. The murderer escaped hours before the deed was discovered. He left behind him the weapon with which he had butchered his victim.

—*New York Times*
April 25, 1891

Carrie Brown, the aging prostitute whom Jennings found, was known to dole out her services regularly at the sleazy East River Hotel. She was the forty-fifth person killed in New York City that year. Jennings raced to the Fourth Ward police station on Oak Street, where he blurted out to police the gruesome spectacle he had found at his hotel. He was still so shaken by the sight of Brown's mutilated body he could barely make sense.

With Captain Richard O'Connor in tow, Jennings led the police back to the hotel room. Even for hardened police officers, the sight of Brown's mutilated body was unspeakable. With Jennings looking on, O'Connor and two of his officers inspected the crime scene. On the floor they discovered Brown's tattered dress and a dark shawl. Her few possessions were still on a bureau in open view. Nothing appeared to have been stolen, including the few silver dollars lying among her things. O'Connor discovered what was then thought to be the murder weapon, a bloody wooden-handled dinner knife, lying on the floor beside the bed. He carefully inspected the knife, taking note of the black painted handle with three notches cut horizontally on either side. O'Connor ran his finger along the knife's dull edge. The point of the knife had been broken off.

It was Jennings, the hotel owner, who first muttered the blood-curdling words: "Jack the Ripper." O'Connor quickly ushered Jennings and the other hotel staff and denizens who had gathered at the door to a room away from the crime scene. He shut the door to room 31 and left a police officer to guard the place. O'Connor knew what he had to do. He bypassed the Fourth Ward station and headed to police headquarters at 300 Mulberry Street to report the murder to Chief Inspector Thomas Byrnes. Byrnes was serving as the acting police superintendent while Superintendent William Murray was out of town. It wouldn't have mattered if Murray was at headquarters or not. O'Connor would still have reported first to Byrnes.

Byrnes was the chief inspector of the city's Detective Bureau, but more than that, he was, for all intents and purposes, the head of the New York City police force. Byrnes received the news of Carrie Brown's murder stoically. He had boasted he would catch Jack the Ripper if he ever struck in New York City, and now he had to prove he could.

The forty-nine-year-old Byrnes was a mostly self-educated Irish immigrant who joined the police force in 1863 and rose through the ranks, quickly overcoming the era's bias against the Irish, by solving a series of highly publicized crimes, including the Manhattan Savings Institution robbery in 1878. Although a powerfully built man with broad shoulders and meaty hands, he moved deftly, almost gracefully. He looked younger than his years despite the huge handlebar mustache and sideburns speckled with gray. Byrnes was credited with turning the Detective Bureau into one of the most efficient crime-fighting departments in the world through his innovative investigative methods. The cigar-chomping, often soft-spoken Byrnes was a master of self-promotion, never missing an opportunity to publicize his exploits and deeds. He had even appeared as a featured character in a series of books, including *A Tragic Mystery* (1887), The *Great Bank Robbery* (1887), *An American Penman* (1887), *Section 558* (1888), and *Another's Crime* (1888), all written by Julian Hawthorne, the son of the famous Nathaniel Hawthorne.

But not every journalist was an adoring fan of Inspector Byrnes or his methods. Lincoln Steffens, a reporter with the New York *Evening Post*, who later went on to national fame as the muckraking author of the book *The Shame of the Cities*, an exposé of local government corruption, described Byrnes as someone who would ". . . buy you or beat you, as you might choose, but get you he would." Another well-known New York City journalist, Jacob A. Riis, a police reporter for the *New York Tribune*, described Byrnes as ". . . tough, effective, unscrupulous, autocratic, and utterly ruthless." Both Steffens and Riis knew full well of Byrnes's often ferocious tactics as a detective. Byrnes had reportedly coined the phrase *the third degree* to describe his technique of eliciting confessions from criminal suspects. He had no scruples about torture and was known to resort to anything necessary, including the infliction of mental or physical pain, to obtain information or a confession from a prisoner.

Under most normal circumstances the murder of a whore along the East River would barely get a rise out of Byrnes. Water Street, where the East River Hotel was located in downtown Manhattan, was overflowing with cheap barrooms, dance halls, and sordid hotels where prostitutes and criminals nightly plied their trade. According to Herbert Asbury, whose book, *The Gangs of New York,* was published in 1928 and later became the basis for director Martin Scorsese's 2002 movie, *Gangs of New York*, practically every block along the waterfront housed at least one dive. "At one time, some tenements had a saloon, dance hall, or house of prostitution on every floor," Asbury wrote.

Murder and mayhem along the East River was a weekly if not nightly occurrence. The discovery of the body of Carrie Brown should have been a routine incident for Byrnes. But Byrnes knew that this murder would be like an albatross around his neck if he didn't solve it, and solve it soon.

Six weeks before the Brown murder, a *New York Times* crime beat reporter had asked Byrnes to comment on the ongoing Scotland Yard investigation of the infamous White Chapel killings—the unsolved murder and mutilation of East End London prostitutes that were attributed to Jack the Ripper. Byrnes told the reporter that the London police had sent him a photograph of the taunting letter with the Ripper's signature scrawled across the page. The return address was simply, "From hell." According to the *Times* reporter, Byrnes, throwing down the gauntlet, said, "It would be impossible for crimes such as Jack the Ripper committed in London to occur in New York and the murderer not be found." Byrnes was even reported to have dared Jack the Ripper to try his luck in New York. Byrnes boasted that if he did he would be under lock and key in less than two days.

Beneath a headline that read AN AMERICAN DETECTIVE'S OPINION, Byrnes laid out in detail how he would go about apprehending the savage, bloodthirsty killer. "I should have gone right to work in a common-sense way, and not believed in mere theories," Byrnes said. "With the great power of the London police I should have manufactured victims for the murderer. I would have taken fifty females from the White Chapel district and covered the ground with them. Even if one fell a victim, I should get the murderer. Men uniformed should be scattered over the district so nothing could escape them. The crimes are all of the same class, and I would have determined the class to which the murderer belonged. But—pshaw! What's the good of talking? The murderer would have been caught long ago."

Taken as nothing more than the usual self-promotion by Byrnes, the story would have disappeared from the public's memory. But then there was the murder of Carrie Brown. It forced Byrnes's hand. He wasn't about to be shown up.

Byrnes had not been alone in his criticism of Scotland Yard's investigation into the Jack the Ripper slayings. For weeks after the killings began in London, the New York City press had a field day disparaging Scotland Yard's unsuccessful and inadequate investigation into the crimes.

The *New York Times* reported, "The four murders have been committed within a gunshot of each other, but the detectives have no clue. The London police and detective force is possibly the stupidest in the world."

The *New York Tribune* was even more condemning when it claimed, ". . . another hacked and mangled body has to be added to the already considerable score which the as yet unknown epicure in laceration has contrived to pile up without fear of any interference on the part of the London police . . ."

Following the brutal murder of Alice McKenzie in London in July 1889, identified as another possible victim of Jack the Ripper, The *New York Times* continued to attack: "There seems to be no more prospect now than there was a year ago that the remarkable criminal who is committing these murders will be detected, unless it be by chance."

Historically speaking, Jack the Ripper murdered and mutilated several prostitutes in the East End of London in 1888, and no one was ever arrested or tried for the murders. "Jack the Ripper" was the name given to the killer because of a series of letters sent to Scotland Yard from someone claiming to be the killer and signing the letters using that name. There remains some dispute about how many victims "Jack the Ripper" actually tallied. Most criminologists agree that he was responsible for the murder and mutilation of at least five prostitutes during his killing spree. Others claim that he may have killed as many as nine. The New York City press was more than happy to have its own Chief Inspector Byrnes poised to show how to catch "the Ripper" the good old-fashioned American way. Byrnes was on the case.

By the time Captain Richard O'Connor arrived at police headquarters, word of the murder and mutilation of Carrie Brown at the East River Hotel had quickly spread across the city. O'Connor informed the coroner's office of the killing and broke the news to Chief Inspector Byrnes.

Already, the city's crime beat reporters had converged on the murder scene.

The East River Hotel was located at the southerly corner of Catherine and Water Streets. Police and newspaper reporters knew it as a "crimp joint," slang for a hotel frequented by criminals who drugged and robbed sailors, often luring them there using prostitutes. According to police reports, sailors were robbed and killed in their sleep at the East River Hotel and places like it along the waterfront, and then their bodies were dumped through trapdoors into the river.

The entire Fourth Ward waterfront district was a basin of misery, disease, crime, and vice. According to a study by the New York Board of Health, it was estimated that within one year, there were approximately four deaths per house or tenement along the waterfront slums, giving the area a death rate of about 10 percent, the highest in the city. According to the report, either the effects of extreme poverty, crime, or disease caused a vast majority of the deaths. The tightly inhabited area was a breeding ground for typhoid, tuberculosis, and cholera. Rats the size of small dogs reportedly roamed the waterfront, living off the piles of garbage and excrement that congested the streets. When the river overflowed or the sewer system backed up, foul-smelling human waste flooded into the streets and cellars of places like the East River Hotel. Some parts of the waterfront were impassable because of the piles of waste and garbage.

By the time Captain O'Connor arrived back at the East River Hotel with several more police officers, reporters were swarming over the place, demanding access to the crime scene. Police detectives searched the fifth floor of the hotel looking for anything that might help in the investigation. According to witnesses, Carrie Brown came to the hotel between 10:30 and 11 p.m. the night before. Brown, who was known as "Old Shakespeare" because she would often blurt out drunken recitations of *Hamlet* or *Macbeth,* claimed to have been a celebrated actress in England during her youth. Brown didn't sign the hotel register, but the man she had picked up signed in as "C. Knick." Mary Miniter, who worked as a housekeeper at the hotel, had caught a glimpse of the man accompanying Brown. According to what was reported in the papers, Miniter claimed he had a foreign appearance and was about thirty years old, with a slim physique and a neat appearance. Miniter told police that the suspect tried to avoid being seen and that he turned away from her whenever she tried to get a better look at him. Still, Miniter was steadfast in her claim that the man appeared to be a foreigner, youngish, and light-haired. Brown and the man were given the key to room 31 on the fifth floor of the hotel.

While the detectives were searching the hotel for clues, the coroner, Dr. Bernard Shultz, began his preliminary examination of the body as reporters crowded around him, taking notes and asking questions. Shultz told reporters that he believed Brown had been strangled first and then mutilated. He estimated that Brown was approximately sixty years old. Shultz let slip his opinion—echoing that of Jennings—that the murder was done by the same person involved in London's White Chapel killings—Jack the Ripper. When asked directly by reporters, Shultz said, "I believe this case is the same as those of London. I do not see any reason to suppose that the crime may not have been committed by the fiend of London."

As word of the murder spread, every available police officer from headquarters and every available detective were assigned to the case on the directive of New York City police commissioner George Washington Walling. City newspapers later called the investigation "the greatest manhunt in the history of the city." Reports of the murder and the vague description of the murderer given by Miniter were distributed to all police stations and neighboring jurisdictions. About twenty detectives from police headquarters—including detectives previously assigned to the Fourth Ward, and a host of uniformed police from across the city—began a dragnet for the suspected murderer, C. Knick. Police canvassed every hotel and lodging house along the waterfront. Byrnes ordered his men to apprehend any suspicious people they might encounter. Police went door-to-door in their search. Other officers began a systematic hunt for anyone who might have known Carrie Brown or had seen her before she checked into the East River Hotel with her killer.

No one at the hotel had any memory of seeing C. Knick leaving the building that night or the following morning. Police suspected that the killer had escaped through a skylight window on the roof and then run off undetected using an outside staircase. The only person of any use to the police was Miniter, who provided investigators with their only real description of the murderer. At Byrnes's urging, Captain O'Connor took Miniter to the Oak Street police station to give her statement again regarding the elusive C. Knick. At the station she repeated the same details about the killer. Miniter was compensated for her help by being arrested and held. Byrnes did not want his only eyewitness to disappear and decided to hold her in protective custody on an outstanding warrant that he had O'Connor concoct.

Then the police discovered another potential witness. Mary Healey, also a known prostitute, had reportedly been seen drinking with Carrie Brown shortly before she was killed. Healey was discovered sleeping off her drunken binge in a room on the first floor of the hotel. Healey was still so drunk that morning that the police had to wrap her in a blanket and transport her to the police station, where they deposited her in a cell and waited for her to sober up.

While the police went about their investigation, the coroner completed his examination of Brown. The body had yet to be moved from room 31. Dr. Shultz told reporters that the killer had carved the abdomen out of her body.

Rumors of the murder swept through the waterfront and then across the city as special editions began flying off the presses. CHOKED, THEN MUTILATED screamed the banner headline of the *New York Times*. The *Tribune* ran with the sensational headline: JACK THE RIPPER STRIKES HOME. The *World* announced: RIPPER'S HORROR REPEATED AT EAST SIDE LODGING. None of the papers could resist running Chief Inspector Byrnes's boast that if ever the Ripper came to New York, he'd have him behind bars within thirty-six hours. It was the last thing Byrnes wanted.

As the day wore on, uniformed police officers were positioned outside the entrance to the East River Hotel to keep the throngs of morbid curiosity seekers from entering the place and disturbing any evidence that might have been uncovered. Crowds of people from the Fourth Ward waterfront and from across the city mingled outside the hotel just to get a glimpse of something, anything—perhaps even the mutilated body of Carrie Brown. By sundown that day, Brown's body still had not been removed to the city morgue. A mood of pending horror swelled through the streets as people discussed the Ripper-like murder and passed on gossip. Most women stayed indoors. The women who did dare to come out of their tenement homes only traveled in pairs or in groups. Even the usually unruly children who raced along the waterfront streets, yelling and chasing rats or playing stickball, were in hiding. Many huddled together in doorways or on tenement stoops, exchanging horror stories about the murder. Fear spread quickly through the East Side.

The waterfront, which made up most of the Fourth Ward slums, was inhabited wall to wall with Irish immigrants, many living in dire poverty and filth. They were usually too busy just trying to survive to care about another murder in their midst, but the words *Jack the Ripper* struck a new kind of fear in them. A monster was loose among them, and no one knew where he might strike next. It would be up to Byrnes to quell their fears and the fears of an entire city.

Canvassing the waterfront churned up more clues and witnesses. Police detectives were able to partly corroborate the true identity of the victim. She had lived for several years in a basement apartment on Oliver Street. The Oliver Street lodging house was operated by Mamie Harrington. Questioning Harrington, detectives learned that the murdered woman's real name was Caroline Montgomery and that she was originally from Salem, Massachusetts. She was called Carrie and had been married to James Brown, a successful sea captain. Following his death, Captain Brown left his wife a small fortune.

According to Harrington, Carrie Brown had moved to New York City fifteen years earlier and settled into a respectable neighborhood where she was able to employ domestic help. She was an attractive, middle-aged woman, well-educated and with refined qualities, including her knowledge of Shakespeare, whom she could recite from memory. However, addicted to alcohol, Brown slowly fell into the depths of misfortune, often drinking herself into stupors or wandering off for days at a time, during which she frequented the seamy waterfront district. Her companions were mostly prostitutes who encouraged her drinking habit since she more often than not paid for everyone's food and drinks. She also took opium and was soon prostituting herself, certainly not for the money, Harrington told detectives. She was arrested several times and sent to the women's home on Blackwell's Island where she would sober up.

Whenever Brown was released from Blackwell's, she would briefly return to her former refined ways but soon would slip back into alcoholism, roaming the saloons and dives along the waterfront, consorting with lowlifes and criminals. She had been released from Blackwell's only two days before her murder.

Harrington told the detectives that Brown had two grown daughters still living in Salem. Ultimately the body of Carrie Brown (Caroline Montgomery) would be sent by train back to her surviving family members in Salem and buried in the family plot.

This information was a far cry from what police had originally gleaned about the victim. Although these facts about Brown's true identity didn't help the police in their pursuit of the murderer, Harrington's further testimony provided the first real clue about Brown's killer. She described how Brown was drinking at the lodging house the night before, when two men came to join her. They had originally come to Harrington's house looking for another woman, Mary Ann Lopez, a local prostitute. Lopez wasn't there, so Brown invited the two men to drink with her. One of the men was known to Harrington as "Frenchy" because he spoke with an accent that most people assumed was French. Harrington did not recognize the other man. She was not sure whether Brown knew "Frenchy" or not since alcohol always made her friendly and outgoing. According to Harrington, at some point in the night, Brown, "Frenchy," and the other man left the lodging house and ended up at John Speekmann's saloon on the corner of Oliver and Oak Streets. There the three eventually met up with Lopez. Detectives were later able to confirm that the four were seen drinking at Speekmann's dive.

Detectives needed to find out more about this "Frenchy" character, but Harrington knew very little about him except that he had what sounded like a French accent. She told police she had never witnessed "Frenchy" using a knife or any other weapon, but said, "Everybody seemed to fear him, and he was said to be a fellow who *would* use a knife." She provided detectives with a description of the suspect that was similar to the description Mary Miniter gave to police earlier. The investigation was hampered by conflicting reports of the suspect's description. After questioning Harrington, detectives returned to the East River Hotel and interviewed the owner, Jennings, and several other people about "Frenchy." Detectives learned that not only did the hotel owner and staff know him, but they also reported that he had spent the night before at the hotel, the same as Carrie Brown. He had taken room 33 directly across the hall from Brown's room. Detectives quickly reported back to Chief Inspector Byrnes that they now had a known suspect who had been seen with the murdered and mutilated victim only hours before her death. "Frenchy" could be directly placed at the scene of the crime and in the company of Brown. This new, intriguing information energized Byrnes. He left the Mulberry Street police headquarters to inspect the scene of the crime himself.

Byrnes had his methods. He liked to work in secret without explaining to anyone what he was up to. This secrecy was a hallmark of Byrnes's rise to fame. Some within the department, like police commissioner George Walling, remained skeptical of Byrnes and his questionable detection methods. Walling's opinion was that the chief inspector's real genius was his talent for self-promotion and not good, hard police work. Walling was on to the ploys used by Byrnes that often baffled and impressed the gullible public and some members of the New York press. One of Byrnes's most famous tricks was to arrest a suspect wanted in a well-publicized crime and hold back the news from the press. Byrnes and his cronies would then extract a "confession" from the secretly held suspect using Byrnes's highly touted "third degree." Byrnes's form of interrogation usually consisted of bringing the suspect into his thickly carpeted office and making him stand in front of the chief inspector. Detectives would stand on either side of the shackled prisoner. As Byrnes began questioning the suspect, he would put on his black leather gloves while he paced back and forth in front of the prisoner. If the suspect didn't give Byrnes the answer he was seeking, Byrnes would whack the suspect in the stomach or the genitals. That way, there would be no visible bruises. The detectives on either side of the suspect would hold him up so Byrnes could continue his interrogation. More "wrong" answers produced another punch. The beatings would stop when the suspect confessed or informed on one of his partners in crime. All this was kept from the press.

Once Byrnes had his confession, he would boast to the press that he knew who committed the particular crime and would vow to capture him in a matter of hours. Of course, he had already beaten a confession out of a suspect being held in secret. A few hours later, the suspect would be hauled out and displayed to the press—proof positive that Byrnes was indeed the best police investigator in the country.

But not every newspaperman was taken in by Byrnes's tricks. Jacob Riis, the reform-minded, crusading *New York Tribune* reporter, knew all about Byrnes's "third degree" techniques. "He would beat a thief into telling him what he wanted to know. Thieves have no rights a policeman thinks himself bound to respect," Riis wrote.

Byrnes's crude interrogation methods might force a suspect to confess to a crime, whether he committed it or not, or to inform on his friends to save himself, but the third degree would have little value in a murder investigation, Police Commissioner Walling thought. According to Walling, Byrnes's methods of interrogation might work on crooks and bank robbers, who might brag about pulling off a certain heist. Other criminals might suddenly turn up with a brand-new bankroll, and there was always a network of shady characters that every criminal came to rely on called *fences*—criminals who received and disposed of stolen goods. All this gave Byrnes plenty of potential suspects and informants to draw on. But based on Walling's experience, a murderer like the one responsible for the sexually motivated mutilation of Carrie Brown usually would not boast about it to anyone; therefore, there was no one who could snitch on the murderer. And even if Byrnes was able to beat a confession out of a murder suspect, there was still the evidence to contend with. Walling was well aware, based on years as a police officer, that anyone might confess to a crime under the threat of torture but that it was the evidence linking the criminal to the crime that really mattered in a case of law. So what if Byrnes could beat a confession out of someone claiming he murdered Carrie Brown. The confession alone needed to be supported by evidence, and Byrnes had no evidence in the case yet.

In his memoir about serving as a New York City police officer and commissioner, *Recollections of a New York Chief of Police*, published in 1887, Walling expressed his concerns about Byrnes's tactics. In it he confesses that he knew Byrnes was an ambitious man who had his eye on the superintendent's job. The murder of Carrie Brown could possibly be the straw that broke the proverbial camel's back—this time showing the true flaws in Byrnes's otherwise untarnished public image.

At sundown on Friday, April 24, the body of Carrie Brown was taken from the blood-soaked room at the East River Hotel to the city morgue. Chief Inspector Byrnes, accompanied by several of his most trusted detectives, including Inspector John "Clubber" Williams, arrived at the hotel to look around the place for himself. Crowds were still gathered in front of the building. Some people had lit small candles, making the throng look like a vigil. A small cheer went up when Byrnes showed up on the scene. Byrnes waved confidently to the people but was in and out in a flash. He and his cadre of detectives proceeded to the Oak Street police station to be apprised of the ongoing investigation from Captain O'Connor and several of his top men. They met in O'Connor's private office. Everyone agreed that Carrie Brown's grisly murder was far more than just another East Side slaying. Although no one dared say it, it was on everyone's mind. Could this really be the work of Jack the Ripper? Had the Ripper taken up Byrnes's challenge? It was at this meeting that Byrnes personally took charge of the murder investigation.

The police theory, however, is that "Jack" is not in New-York, but that an imitator, perhaps a crank, committed the murder. A strict policy of not saying a word about the case was kept up last night. At midnight the temporary detective headquarters at the Oak Street Station were closed for the night, but the night squad were told to look out for a man about 5 feet 8 inches high, rather thin, with a light moustache, light hair, and hooked nose, and dressed in a dark cutaway coat and derby hat. . . .

—*New York Times*
April 25, 1891

There was a collective sigh of relief among the officers present for several reasons. First, if anyone could solve the case, it would be Byrnes. He was a celebrated and savvy police detective. He had made his reputation by solving some of the city's most sensational crimes. Byrnes was incredibly knowledgeable about the degenerate lowlifes who inhabited the city's criminal underworld. If someone knew something, Byrnes would hear about it. And perhaps more importantly, there was relief that with Byrnes taking over the case, if he failed, he did so on his own. Everyone, including Byrnes himself, knew the consequences of not finding Carrie Brown's killer. Byrnes had work to do, and at the top of the list was finding "Frenchy."

Byrnes met with the Brooklyn police commissioner on Saturday, April 25. The Brooklyn police had offered to help the inspector, but Byrnes told them he was sure that Brown's killer was not hiding out in Brooklyn. He gave no reason for his assumption.

The Brooklyn police had been notified of Brown's murder by the late afternoon of Friday, April 24, and had begun an intense investigation of their own. By that evening, a Brooklyn police officer and mounted patrolman John Frank of the Tenth Precinct had made an arrest in connection with the murder.

Officer Frank had arrested two vagrants, charging them with loitering. The real reason Frank had arrested the two men was because one of the vagrants, a man who gave his name as John Foley, looked like the man that the New York police reported they were seeking in connection with Brown's murder. According to unconfirmed police reports—Byrnes had issued a communication blackout on any news to the press—the suspect they were looking for was a tall, slender, olive-skinned man with a shock of black, curly hair. The suspect was a foreigner who reportedly spoke with an accent and went by the nickname, Frenchy. Foley and the other man were locked up in a cell at a Brooklyn police station until someone from the New York City Police Department showed up to question them. Byrnes didn't want to share the limelight with anyone, especially in this case. He thanked the Brooklyn police but didn't accept their offer to help in the investigation. After being interviewed, New York City police had Foley released. By that time, Byrnes had his own suspect in custody.

Not to be shown up by the Brooklyn police, the New York police had also apprehended a man fitting the description of the suspect. Sometime around nine o'clock on Friday night, New York police officers arrested an immigrant who had been, according to police, suspiciously loitering near the East River Hotel. One theory that Byrnes had developed and expressed in many newspaper interviews regarding criminal detection was that most criminals were not apt to flee the scene of their crime, but rather, out of some morbid curiosity, they often skulked around the crime scene. The immigrant arrested by the police that evening, a man of either Greek or Italian heritage, who spoke in broken English, fit the bill on both counts: He physically fit the description of Frenchy, the man they were looking for, and he was suspiciously hanging around the hotel.

———•◦◦•———

IT IS YET A MYSTERY
The Police Still At Sea In
The East River Hotel Murder Case

There was no startling development in the East River Hotel murder yesterday. The police seem to be absolutely at sea. They will say nothing perhaps because they have nothing to say. They display an irritability that is in itself strong evidence that they are completely baffled.

The official statement made by Inspector Byrnes late Saturday night to the effect that he was almost satisfied that the perpetrator of the crime was a man known as "Frenchy," a cousin of George Francis, also known as "Frenchy," the last named now being in the hands of the police. It is generally believed to have been what in police circles is called a "throw-off." Byrnes as much said he would be able to put his hands on Frenchy as soon as he wanted him. He has not got him yet. . . .

Byrnes himself said yesterday that "Frenchy" had not been arrested. This and the statement that the description of the murderer were conflicting thus rendering identification extremely difficult were the only statements that the Inspector would make for publication.

The manner in which the police are working is almost conclusive evidence that they are just where they started, so far as the actual capture of the murderer is concerned. They are simply pursuing a drag-net policy. . . .

Mysteriously as the police are moving it is known that they made a number of arrests yesterday. Most of the prisoners, after examination, were discharged. . . .

—*New York Times*
April 27, 1891

———•◦•———

The problem with identifying the suspect lay in the conflicting descriptions being circulated. An unconfirmed report by the police was that the suspect was a dark-skinned foreign-born man, tall and slender. This conflicted with the description given to police by Mary Miniter, the only person to have seen Carrie Brown's killer, who had described the suspect as a foreigner, youngish, and light-haired. Some newspapers published a description of the killer as tall, blond, and Germanic-looking—descriptions guided more by editorial speculation than eyewitness testimony.

The man arrested by the New York police on Friday evening, whom they referred to as "The Greek," was taken to the Oak Street police station for questioning. A series of witnesses was brought in to view "The Greek," who was not of Greek heritage at all, the police later learned. He was an Algerian immigrant named Ameer Ben Ali. Ben Ali was known in and around the East River Hotel neighborhood as "Frenchy." Ben Ali denied ever being near the hotel the night of the murder and denied any knowledge of Brown. After questioning he admitted knowing Brown and being with her the evening she was murdered.

Miniter was brought in to identify the suspect. She told police that Ben Ali was not the man who had rented the room at the hotel with Brown. When informed of the disappointing news, Byrnes decided it didn't matter and kept Ben Ali locked up anyway as a material witness in the case.

By the end of Friday night, a succession of suspects had been arrested, detained, questioned, and released. On Saturday morning a new description of the suspect was circulated to various police departments. After questioning Miniter—his only real witness—again, Byrnes was able to further jog her memory. She told Byrnes she recalled other important details about the man police were looking for. She added to her original description—foreign-looking, youngish, perhaps in his thirties, and light-haired—that the man had been sporting a mustache, appeared to be slender, under six feet tall, had a prominent hooked nose, and had been wearing a derby. The new information was added to the original description and circulated throughout the police department.

It didn't take the overly zealous police long to find someone who matched that description. German immigrant Adolph Kallenberg was arrested and brought to the Oak Street police station for questioning.

Miniter was again brought in to confront the suspect and again she told the police that Kallenberg wasn't the man she saw with Brown. Kallenberg was released shortly after.

———•••••———

Eight little whores, with no hope of heaven,
Gladstone may save one, then there'll be seven.
Seven little whores beggin for a shilling,
One stays in Henage Court, then there's a killing.
Six little whores, glad to be alive,
One sidles up to Jack, then there are five . . .

—"Jack the Ripper" poem appearing in the 1959 book,
The Identity of Jack the Ripper, by Donald McCormick

———•••••———

Despite the press's assertion that the police were baffled by the case, a break came late on that Saturday when the night clerk at the Glenmore Hotel in Chatham Square, a flophouse located just off Catherine Street, a few blocks from the East River Hotel, was brought in for questioning.

The clerk, John Kelly, informed police that a man came into the Glenmore between 1 and 2 a.m. Friday morning wanting to rent a room. Kelly told police that the man's hands, face, and clothes were stained with what looked like blood. According to Kelly, the man was wearing a derby that he had pulled down to conceal portions of his face. He spoke in broken English and had a thick accent of some sort.

"He asked me if I could give him a room," Kelly told police. "There were also two blotches of blood on his right cheek, as though he had put the bloody hand to his face. There was also blood on his right coat sleeve and it was spattered on his collar."

When Kelly told the man the prices of the rooms, the man became agitated and demanded that Kelly give him a room for the rest of the night for free. He claimed he had no money. At that point Kelly told the man to leave. The man didn't put up an argument, but instead of leaving, he tried to make his way to one of the washrooms downstairs at the hotel, saying he had to clean up. Kelly called for the night watchman, and the two men led the strange blood-stained man out of the hotel, where, according to Kelly, he bounded up the street and disappeared into an alley.

Under normal circumstances, the appearance of a bloodied stranger at that time of night in the Chatham Square neighborhood, with its flophouses, saloons, and houses of prostitution, teeming with every imaginable crime and vice, would not have piqued the interest of the police. But Kelly's description of the man coming so close on the heels of Brown's murder at the East River Hotel nearby, clearly raised their concern. Kelly's description of the man was nearly identical to that of Miniter's.

According to Kelly, the stranger spoke with a thick German accent. He was just under six feet tall, had a fair complexion, a long nose, and wore a pencil-thin mustache. He was wearing a worn cutaway coat and a derby, exactly as Miniter had described.

More remarkably, Kelly's description of the man was given to the police before Miniter gave her new description to Byrnes and it was released to the newspapers. Therefore, Kelly couldn't have known about Miniter's description beforehand.

The information was immediately relayed to Byrnes, who saw in Kelly's description corroboration of the suspect's identity. The police department was put on alert for a man fitting the combined descriptions given by Miniter and Kelly. Byrnes refused to divulge much about the Carrie Brown murder case to news reporters. That was his modus operandi. He had ordered all the men assigned to the case to do the same—keep their mouths shut. Even when asked if he thought that Brown's murder was the work of Jack the Ripper, Byrnes refused comment. Within the Detective Bureau it was generally assumed that Brown's brutal murder was the work of a Jack the Ripper copycat, and not a very good one at that. Byrnes did admit to the press that the police were searching for a sailor named Isaac Perringer, who reportedly had been seen drinking with Brown earlier in the evening of her murder.

The police had cobbled together a scenario covering Carrie Brown's last few hours based on various reports given to them by witnesses, including Miniter. What they knew was that Brown had been seen drinking with Ameer Ben Ali, who was still being held in custody but not charged. Brown and Ben Ali had been joined by another man. What the police did know about the second man was that he too spoke French as well as English and also went by the nickname "Frenchy." The police were still unable to find the man. With one person of interest, Ben Ali (nicknamed "Frenchy") being held, the police intensified their search for the second Frenchy, who was nowhere to be found. Ben Ali freely admitted to the police that after a bout of drinking, he had rented a room with Brown at the East River Hotel. He also admitted to being in the hotel at the time of Brown's murder. But he disavowed any involvement in it.

According to the police, Ben Ali had a cousin who was also known by the same nickname. Both Ben Ali and his unnamed "cousin" had reputations as waterfront thugs and were known to consort with a variety of prostitutes who inhabited the waterfront. On the night of the murder, Frenchy I (Ben Ali) and Frenchy II (his cousin) had been drinking with Mary Ann Lopez and Carrie Brown. It was Byrnes's contention that, if and when the police found Frenchy II, they would have their murderer. Still, Byrnes gave no details of how close the police were in determining the location of Frenchy II. Byrnes boasted to newspaper reporters who had gathered at police headquarters since the discovery of the vicious murder that he could put his hands on Frenchy II whenever he wanted. If that were true, reporters wanted to know, why wasn't the mysterious Frenchy II in custody? Reporters who knew Byrnes's methods understood that the chief inspector was not showing all his cards. Some even suspected that Byrnes already had Frenchy II in custody. It did not seem like professional detective work by Byrnes to announce to the world that he was in pursuit of a suspect, thereby giving the suspect time to escape. Most reporters agreed there was something fishy about the whole investigation.

For a man who professes to have so much confidence in his own ability Inspector Byrnes betrays singular evidence of weakness . . . he talks too much. He has seen fit to name the perpetrator of the horrible murder . . . and has not been slow to ventilate his theories in the public prints. . . . Less promise and more performance would be a good motto for the inspector to heed.

—*Brooklyn Daily Eagle*
April 27, 1891

It didn't take very long for the crazies to come out of the woodwork when the story broke in the newspapers. Police were deluged with false claims regarding the whereabouts of the suspected murderer. One of the most spectacular claims came from Steve Brodie, a New Yorker who had become famous for jumping off the Brooklyn Bridge in 1886 and surviving. An outspoken publicity hound, Brodie informed the police that he had found pieces of Carrie Brown's intestines in the gutter outside the East River Hotel. The intestines were sent to New York City deputy coroner James Jenkins, who had conducted the autopsy on Brown. Jenkins determined that the intestines were those of a dead cat.

Jenkins had previously been questioned by reporters and had been asked whether he thought Jack the Ripper had committed the brutal crime. Jenkins told reporters that he was "not advancing any theories" regarding the killer's identity. Jenkins was asked whether Brown's mutilations were done at the hands of someone who might have been a surgeon. Speculation had been reported that Jack the Ripper might have been a skilled surgeon based on the precise way he had mutilated his victims' bodies. Jenkins told reporters, "If it was done by a surgeon, he was a butcher."

A LEAP FROM THE BRIDGE
STEVE BRODIE'S PLUNGE INTO
THE EAST RIVER
THE RISK TAKEN ON A BET OF $200
—BRODIE NOT HURT, BUT UNDER
ARREST AND IN THE TOMBS

A tall slim man, who looked very much like an overgrown street boy, stood talking to a young woman at the New York end of the Brooklyn Bridge a little after 2 o'clock yesterday afternoon. He bade her good-bye and kissed her. She responded by saying, "Good-bye, Steve; take care of yourself, and may you be successful and scoop in dose $200 so we kin have a good time." The man, who was Stephen Brodie . . . has been rather unlucky lately in betting on horse races, and to retrieve his losses he took up a bet that he would jump off the East River Bridge. . . .

Brodie swung to and fro in the breeze, and steadied himself as well as he could. When he swung perpendicular over the river he let go his hold, and shot down like an arrow. It was but a few seconds before he struck the water. . . . The distance which Brodie jumped or dropped was probably about 120 feet. . . .

"I was in training for a long time to make this jump. I tried various distances from piers and from masts in the East River, and concluded I could jump without injury to myself or the Brooklyn Bridge. I wasn't afraid. I told my wife all about it. She gave birth to a youngster a few days ago, and she was anxious to see me win the bet."

—*New York Times*
July 24, 1886

The Jack the Ripper case in New York City was about to come to a convenient end. Most reporters had covered the city's crime beat long enough to realize that Byrnes was too smart to announce publicly that he was looking for a prime suspect in the case, and yet he had done just that, giving the suspect an opportunity to escape his grasp, by divulging to the newspapers that he was looking for Frenchy II—Ben Ali's cousin. It had to be a ruse of some sort. Byrnes never gave out information unless he had some clandestine motive. Many reporters felt that Byrnes was leading them on and that he had the man he wanted, Frenchy I—Ben Ali—behind bars. Still, they played along with the charade. Even some of the police investigators, who spoke to reporters privately, were of the opinion that Byrnes already had his man and that now it was just a matter of proving it. No one, not the police officers who worked for him or the newspaper reporters, thought Byrnes couldn't come up with the proof he needed. He always had, one way or the other. Even if the mysterious Frenchy II had murdered Carrie Brown, if Byrnes couldn't find him, then as sure as the sun rose over Brooklyn, Byrnes would find a way to charge the man he did have in custody. The police continued their investigation over the next several days without turning up the whereabouts of the reported Frenchy II. Dozens of suspects were arrested, brought in for questioning, and subsequently released.

Based on evidence Byrnes had gathered from various sources, it became clear that, if indeed there was a Frenchy II and he was a cousin of Ben Ali, and if both men were known as sailors, then the second suspect might be hiding somewhere along the East River piers. Byrnes followed up on his hunch and boarded the steamship *Philadelphia* docked along the East River. On board Byrnes found and arrested the second engineer of the ship. Checking the shipping schedules, Byrnes discovered that the *Philadelphia* had arrived in New York on the day Carrie Brown was last seen—Thursday, April 23. The man he arrested was a blond-haired German who spoke little English. He fit the description that Miniter had given to the police. Byrnes himself interrogated the engineer from the *Philadelphia* but he was eventually released. It seemed like another dead end for Byrnes. By Monday, April 27, nearly four days after the murder, the police were still stymied.

That afternoon, Byrnes gave reporters a statement. In it, Byrnes completely contradicted his earlier premise. Byrnes claimed he had no positive proof that Frenchy II was the murderer of Carrie Brown. Byrnes's revelation left both reporters and his own men in a state of utter confusion. So now, it appeared, Byrnes's ruse was up. The question that remained for reporters and police who were wise to Byrnes's tricks was this: Why, exactly, had he put so much energy into capturing Frenchy II if he wasn't the killer? Byrnes told reporters, "I don't know anything more about the murder than you do."

So much for a satisfactory answer. New York City and Brooklyn police were apprehending every man they could find who fit the description of the missing Frenchy II, or who had ever gone by the nickname of Frenchy—an endless stream of arrests leading nowhere. All Byrnes could give the public was "I don't know."

It wasn't until later in the afternoon of the 27th that police arrested Eli Commanis, alias John Williams, alias Frenchy. Police arrested Commanis in his room at a lodging house on Furman Street. Commanis was picked up on the flimsiest of evidence, but as the case dragged on and no charges were brought against anyone, the police had resorted to using any excuse to make an arrest. Commanis was a dock worker, short, with dark hair, not fitting the description of the man police were after. What the police did know about Commanis was that he knew Carrie Brown and had, for a time, lived next door to the East River Hotel. He had moved to his new Furman Street address right after Brown's murder. On top of all that, police discovered that two years earlier, a woman had been murdered at a rooming house where Commanis had been staying. The case remained unsolved. The arrest of Commanis might have been a break for police if Miniter hadn't been brought in to identify him and told police she had never seen the man before. After a particularly grueling interrogation by Byrnes and others, Commanis was released. Monday, April 27, ended as it had begun: no Frenchy II, and no charges brought in the case. The investigation lumbered on. More arrests were made, more interrogations, and more suspects released from police custody.

On Wednesday, April 29, police in New Jersey managed to steal the spotlight from Byrnes and the New York City police. They told reporters that they had apprehended Frenchy II, a man named Arbie

La Bruckman, whose list of aliases included John Frenchy and Frenchy. He was, according to New Jersey police, the Frenchy II whom Byrnes and his department had been seeking.

———•••••———

Police described La Bruckman as a strong, villainous-looking man approximately thirty years old. According to New Jersey police, he was "about 5 feet 7 inches in height and weighs about 180 pounds . . . has black hair and a dark brown mustache." La Bruckman had been born in Morocco. Although he didn't fit the description of the man Mary Miniter had provided the police, under questioning by New Jersey authorities, La Bruckman admitted he was the man they were looking for—Frenchy II. He told the New Jersey authorities that he hadn't been in hiding, as newspaper reports claimed. According to La Bruckman, who was a merchant seaman, he had been arrested by Scotland Yard on his last trip to London, suspected of being Jack the Ripper. He was held for more than two weeks and intensely interrogated, but he was released because there was not sufficient evidence to hold him.

La Bruckman was questioned but was not considered a major suspect in the Jack the Ripper case. La Bruckman's opinion of himself as a suspect in either case, the murder of Carrie Brown and the murders done at the hands of Jack the Ripper, was not substantiated by any facts of consequence. It appeared La Bruckman enjoyed the notoriety, but he wasn't the man Byrnes was looking for. Byrnes was not interested in interrogating La Bruckman, who was ultimately released from police custody. Another dead end.

Byrnes's case—or what little he had of it—was unraveling right before his eyes, so he decided on a different approach, one with far-reaching legal implications, at least as far as Ameer Ben Ali was concerned. Byrnes turned his attention to the only piece of evidence he had left in the case: Ben Ali, who had been held in custody as a material witness since the Friday before.

The Queens County sheriff contacted Byrnes and informed him that he had evidence that, before being arrested as a material witness in the Brown murder, Ben Ali had been recently arrested and held at the Queens County jail, charged with vagrancy. At the time, Ben Ali was going under the name George Frank. If the Ben Ali being held in custody by Byrnes and the reported George Frank were one and the same, then the Queens County sheriff assured Byrnes that he had some incriminating evidence regarding Ben Ali. Byrnes wasted no time in transporting his prisoner to the Queens County jail for identification.

According to the Queens County sheriff, George Frank and Ameer Ben Ali were the same man. More importantly, at least to Byrnes, was that while Ben Ali was being held in the Queens County jail for vagrancy, he reportedly had a knife in his possession that could have been used to murder Carrie Brown. For Byrnes, locating the murder weapon had been a hindrance to his investigation. Now, he had Ben Ali in custody and a potential murder weapon, a knife, accounted for. Although the knife was no longer in the possession of the Queens County sheriff, because it had been returned to Ben Ali after he was released from custody in Queens, Byrnes could at least connect his prisoner to owning the kind of weapon that might have been used in Brown's murder.

By Thursday of that week, the process of elimination in the investigation of Brown's sensational murder had concluded as far as Byrnes was concerned. According to Byrnes's theory, and information that he had intentionally withheld from reporters and even many of his own men, circumstantial evidence pointed directly to the man Byrnes had had in custody from the start—Ameer Ben Ali. A trail of blood had been discovered coming from the room Brown had been killed in, room 31, to the room across the hall, room 33—where Ben Ali had reportedly spent the night of the murder. Investigators discovered blood smeared on both sides of the door to room 33, and blood was found on the bed and sheets in the room. Byrnes contacted the New York City Board of Health and had Dr. Cyrus Edson conduct several reportedly scientific examinations of blood found on Ben Ali's clothes and blood found under his fingernails.

Although Byrnes and Edson claimed the examination scientifically proved that the blood on Ben Ali's clothes and under his nails was human blood, there was no way to prove that the blood belonged to Carrie Brown. Edson's conclusion that it was human blood under Ali's nails still did not connect Ali to the murder. Edson had no scientific way to make that connection. It wasn't until 1900 that Karl Landsteiner, a professor of pathological anatomy at the University of Vienna, first discovered human blood groups. It was Landsteiner's discovery that allowed forensic scientists to identify various blood groups. Edson would not have been able to perform such an analysis prior to that time.

As Byrnes intensified his investigation aimed at proving Ben Ali as Brown's murderer, he began to accumulate more circumstantial evidence, primarily dealing with Ben Ali's character. Several sources came forward to claim that Ben Ali was a dangerous man who, on more than one occasion, had threatened and abused women, including Brown on the night she was murdered. Why this evidence had not come out at the beginning of the investigation was perfectly clear— Byrnes's investigation had reached a dead end and now he needed to come up with a suspect one way or another. Adding fuel to the fire, Byrnes later pointed out to reporters that Ben Ali was a merchant seaman who traveled back and forth between New York City and London, the operative word being London. In this way Byrnes was attempting to associate Ben Ali with the London-based Jack the Ripper. Byrnes proudly declared that Frenchy, Ameer Ben Ali, was the killer. The illustrious chief of detectives Thomas Byrnes had got his man once again. Almost.

Byrnes had a new theory of what had happened. The man who had come to the East River Hotel with Carrie Brown and who signed his name as C. Kniclo had no connection to the murder. According to Byrnes's theory, Kniclo left the hotel before midnight, and Brown was murdered after he had left. It had already been established that Ben Ali spent the night in room 33, across the hall from Brown's room. Byrnes's scenario had Ben Ali entering Brown's room and killing her. Blood had been found in the hall between rooms 31 and 33; on both sides of the door to room 33; on the floor of room 33; and on Ben Ali's socks and beneath his fingernails. Everything pointed to Ben Ali as Brown's killer. The motive, according to Byrnes, was simple: money. Ben Ali had stolen what little money Brown had on her. The case was solved.

Ben Ali was taken to the Court of General Session, where he was provided with pro bono counsel. Ben Ali pleaded not guilty to the crime, maintaining his innocence. He was committed into the custody of Byrnes and taken back to police headquarters on Mulberry Street. He was arraigned on April 30, 1891, and held in the Tombs until his trial began on June 24. "The Tombs" was the nickname given to the New York Halls of Justice and House of Detention located in lower Manhattan. It housed the city's courts, police, and detention facilities. Since Ben Ali did not speak English, the court provided him with an Algerian interpreter. District attorney De Lancey Nicoll served as the prosecutor. Abraham Levy was Ben Ali's court-appointed defense attorney. Inspector Byrnes and four officers testified for the prosecution. Dozens of denizens of the East River waterfront were called by the prosecution to testify against Ben Ali, stating he was a frequent lodger at the East River Hotel and was often caught entering occupied rooms. Several medical experts were called to testify. They all indicated that the blood found on Ben Ali's socks and under his nails was consistent with blood found fundamentally in human intestines and consistent with the blood flowing from the gruesome abdominal injuries inflicted on Brown. Levy only had his client, Ben Ali, as a rebuttal witness. Through his interpreter Ben Ali unfailingly denied killing Brown, but he provided the jury with no explanation for the blood found on his socks and fingernails and offered no alibi for the night of the murder. The trial lasted less than a month, and on July 10, 1891, Ameer Ben Ali was found guilty of second-degree murder and sentenced to life imprisonment in Sing Sing.

Although the case was closed and Ben Ali was in prison, rumors about the murder persisted. Byrnes offered no explanation for why Ben Ali would have disemboweled the aging prostitute, or why he would have carved an X on her body like the London Jack the Ripper. Ben Ali was not an educated man, and he couldn't speak or read English, so there was no way he could have read any of the American newspapers describing the crimes of the London Ripper. Many, especially in the press, felt Ben Ali had been framed in order to save Byrnes's reputation as the city's preeminent crime fighter.

Other facts in the case had been conveniently ignored. Crusading newspaper reporter Jacob Riis, who had been one of the first reporters on the crime scene, filed an affidavit stating that he never saw any blood on the doorknob of room 33, where Ben Ali reportedly spent the night. However, evidence presented during Ben Ali's trial was based on the premise that Ben Ali had gone into room 31, slaughtered Carrie Brown, left the bloodied room covered in blood, and returned to his room across the hall—and all this was supposedly done without Ben Ali once touching the doorknob of either room 31 or 33. A key ring with room number 31 on it and a bloody shirt were later found in a New Jersey flophouse. The key belonged to room 31 at the East River Hotel. Ben Ali had no way of getting to the New Jersey hotel where the key and bloody shirt were discovered. None of it added up.

Based on new evidence, New York governor Benjamin B. Odell issued a pardon for Ameer Ben Ali in 1902. Ben Ali had served nearly eleven years in prison. He was subsequently deported to Algeria. No investigation into the prosecution of Ben Ali was ever conducted, and the immaculate reputation of Chief Inspector Thomas Byrnes remained untarnished. Byrnes had displayed a pioneering investigative technique in the Ben Ali case, attempting to connect Ali to the crime through the rudimentary examination of blood samples. Although his technique was flawed, the process remained a prototype for future forensic practice. Less than a year after the Ben Ali case, in April 1892, Byrnes was appointed superintendent of the New York City Police Department. He had come a long way from his humble beginnings in Ireland and his childhood of poverty on the streets of New York City.

AMERICAN ALMANAC, 1854

By the end of 1854 nearly two million Irish immigrants, approximately one-quarter of Ireland's population, had fled to the United States, with a majority settling in New York City. Nearly half of the reported thirty thousand abandoned children in New York City were Irish. Notorious areas in the city like Five Points, called one of the worst slums in the world by Charles Dickens on his trip to America, were reportedly close to 75 percent Irish. Young Thomas Byrnes and his family were among those poor Irish immigrants living in New York City squalor.

———

NO IRISH NEED APPLY

Byrnes and his family, like other Irish immigrants in New York City, faced oppressive discrimination in jobs and housing. Songs and laments exposing the plight of the Irish in America were common, such as the following song written by Kathleen O'Neil:

I'm a simple Irish girl, and I'm looking for a place,
I've felt the grip of poverty, but sure that's no disgrace,
'Twill be long before I get one, tho' indeed it's hard I try,
For I read in each advertisement, "No Irish need apply."
Alas! for my poor country, which I never will deny,
How they insult us when they write, "No Irish need apply."
Now I wonder what's the reason that the fortune-favored few,
Should throw on us that dirty slur, and treat us as they do,
Sure they all know Paddy's heart is warm, and willing is his hand,
They rule us, yet we may not earn a living in their land,

Ah! but now I'm in the land of the "Glorious and Free,"
And proud I am to own it, a country dear to me,

I can see by your kind faces, that you will not deny,
A place in your hearts for Kathleen, where "All Irish may apply."
Then long may the Union flourish, and ever may it be,
A pattern to the world, and the "Home of Liberty!"

And the poor and destitute developed their own laments.

Hot corn, hot corn
Here's your lily white corn
All you that's got money
Poor me that's got none—
Buy me lily white corn
And let me go home.

—SONG SUNG BY HOT-CORN GIRLS WHO PEDDLED THEIR CORN TO CROWDS
ALONG NEW YORK CITY'S MERCHANT'S EXCHANGE AND FERRY LANDINGS

———•••———

Despite the plight of the Irish and the poor in general in New York City, art and culture flourished in well-to-do sections.

O sole mio . . . Opera was thriving in New York. The Academy of Music opened on Fourteenth Street at Irving Place at a cost of more than $300,000. The first performance, Bellini's *Norma,* was presented there in early October.

The Astor Library in New York City was officially opened. It was funded by a $400,000 bequest from John Jacob Astor, who died in 1848. Astor, one of the richest men in the country at the time of his death, had little formal education but retained a love of literature. The Boston Public Library also opened this year.

The hoop skirt became the fashion rage for women—a style set by Paris fashion designers and promoted by the Empress Eugenie of France.

———•••———

Along with the sad laments of the city's lowly, other popular music was a mainstay in New York City in 1854, and among the most popular songs were those written by Stephen Foster.

Jeanie with the Light Brown Hair

I dream of Jeanie with the light brown hair,
Borne, like a vapor, on the summer air;
I see her tripping where the bright streams play,
Happy as the daisies that dance on her way.
Many were the wild notes her merry voice would pour,
Many were the blithe birds that warbled them o'er:
Oh! I dream of Jeanie with the light brown hair,
Floating, like a vapor, on the soft summer air.

—WORDS AND MUSIC BY STEPHEN FOSTER

Oh! Susanna

I come from Alabama with my banjo on my knee;
I'm goin' to Lou'siana, my true love for to see.
It rained all night the day I left,
the weather it was dry;
The sun so hot I froze to death,
Susanna don't you cry.
Oh! Susanna, don't you cry for me;
I come from Alabama,
with my banjo on my knee.

—WORDS AND MUSIC BY STEPHEN FOSTER

Stephen Foster was born on July 4, 1826, in Pittsburgh, Pennsylvania. He was educated at Jefferson College and became a full-time musician in 1850, working for several musical groups, including Christy's Minstrels and the New Orleans Serenaders. His many songs became popular favorites with the public. He moved to New York City in 1860 but became an alcoholic. Living alone and in dire poverty in a run-down hotel in the Bowery, he died in January 1864 at Bellevue Hospital from injuries he suffered in a fall. He was thirty-seven years old.

LIVING IN NEW YORK CITY

Average wage for shoemakers: $5.00 per week

Laborer's daily wage: $1.00

Laborer's average yearly wage: $200.00

Average weekly wage for women: $2.00

Average daily wage for tailors: 75 cents

Average weekly wage for seamstresses: $1.50–$2.00

Number of asylums: 22

Number of hospitals: 8

Number of benevolent societies: 90

Number of inmates at Bellevue: 1,400

Number of hotels: 45

Number of men worth over $3 million: 15

Amount John Jacob Astor invested in land: $2 million

———

For young boys like Thomas Byrnes, growing up in the slums of New York City in 1854, the dark clouds of war were forming on the horizon. Byrnes and young men like him would be drawn into America's most bloody conflict, the Civil War.

The Kansas Nebraska Act was signed into law by President Franklin Pierce. The act only served to incite violence and bring the Civil War a step closer. It created two new territories governed by popular sovereignty—each territory was free to decide whether it would be a slave or free state when it was ultimately admitted into the Union. The act's sponsor was Senator Stephen A. Douglas, who would run for and lose the presidential election of 1860 against Abraham Lincoln.

———

QUIPS & QUOTES

The price of anything is the amount of life you exchange for it.

—Henry David Thoreau

Could I begin life again knowing what I know now, and had money to invest, I would buy every foot of land on the Island of Manhattan.

—JOHN JACOB ASTOR

I wish I could indulge higher hope for the future of our country, but the aspect of any vision is fearfully dark and I cannot make it otherwise.

—FRANKLIN PIERCE

Slavery is not the only question which comes up in this controversy. There is a far more important one to you, and that is, what shall be done with the free Negro?

—STEPHEN A. DOUGLAS

All the world is sad and dreary, Everywhere I roam.

—STEPHEN FOSTER

2
NO IRISH
NEED APPLY

In which the Byrnes family emigrates from Ireland during the Potato Famine and settles into one of New York City's worst slums, Five Points, where they struggle to survive amid vast prejudice and poverty.

NEW YORK CITY, 1854

A picture of James Byrnes, his father, remained on the fireplace mantle in Thomas Byrnes's apartment for much of his life. It served as a constant reminder of the struggle his father had gone through. Byrnes would forever remember the day his father came home, fired from his job as a stitcher at the Whitman Garment factory.

James Byrnes railed that he could have shown the Whitman bosses how to beat the truth out of the culprits. His fists were clenched into tight balls. He threw his coat onto the broken chair next to the kitchen table, and it fell to the floor.

James Byrnes could thread a needle with his eyes closed. His hands never trembled. He worked quickly and all his work was impeccable. His former boss would hold up the elder Byrnes's work to the other stitchers in the factory as an example of how to properly line the sleeve of a topcoat.

He had labored at the factory his whole life in America and had never stolen a thing, James Byrnes ranted to his young son, his voice booming through the small apartment. Tears were welling up in the father's eyes. James explained to his son that someone had been stealing buttons at the shop.

The workers were told that if one of them didn't confess to stealing the buttons, they'd all get fired. James Byrnes spoke up. He told them it wasn't fair. He told them he had never stolen anything in his life. They wouldn't listen. They called him a socialist. A rabble-rouser. When no one confessed, they fired the lot of them. James Byrnes was without a job.

James raised his clenched fists and waved them at the kitchen ceiling, swearing at the factory owners, raging at whoever it was that stole the buttons and wouldn't confess. He swore that if he ever found out who it was, he'd kill the person for making him lose his job. He kicked the broken chair across the small room, and Thomas let out a shriek. Then James grabbed the chair, pulled it to the kitchen table, and sank down on it, burying his head in his hands, sobbing.

The harsh reality for Irish immigrants like James Byrnes was that their primary source of work was usually in the least-skilled, lowest-paying jobs New York City had to offer. They labored on the docks as longshoremen, in factories as unskilled workers, in hotels as porters, on the sea as boatmen, and as common laborers. They did the jobs that demanded physical strength. In 1854, two years after the Byrnes family had arrived in America, the major working group among New York's Irish population was made up of menial day laborers who earned about $1 for a ten-hour workday. Like James Byrnes, they worked six days a week and were glad to have a job.

Irish Emigration Society

A Society has recently been established in this City for the purpose of sending Westward destitute Irish families who have resided for some time in New York. It is the business of the Commissioners of Emigration to dispatch these emigrants to the interior who have recently arrived and are not inclined to remain in the City. The object of the present Society is to aid a different class, who are frequently in more need of assistance than those who have been only just landed on our wharves. There are many poor families in this City whose support is entirely dependent on the daily earnings of the parent, and, should sickness occur, or any accident throw him out of employment, the hardships which some families endure and the devices to obtain livelihood to which they must be driven, are very deplorable indeed . . . but once sunk in the slough of poverty, they are unable to extricate themselves and must perish—miserably perish there . . .

—*New York Times*
July 11, 1855

As a skilled garment worker, the elder Byrnes made $9 to $10 per week. But now it was all gone in one fell swoop. Someone at the factory had been pilfering buttons, and the owner wouldn't stand for it. Like any good businessman of the times, the boss kept track of even the most minute inventory, and he knew exactly how many buttons there should be for every one of his workers.

The work was not easy. Sewing was usually the province of Irish women in New York City, but some skilled men, like James Byrnes, managed to find employment in the garment factories. Many Irish women worked as seamstresses, milliners, dressmakers, shirt and collar makers, embroiderers, and pieceworkers in the factories and sweatshops. By the 1850s, 40 percent of all Irish women age fifteen to nineteen sewed or stitched for a living in the garment trade. The jobs were among the worst-paying in the city, since women occupied most of the positions, but someone of James Byrnes's caliber—a man who knew the tedious ins and outs of sewing—was a treasure for any garment business. James Byrnes had been a tailor in Ireland before fleeing his country for the New World. Still, he labored under poor conditions, with long hours, bad lighting, and demanding bosses, like the one who had fired him.

Six workers besides James Byrnes had been singled out as the culprits. The boss gave them all an ultimatum: If whoever stole the buttons came clean, only that person would suffer the consequences of being fired. If not, all seven stitchers would be given the boot.

"You won't get it out of them that way," Byrnes protested. "You got to make them confess. Beat it out of them."

Since none of the stitchers, six women and Byrnes, came forward to admit to the theft, they were all fired. If Byrnes couldn't find another job, he faced the prospect of having to accept charity or go to the poorhouse, neither of which were suitable alternatives for him to consider.

Young Thomas shook with fear—not of his father, but of the fate that he knew lay in store for him unless things changed.

Thomas Byrnes was born in Ireland in 1842. He was the older of two sons born to James and Ellen Byrnes. The Byrnes had two daughters as well. The Byrnes family immigrated to America in 1852. James Byrnes, his wife, two daughters, Kate and Molly, and two sons, Thomas and Deven, settled into one of the tenement houses in the notorious Five Points neighborhood. This dangerous area was the scene of a murder a night, according to police reports. Populated largely by the working-class Irish who had fled the Great Potato Famine, the dirty, dark streets were the home of prostitutes, thieves, and murderers. James Byrnes, a gentle man, was not about to let his sons and daughters be drawn into the lurid life of crime and violence that surrounded them. He kept close tabs on his children and, as a Catholic, depended upon the church for help and guidance in keeping his young ones from going astray. He made all four of his children attend daily Mass regardless of the weather. Thomas often had to share a topcoat with his younger brother on winter treks to the nearby church.

New York City had grown from a population of about forty thousand inhabitants in 1800 to a major metropolis of nearly a half-million people by 1852, the year the Byrnes family arrived.

The New York that the Byrneses settled into was actually five separate boroughs. It was not until a new charter was adopted in 1898 that the five boroughs were incorporated into the single metropolis now known as New York City. Brooklyn and Queens made up the western portion of Long Island, with Staten Island and Manhattan their own separate land masses. The Bronx, to the north, was attached to the New York State mainland.

The Byrnes family joined thousands of destitute immigrants huddled together in overcrowded, unsanitary slums like Five Points, which was named for the five points created by the intersection of Anthony, Orange, and Cross Streets. Poor immigrants arrived by the boatload and settled into this rat-infested, crime-ridden neighborhood. Although a predominantly Irish neighborhood, Germans, French, African Americans, and English also settled into Five Points.

More than 3,500 people populated a mere half-square-mile area. Garbage was discarded out of tenement windows and onto the streets, piling up so high that it surged over the tops of pedestrians' boots. Chamber pots were also emptied into the streets, producing vast lakes of human excrement and clouds of stinking odors. The stench permeated the streets and buildings.

Whole families of half-starved and sickly immigrants moved into decrepit tenements with names like Jacob's Ladder, Gates of Hell, and Mulberry Bend. Many of these families were fortunate to have a single room to live in. Others without families lived in boardinghouses that were nothing more than grimy dirt floors on which throngs of people slept on straw mattresses. They were charged inflated rates, and if they could not pay, their possessions were stolen from them.

Surviving in this environment of dire poverty meant that all members of the family had to try to earn a living by whatever means possible. Some were forced to resort to a life of crime or prostitution in order to survive. Alcoholism was rampant, and frequently children were left to fend for themselves, roaming the streets, joining criminal gangs, destined for a life of misery. During this time, nearly 75 percent of the children under the age of two died each year. Disease—typhus and cholera epidemics caused by unsanitary conditions—killed many of these poor immigrants and their children. Still others died from poor nutrition.

The Byrnes family settled into the steamy cesspool of Five Points, and young Thomas received his education on the mean streets of New York City. Thomas's mother, Ellen, made a little money doing laundry to help support the family. Since most tenements didn't have indoor plumbing, water had to be brought in for baths, washing clothes and dishes, or cleaning the apartment. If hot water was needed, it had to be heated on the stove. It became young Thomas's job to haul buckets of water up the six flights of stairs to their apartment, where his mother washed and ironed bedsheets and other laundry on consignment. In the summer when the weather permitted, the laundry was washed outside by the water pumps to save the labor of hauling it up and down dark tenement stairways. Under the best of conditions, the wet laundry was hung to dry on the roof or on clotheslines strung between buildings. But poor weather, water dripping from clothes on higher lines, pollution, falling refuse, and thieves frequently made it necessary to dry laundry in the kitchen. Ironing was done by heating several irons on the stove and then using them alternately as they cooled. It was hot and exhausting work for young Thomas, who was also assigned the responsibility of caring for his sickly brother, Deven, who was two years younger.

The Byrnes girls, Molly and Kate, did the housework and attended Mass regularly. They were not allowed to go out of the house unattended, and they kept to themselves, having no friends. In America, unlike Ireland, where women seldom worked once they were married, jobs sewing and doing laundry allowed young daughters and married women the chance to contribute to the family income. Despite the low pay, sewing was one of the few means women had to earn money. They performed piecework on a contract basis, for very little pay, and enlisted their children's help in finishing buttons and seams. Ellen Byrnes was already doing laundry as a way of earning extra income for the family.

After he was fired, James Byrnes thought about the possibility of taking in a boarder, but where would they all live? The tiny three-room apartment was barely enough for the Byrnes family.

Seeing his father break down in tears, filled with anger about his treatment, made young Thomas Byrnes promise himself that he would never suffer the same consequences. He vowed that, when he was old enough, he would get a job that no one could ever take from him—a job for life.

TENEMENT HOUSES
Full Statistics of Their Inmates
Human beings Crowded like Sheep into Pens
112 Families in One House

A committee of the Legislature having been appointed to visit the City to make examination as to the propriety of legislation in the matter of tenement houses, they have applied to the Mayor for information wherein to base their calculations. The Mayor accordingly issued a general order to the Police, requiring a report of "the legality, and street, and number of houses, of the most populous tenement in each patrol, district or ward." The returns have been received at the Central Office, excepting only that from the Eleventh Ward. . . . In the Fourth Ward there were reported 47, one of which, Capt. Ditchett remarks, (No. 38 Cherry street) when full has 112 families in it. . . . In the Seventh District are 65 front and 10 rear tenement houses, containing in the aggregate 1,232 families, averaging 16 families in each house. . . . Cherry-street has 233 families penned up in a dozen houses.

—*New York Times*
March 14, 1856

The dilapidated tenement where the Byrnes family lived was a brick building, six short stories high with a basement. Each of the six floors contained four three-room apartments, which were reached by an unlighted wooden staircase that ran through the center of the building.

Like the rest of the apartments in the building, the largest room in the Byrnes's flat was ten by twelve feet and served as the main living room. Ellen Byrnes called it simply the "big room." Behind it were a kitchen and one tiny bedroom. The entire apartment totaled about 325 square feet. Only the "big room" received direct light and ventilation from the two front windows facing the street. The other rooms were darkened by the closeness of the tenements on either side. The bedroom had casement windows, opening onto the hall. There was no toilet, no shower, and no bath—no direct source of water into the building. Several clapboard outhouses were located in the backyard. Luckily for the Byrnes family, the small apartment did have heat. The kitchen had a fireplace where they burned either coal or wood, depending on what James was able to get his hands on.

Garbage was thrown out in boxes set aside in front of the building. According to an 1856 *New York Tribune* article, these boxes were filled with ". . . potato-peelings, oyster-shells, night-soil, rancid butter, dead dogs and cats, and ordinary black street mud; [the garbage boxes formed] one festering, rotting, loathsome, hellish mass of air poisoning, death-breeding filth, reeking in the fierce sunshine, which gloats yellowly over it like the glare of a devil whom Satan has kicked from his councils in virtuous disgust."

Without running water, cleanliness for the Byrnes family and others like them was impossible. Sewage backed up in backyard privies, and rats ran wild through the muck and mire. Cholera epidemics broke out constantly. According to sociologists and historians, ". . . no Americans before or since have lived in worse conditions than the New York Irish of the mid-nineteenth century."

The illusion of America as the land of opportunity, hope, and family unity was shattered for most immigrants, the Irish especially. Thomas D'Arcy McGee, an exiled Irish political radical, wrote in *The Nation* in 1850: "In Ireland every son was a boy and a daughter a girl till he or she was married. They were considered subjects to their parents till they became parents themselves. In America boys are men at sixteen. . . . If [the] family tie is snapped, our children become our opponents and sometimes our worst enemies."

Under these conditions, family life for the Irish disintegrated. It was all James Byrnes could do to hold his family together. Until he was fired from his job, Byrnes was doing the best he could to maintain some normality in his family. But his untimely firing led quickly to the demise of family life as he had known it.

New York City had a booming hotel, restaurant, and entertainment business. There were opportunities for waiters and bartenders, and there was a plethora of Irish pubs and saloons where James Byrnes thought he might try to get a job. If he had a steady hand for threading a needle, he saw no reason that this same steady hand could not serve drinks and meals from a tray. Irish waiters and bartenders made about $5 a week. Because of the male-dominated Irish drinking culture, working-class saloons and restaurants were filled year-round. Many saloons offered a free lunch, usually of cold meat, pickles, tomatoes, and onions. Beer by the glass cost a nickel. James decided to try his luck at one of the many Irish saloons and restaurants on the Lower East Side.

Following the customs of their native land, Irish immigrants spent much of their time in saloons and pubs, which were informal clubs for them. Bartenders and waiters often served as their customers' spiritual, political, and social advisors. Irish owners hired their own countrymen whenever possible, realizing that their customers would feel most comfortable with people of their own background and heritage.

Opening a saloon was the peak of success for many Irish immigrants. The saloons were located in small cellars or in extravagant hotels. It didn't matter. These places lined the Bowery and Broadway, catering to working-class Irishmen. Successful saloonkeepers gained influence in Tammany Hall—the city's Democratic Party political machine—and sometimes became politicians, while politicians opened saloons with the profits they gained through graft and political bargaining. The fired James Byrnes, though, had no one to turn to within the political machinery of the city. The prospect of going to the city's poorhouse, of his family being separated, or of any of them being drawn into a life of crime or prostitution forced the otherwise-proud Byrnes to beg for work.

An estimated 2,000 prostitutes worked the streets in Five Points. They were called "nymphs of the pave," in the popular Irish slang known as "flash talk." Flash talk was the profanity-filled street lingo many Irish immigrants spoke to each other. Besides prostitution, alcoholism as well as addiction to opium and laudanum reached epidemic proportions in Five Points. Criminal gangs fought each other for control of the streets. The gangs robbed houses and small businesses and trafficked in stolen property. According to police records, over half the people arrested in New York City in the 1840s and 1850s were Irish. Police vans used to round up Irish criminals were christened "paddy wagons."

New York City's Irish seemed a lost community, mired in poverty and ignorance, destroying themselves through drink, idleness, violence, and criminality. They faced overt discrimination at every turn. Some native New Yorkers suggested the Irish were an inferior race.

Angered by the spectacle of social ruin, the opinion of native New Yorkers grew nastier, and prejudices that once might have been concealed were overtly expressed. Signs proclaiming NO IRISH NEED APPLY appeared in shop windows. Newspaper writers and cartoonists ridiculed the Irish in print. A former New York City mayor, George Templeton Strong, wrote in a city newspaper article that ". . . the gorilla is superior to the Celtic in muscle and hardly their inferior in a moral sense." In the same vein, *Harper's* in 1851 described the Irish as ". . . simian-like, with protruding teeth and short upturned noses." Celebrated cartoonist Thomas Nast constantly depicted the Irish as closely related to apes.

———•••••———

WANTED.—A smart active girl to do the general housework of a large family, one who can cook, clean plates, and get up fine linen, preferred. N. B.—No Irish need apply.

—*London Times*

February 1862

———•••••———

One of the only comforts the Irish found was in the Catholic Church and their religious beliefs. Like many before him, James Byrnes threw himself on the mercy of his parish priest, Father Patrick Coogan, who knew the plight Byrnes faced. Hundreds of his parishioners suffered the same dire circumstances. As luck would have it, Coogan was entertaining William F. X. O'Neill, a well-connected Tammany Hall insider who happened to own a small bar along Broadway. Coogan immediately advocated for Byrnes to O'Neill. Unable or unwilling to turn down the priest, O'Neill told Byrnes to report to his bar, The Billy Club, to begin work as a bartender the next day. Byrnes had been saved, or so he thought.

Although the job as a bartender provided the Byrnes family with an income, it was not nearly enough to survive on. James Byrnes was forced to let his two daughters look for work as domestic help, which he found demeaning. After sewing, domestic service was the most frequent form of employment for single Irish women. Native-born women shunned such service as too undignified, particularly as the Irish came to take over the field, while other immigrant groups did not wish their daughters to live away from home.

Neither Kate nor Molly Byrnes saw any social stigma in domestic service. By 1854, nearly 80 percent of all domestic help in New York City was Irish. The two girls quickly found jobs as servants, and both received free room and board in their employers' homes. They earned regular paychecks at rates much higher than factory work, allowing them to not only contribute to the family, but to save some money as well. With the two girls gone, the Byrneses' small apartment became almost livable.

Although the girls were paid well and given room and board, living in an employer's home proved to be restrictive. Kate experienced frequent tensions with the mistress of the home over the way she did the housework. Kate was able to hang on to her lucrative job by giving in to the sexual demands of the master of the house. The affair went undetected by the wife.

With James Byrnes working as a bartender, and his two daughters working in domestic service and contributing to the maintenance of their former home in Five Points, the financial situation at the Byrnes household stabilized, but more misery was looming on the horizon for them. Deven, the youngest son, was sick and not getting better.

The unsanitary and overcrowded conditions of the tenement slums were the leading contributing factor to outbreaks of disease in Five Points and other congested ethnic neighborhoods. Most native-born New Yorkers from the middle and upper classes blamed the immigrants for bringing disease to America, endangering the well-being of their innocent hosts. Whenever an epidemic broke out, the most convenient scapegoat was whatever immigrant group was the largest, most feared, and most visible at the time. Tuberculosis became known as a "Jewish disease." Polio was an "Italian disease." The cholera epidemics that broke out in Five Points were deemed an "Irish disease."

Young Deven Byrnes died of cholera at the age of eleven. He died in his father's arms, lying by the poorly lit kitchen stove. Thomas

Byrnes was thirteen years old. James Byrnes never recovered from the loss of his youngest boy. He began drinking heavily and missing work. Finally, one evening James never returned home from work. Thomas and his mother were left to fend for themselves.

Although Thomas was never formally schooled, he read a great deal, thanks to the continued support of Father Coogan of St. Patrick's Cathedral. Coogan lent Thomas many books from his personal library at the church rectory, and Thomas developed a voracious appetite for reading.

When Ellen Byrnes and her young son finally realized that James was never coming back home, Father Coogan intervened again, helping Thomas get a job in one of the firehouses, where he swept and cleaned and kept the fire wagons ready. It did not pay much, but with his two sisters working and his mother now employed full-time as a seamstress, they managed to get by.

The mushrooming of photographic establishments reflects photography's growing popularity. . . . In America the growth was just as dramatic: in 1850 there were 77 photographic galleries in New York alone . . .
—ROBERT LEGGAT, *A HISTORY OF PHOTOGRAPHY,* 1995

How charming it would be if it were possible to cause these natural images to imprint themselves durably and remain fixed on the paper!
—WILLIAM HENRY FOX TALBOT, 1839

Long after Thomas Byrnes moved from Five Points, he kept his father's picture with him, right there on the fireplace mantle. Photographs would come to play an important part in Byrnes's later life when he became the chief of detectives in New York City.

AMERICAN ALMANAC, 1863

Thomas Byrnes joined the Eleventh New York Volunteer Infantry Regiment in 1861. The regiment was nicknamed the "Zouaves." It was known for its unusual dress—bright jackets, baggy trousers with colorful sashes, and oriental headgear. The regiment was organized by Colonel Elmer E. Ellsworth, a close friend of President Abraham Lincoln's. Byrnes saw little combat during his two years of service in the Union Army. He joined the New York City Police Department as a patrolman following his discharge from the service in 1863. The war raged on for another two years with Lincoln serving as commander in chief.

President Abraham Lincoln issued the Emancipation Proclamation on January 1, 1863. The proclamation only applied to slaves living in the Confederate states and did not apply to slaves living in Union-controlled states or the Southern states that did not secede from the Union. Southerners viewed Lincoln's proclamation as an attempt to incite a slave rebellion in the South.

General Robert E. Lee won the most decisive battle for the Confederacy at the Battle of Chancellorsville in Virginia. Despite being outnumbered, Lee's troops inflicted approximately 17,000 casualties—deaths and injuries—on the Union forces, under the command of General Joseph Hooker. Lee's rebel forces suffered close to 13,000 casualties in the battle.

Stonewall Jackson, one of the Confederacy's most distinguished generals, was wounded during the Battle of Chancellorsville and died a few days afterward. It was a tremendous loss to the Confederate Army.

The Battle of Gettysburg was an enormous defeat for General Lee. Fresh from his victory at Chancellorsville, Lee made a desperate attempt to smash through the Union forces at Gettysburg, Pennsylvania. The Confederate forces suffered approximately 30,000 casualties during the battle, including soldiers who were killed, wounded, or missing in action, while the Union forces had approximately 23,000 casualties. Lee was forced to retreat south across the Potomac River after losing the battle at Gettysburg, marking the last time Lee and the Confederate Army fought a battle in Union territory.

The Gettysburg Address, a brief three-paragraph dedication, was delivered by President Abraham Lincoln in November 1863 to commemorate the bloody battle fought on Pennsylvania soil. Lincoln wrote the 272-word speech on the back of an envelope. Over the years Lincoln's brief address has continued to inspire Americans and is considered one of the greatest speeches of all time. In it Lincoln was able to articulate the costly price that must be paid for freedom. The Soldiers' National Cemetery at Gettysburg was created, and 3,577 Union troops who died in the Battle of Gettysburg are buried there. The identity of many of them remains unknown.

Four score and seven years ago our fathers brought forth on this continent, a new nation, conceived in Liberty, and dedicated to the proposition that all men are created equal.

Now we are engaged in a great civil war, testing whether that nation, or any nation so conceived and so dedicated, can long endure. We are met on a great battle-field of that war. We have come to dedicate a portion of that field, as a final resting place for those who here gave their lives that that nation might live. It is altogether fitting and proper that we should do this.

But, in a larger sense, we can not dedicate—we can not consecrate—we can not hallow—this ground. The brave men, living and dead, who struggled here, have consecrated it, far above our poor power to add or detract. The world will little note, nor long remember what we say here, but it can never forget what they did here. It is for us the living, rather, to be dedicated here to the unfinished work which they who fought here have thus far so nobly advanced. It is rather for us to be here dedicated to the great task remaining before us—that from these honored dead we take increased devotion to that

cause for which they gave the last full measure of devotion—
that we here highly resolve that these dead shall not have died
in vain—that this nation, under God, shall have a new birth of
freedom—and that government of the people, by the people,
for the people, shall not perish from the earth.

—GETTYSBURG ADDRESS

ABRAHAM LINCOLN

NOVEMBER 19, 1863

In October 1863, in the midst of the grueling and seemingly endless horrors of the Civil War, Lincoln issued a presidential proclamation declaring the traditional Thanksgiving observance as a national holiday to be commemorated each year on the fourth Thursday of November. Lincoln urged every American to give thanks on this day for their many blessings. Thomas Byrnes, who was serving as a New York City police officer, had much to be thankful for.

Thanksgiving was named as a national holiday by President Lincoln. The holiday was to be celebrated on the last Thursday in November. In 1939 President Franklin Roosevelt changed the date, and in 1941 Congress passed a resolution naming the fourth Thursday of November as Thanksgiving.

Sarah Josepha Hale was the driving force behind making Thanksgiving a national holiday. Hale, who was a successful novelist, editor, and children's poet, spent nearly forty years lobbying Congress and various presidents to establish a national day of thanks. Hale was a tireless crusader for women's rights, urging that women be given equal pay and job status in the workplace. She was also instrumental in raising money to help complete the Bunker Hill Monument in Boston. She was the first editor of the first women's magazine in America, and as the editor of *Godey's Lady's Book,* she helped turn it into one of the most successful magazines in the country with a circulation of 150,000. She wrote an abundant number of editorials in her campaign to have Thanksgiving Day declared a national holiday. Hale was also the author of the famous children's poem, "Mary Had a Little Lamb."

Mary had a little lamb,
little lamb, little lamb,
Mary had a little lamb, its fleece was white as snow.
And everywhere that Mary went,
Mary went, Mary went,
and everywhere that Mary went, the lamb was sure to go . . .
—"Mary Had a Little Lamb"
Sarah Josepha Hale, 1830

QUIPS & QUOTES

No human counsel hath devised, nor hath any mortal hand worked out these things. They are the gracious gifts of the Most High God, who, while dealing with us in anger for our sins, hath nevertheless remembered us in mercy.
—Abraham Lincoln

It is well that war is so terrible—lest we should grow too fond of it.
—Robert E. Lee

Let us cross over the river, and rest under the shade of the trees.
—Stonewall Jackson's dying words

If every state would join in Union Thanksgiving on the 24th of this month, would it not be a renewed pledge of love and loyalty to the Constitution of the United States?
—Sarah Josepha Hale

3

NEW YORK
UNDER SIEGE

In which Thomas Byrnes, as a new police officer, distinguishes himself during the New York City draft riots, when mobs go on the rampage for three straight days, burning buildings, looting stores, causing more than $3 million of property damage, and lynching a dozen African Americans. Byrnes rises through the ranks of the police force.

———

Thomas Byrnes was just twenty-one years old when he joined the New York City Police Department as a patrolman in 1863, just in time to help quell the New York City draft riots that July. Beginning on July 13, a mob of fifty thousand people, mostly Irish immigrants like Byrnes himself, banded together and terrorized the city for a full week, burning and looting stores, churches, and even an orphanage, attacking citizens, and lynching and killing a dozen blacks. The mob caused nearly $3 million of damage, four police officers were killed, and twelve hundred rioters were either killed or wounded. Eventually, President Lincoln was forced to send Union troops to restore order, and the troops stayed, encamped around New York City for several weeks.

———

QUIET AND ORDER UNIVERSAL ARRIVAL OF THE VERMONT BRIGADE MILITARY MOVEMENTS
Arrest of Prominent Ringleader.
FURTHER INCIDENTS OF THE LATE RIOTS

There were no indications in any position of the city yesterday of the return of the spirit of lawlessness. The Districts so recently and seriously incited were free from anything like an excitement, and all the indications are that law and order have returned in a way not again to be interrupted. Those who have participated in the riots have realized the horror of the struggle with the authorities and seen the folly of the conflicts. They are bringing good common sense to bear upon the distasteful question of the draft, and while their opposition to it is as dedicated as ever, and their denunciation bitter, threats of another resort to violence are but seldom heard, and when heard are not from those whose connection with the mob was from sympathy with its prejudices, but because of the opportunity it afforded them for murder and plunder. . . .

—*New York Times*
July 31, 1863

As his first official duty as a police officer, Thomas Byrnes was forced to align himself against a riotous faction of his own Irish immigrant brethren. It was not an assignment he relished any more than other Irish police officers at the time, but he carried out his orders loyally and systematically—a trait that would become part of his lifelong character.

Byrnes had grown into a formidable young man. He stood over six feet tall, was lean and spare, a mere cluster of bone and sinew, but strong as an ox and hardened by his life in the Five Points neighborhood. He was good-looking, with a high forehead and prominent cheekbones. He had a rugged-looking face, clean shaven except for the beginnings of what would become a handsome handlebar mustache that he wore all his life. His complexion was clear, his brown eyes sincere and bright. Between his good looks, impeccable manners, and outgoing personality, Byrnes had turned into a fine upstanding gentleman.

Although he had grown up in the midst of poverty and crime, Byrnes had developed no vices except for his love of cigars. He did not drink or carouse, and he did not gamble or engage in any sort of mischief, due in part to the watchful eye of his mother. At nineteen years old, Byrnes was appointed to the New York City Fire Department. Although it was a fairly safe and secure job, Byrnes had his

sights set on another line of work. He wanted to become a police officer. Every municipal job was controlled by Tammany Hall—especially
the Tammany chief Boss Tweed, who controlled all the municipal jobs
in the city by 1863. In order to get a job working for the city, job appli-
cants like Byrnes had to prove their worth by working for the political
bosses during elections. Byrnes was appointed to the New York City
police department in 1863.

———

Tammany Hall, started in 1789 for patriotic and fraternal purposes,
wedded the city's Democratic Party and the Society of St. Tammany.
The New York City Mayor's Office, the Democratic Party, and the Tammany Hall organization were intertwined. At the head of this intricate
political machine was William Marcy Tweed—Boss Tweed—a huge,
barrel-chested man who stood nearly six feet tall and weighed close to
three hundred pounds. Tweed started out as a bookkeeper and a volunteer fireman, and was later elected alderman. He progressed through
various municipal positions, secured control of the Seventh Ward in
the city's Lower East Side, and became the first "Boss of New York"
when he was crowned the grand sachem of Tammany Hall in 1863. By
1869, he was so powerful and had so many of his cronies—known as
the "Tweed Ring"—in political positions throughout the city that he
was able to control practically everything, including the city treasury.
It is estimated that, between 1865 and 1871, Boss Tweed and his gang
stole $30 million to $200 million from the city.

———

In his Emancipation Proclamation in September 1862, President Abraham Lincoln declared that the freeing of slaves would begin in January 1863. The historic announcement was not universally greeted
with approval. Lincoln's proclamation freed slaves in states that were
rebelling against the Union. Abolitionists across the country lauded
the proclamation. It brought official acknowledgment that the Civil
War was being fought, in part, for a cause other than saving the Union.
But even as far back as Lincoln's election in 1860, the Democratic

Party had warned the Irish and German immigrants in New York City that freeing the slaves would result in fewer jobs. For the Irish, Lincoln's Emancipation Proclamation spelled doom—a potential influx of new laborers to an already-distressed job market. Why would an Irish immigrant risk his life fighting for a future such as that? Then came the March 1863 draft law, which required that all men between the ages of twenty and thirty-five and all unmarried men between thirty-five and forty-five years of age be subject to being drafted into the Union military. Meanwhile, slaves were exempt from the draft because they were not considered American citizens.

As the names of eligible men were entered into a draft lottery, a surge of antiwar sentiment flooded the newspapers. Writers and editors condemned Lincoln and his Republican administration for intruding into local practices in order to fight what many decried as "the nigger war."

The first military draft in New York City was held on Saturday, July 11, 1863, and the names of the draftees were published in the newspapers. At first nothing happened and the city breathed a sigh of relief, but it was too soon. Within a day, groups of irate citizens, most of them Irish immigrants, banded together across the city, forming an angry, bloodthirsty mob. Eventually almost fifty thousand people terrorized city neighborhoods and descended on military and government buildings. Roving mobs attacked anyone—police, soldiers, or civilians—who tried to stop them. Later on the first day of the riots, the angry mobs began to randomly attack black people.

Newly appointed police officer Thomas Byrnes, along with a new police recruit, Jimmy Williams, was assigned to mob control as part of a large police action on Fifth Avenue between Forty-third and Forty-fifth Streets at the site of the Orphan Asylum for Colored Children. Police were certain that the orphan asylum would be a target of the rioters, and they were right. Hundreds of angry immigrants made their way toward the asylum, where they would be confronted by Byrnes, Williams, and a dozen other police officers stationed outside the building.

One angry mob, in another part of the city, attacked police superintendent John A. Kennedy. The sixty-year-old superintendent had learned through operatives that something was brewing in the city because of the draft lottery, and he immediately began to shore up his police force. Altogether Kennedy arranged for sixty uniformed police officers under his command to surround police headquarters, positioning some in front of the building and some inside. The crowds throughout the city were growing by the minute, and so extra police details were sent to guard City Hall and the various marshals' offices throughout the city. But the meager police presence was not enough to stem the tide.

Another mob attacked the marshals' office on Third Avenue, overrunning police and staff and setting fire to the building. The fire department arrived as soon as the flames were lapping the sky. The mob tried to stop firemen from dousing the fire, causing two adjacent buildings to go up in flames as well.

Hearing of the conflagration, Kennedy made his way across town in his personal carriage. Kennedy was unarmed and dressed in his civilian clothes as he sped across the city to inspect the damage. He was forced to leave his carriage farther up the street because crowds and firefighting apparatus clogged his passage. Someone in the hostile mob recognized Kennedy, and before he had a chance to defend himself, a dozen men seized him, viciously punching and kicking him. Kennedy was knocked to the ground but somehow managed to get back on his feet. He took off, running down an embankment into a vacant lot pursued by an angry crowd chanting, "Kennedy! Kennedy!" When the first gang of rioters didn't follow him into the empty lot, Kennedy thought he was safe. He wasn't. Another crowd, as brutal and intent on doing him harm as the first, suddenly appeared and set upon him. Kennedy struggled to protect his head from the onslaught of blows. Miraculously he managed to escape this mob as well, running toward Lexington Avenue, where he hoped he might find refuge in the police station.

Kennedy had outdistanced his pursuers, but dazed and injured, he stumbled and fell face-first into a pool of muddy water that covered much of the street where the roadway had caved in. He struggled to get up, fearing he might drown. In a mad frenzy the mob cried,

"Drown the bastard! Drown him!" Things might have ended badly for the superintendent if the mob had decided to follow him into the muck and mire of the huge city pothole. They didn't. Luckily for Kennedy, a young police officer, newly sworn in and headed for duty, happened on the scene. Although young Thomas Byrnes didn't know that the man struggling in the water was his superintendent, he waded into the muddy water to rescue Kennedy. With his revolver drawn and trained on the mob at the far end of the pothole, Byrnes lifted Kennedy to his feet and led him to safety.

Still not knowing the identity of the man he had just saved, Byrnes elicited the help of the first person he found on Lexington Avenue, who happened to be John Eagan, a prominent New Yorker. Although he knew Kennedy personally, he didn't recognize the dirty, battered, and bleeding man that Byrnes was supporting. Knowing his civic duty, Eagan, with the help of Byrnes, was able to get Kennedy onto the back of a wagon and have him taken to police headquarters. Byrnes left Kennedy in the care of Eagan before proceeding to his assigned duty.

It wasn't until he arrived at police headquarters that Eagan realized the man he had helped was his friend. A doctor was immediately called, and Kennedy's wounds were treated. No bones were broken, but Kennedy suffered a large gash on his head. Gaining his composure, Kennedy thanked Eagan for saving him from the crowd. Eagan was quick to inform the injured Kennedy that it was one of his own police officers who had saved him. But Eagan did not immediately know the young man's name. Kennedy, lucky to be alive, swore he would find out who the police officer was and reward him generously.

With Superintendent Kennedy out of commission because of his injuries, the direction of the police department fell squarely on the shoulders of police commissioner William Acton and police inspector Daniel Carpenter. Acton decided to run the central command out of headquarters for the duration of the riots, while Carpenter took control of the field operations. Both men were later commended for their devotion to duty during the riots.

After the Kennedy incident, Byrnes joined his police detail guarding the Orphan Asylum for Colored Children on Fifth Avenue. The four-story asylum was large enough to care for more than two hundred children. The building was well stocked with food, clothing, and other necessary provisions. To the rioters it was a symbol of white generosity toward blacks and another cruel example of blacks usurping their political and economic power. There were 233 children in the building when the angry mob descended.

Armed with clubs, shovels, and bats, the infuriated mob stormed through the police barrier, swinging wildly at the police officers, knocking some to the ground, and stampeding over them. Byrnes was kicked and punched but managed to stay on his feet, even if he wasn't able to stop the advancing horde. His friend and fellow police officer, Alexander Williams, who was also of Irish descent, had willingly stepped aside when the mob surged forward. Williams didn't have a scratch on him, but Byrnes took his bruises because he had orders to follow, and he would follow them to the letter of the law.

Once they broke through the meager police barrier, the rioters stormed into the building and looted it of everything not tied down. They stole food, clothing, and medicine. Several of them set the building on fire. By then teachers and nurses at the orphanage had herded the children into the basement, hoping to escape the mob.

As the building went up in flames, firefighters vainly tried to save it, but even they were hampered by the throngs of angry rioters. The destruction only took twenty minutes. The orphan asylum burned to the ground, but not before Byrnes, in a heroic and dangerous effort, led the 233 children who were cowering in the basement to safety. The rioters didn't attack the children. According to a newspaper account, when someone at the scene tried to assist Byrnes in helping the children out of the burning building, several members of the mob grabbed him and appeared ready to tear him to pieces. They probably would have, had Byrnes not intervened. Byrnes pulled his revolver from his holster and fired several shots in the air. When one rioter started toward Byrnes with a club, Byrnes pointed his gun straight at the man's forehead and warned the man that he would shoot him first, even if the others managed to get him.

The man stopped in his tracks. He immediately recognized Byrnes from the neighborhood and threatened to remember him. Byrnes stood his ground, telling the rioter that he would remember him too when the riots were all over. Byrnes stared the bat-wielding man down with a steely gaze that told the rioter that, even if they knew each other, and even if they were both Irish, Byrnes had a job to do, and if it involved shooting the man, he would. The rioter fled, disappearing into the crowd and smoke that engulfed Fifth Avenue.

Byrnes was able to lead the poor frightened children to the Thirty-fifth Street police station, where he hoped they would be safe. Byrnes left before anyone connected to the orphanage could thank him. The children, burned out of their home, stayed at the police station for three days. When the rioting was quelled, they were taken to the safety of the almshouse on Blackwell's Island. Ironically, the purpose of the orphanage had been to prevent orphaned black children from ending up at that very almshouse.

The mob went wild throughout the city, attacking men who were sympathetic to blacks and even women who were married to black men. Along the waterfront, a gang of one thousand rioters attacked two hundred black longshoremen. A majority of the longshoremen managed to defend themselves or hide until the police arrived to break up the melee, but not before the mob had killed five. The mob hanged William Jones and burned his body. They nearly beat to death and almost drowned Charles Jackson. Jeremiah Robinson was beaten to death, and his mangled body was thrown into the East River. What happened to the other two victims is not known.

A VICTIM OF THE NEW YORK MOB

A colored man, whose name is unknown, came to the premises of MR. LANSING, a farmer living near Cohoes, Thursday night, and represented that he had been set upon by the mob in New-York, and severely injured. He asked permission of MR. LANSING to sleep in his barn, which was granted. On going into the barn yesterday morning, MR. LANSING discovered the poor

Negro lying upon a bundle of straw, dead. On examining the
body, it was found that it had been stabbed in various places,
and how the man lived long enough to get to Cohoes, was the
wonderment of everybody. CORONER BRENNAN held an inquest.

—*Albany Times*,
July 21, 1863

Moving across the city, the white mob assaulted black men of every
profession. Rioters destroyed whorehouses, saloons, and tenements
that accommodated blacks. They also made a sport of mutilating the
black men's bodies, sometimes sexually. A group of white men and
boys assaulted a black sailor, stomping on his body and finally plung-
ing a knife into his chest. White men, women, and children watched
the mob kill the sailor, but not one of them interceded, fearing for their
own lives. According to a newspaper account, one unnamed rioter
vowed to seek revenge "on every nigger in New York."

Black coachman Abraham Franklin was randomly chosen and
dragged from his small tenement apartment and paraded down the
street. The mob strung Franklin up from a lamppost and left the life-
less body hanging there with a noose around his neck.

Another black man, James Costello, kept the mob at bay by defending himself with a gun. After emptying six shots into the crowd of men
who were pursuing him, a gang of men and boys finally subdued him.
More than a dozen men punched and kicked Costello, pelting him
with stones and finally hanging him.

White laborers declared their dominance over black workers and
citizens through the riots. Because of the Civil War, the military draft,
Lincoln, and the Republican Party's rise to power, the mostly poor
Irish Democratic workers viewed their jobs, homes, and livelihood as
being ripped out from beneath them. Black men were not their equals,
no matter what Lincoln proclaimed. They set out to prove it through
mob violence.

After the destruction of the Orphan Asylum for Colored Children,
Officer Byrnes was reassigned to keep peace in his own Five Points

neighborhood with a contingent of fellow police officers. Byrnes was happy to be heading back to his home turf. He knew every avenue and street, back alley and dive in the neighborhood. He also knew most if not all the black men and their families who lived in Five Points. He was intent on protecting them from the mob. Five Points remained comparatively quiet throughout the riots. No mobs destroyed any buildings, nor did they harm or kill any black people there.

The most violent neighborhood in New York City turned out to be the least violent during the draft riots, and it had nothing to do with the police presence sent there to keep order.

When rioters took aim at a black drugstore owner in Five Points, his Irish neighbors defended him and scattered the angry mob. When a gaggle of bloodthirsty rioters became lost and found themselves trapped on a dead-end street, both black and white men and women living in the tenements alongside the dead end poured boiling water and oil on them, making the rioters flee for their lives. It turned out to be easy duty for young Byrnes, and he was thankful for it.

In the end, after five days of rioting, the mob had lynched a dozen black men. Hundreds of blacks were driven out of New York City. In lower Manhattan, rioters attacked and set fire to Horace Greeley's *New York Daily Tribune*, the city's most pro-Republican newspaper. They ransacked the homes of wealthy citizens, which the mob imagined were owned by Republicans. Rioters continued to attack the outnumbered police force, not only because the police tried to control the mobs, but also because the rioters assumed that the police department was connected to the Republican Party. The mob singled out the Brooks Brothers store in lower Manhattan because the rioters decided it was the principal clothier for the city's richest and most prominent citizens. Brooks Brothers also made uniforms for the Union Army. The store was looted and nearly destroyed.

Buildings and businesses throughout the city were besieged because they symbolized the Republican Party's interests and because they represented the city's wealthiest and most privileged citizens. The mob also attacked and destroyed draft offices and the homes of police officers and businessmen. A band of rioters even burned the

Armory on Second Avenue because it represented the military draft instituted by President Lincoln. The Armory was burned in such a state of frenzy that several rioters became trapped in the blazing building and ultimately died in the fire they had set.

Finally, after five days of mob chaos and violence, Lincoln ordered more than four thousand federal troops to occupy the city and quell the rioting. Although the troops managed to bring some semblance of order, there were still sporadic outbreaks of violence. Police and army regiments occupied the city streets and drove the mobs into retreat.

Thomas Byrnes and his police unit were reassigned from the relatively calm Five Points neighborhood to a cavalry unit commanded by Colonel Thaddeus Mott. The Fourteenth New York Cavalry marched through the downtown streets with police officers on foot, patrolling the sidewalks and doorways and alleys, rousting and arresting rioters. On the last day of rioting, the contingent of cavalry and police marched along Twenty-second Street. Out of one alley sprang a mob armed with bats, shovels, and anything it could use to inflict damage. The mob descended on the military unit, but the soldiers were able to beat back the attackers. Colonel Mott, hoping to round up the rioters, ordered several of his men who remained on horseback to split up and pursue the angry crowd as it divided and ran in different directions. Byrnes, who had come to know the mob's tactics over the past five days of fighting, advised his commanding officer that pursuing the men down dark alleys and side streets on horseback was useless and dangerous.

Mott's soldiers deployed down the small alleys and narrow side streets on horseback, and just as Byrnes had warned, one of Mott's men, Sergeant Charles Davids, was jumped by a band of rioters who had been hiding in the dark cubbyholes and entranceways along an alley. They knocked Davids off his horse and beat him to death before reinforcements could arrive to help.

Mott sent a unit of infantrymen into the alley to retrieve Davids's body. As they tried to carry the body out, they were attacked by an even larger mob. This time, with the help of armed police officers, Byrnes among them, they drove the rioters off, sending them running toward Thirty-first Street, where they took refuge in a series of homes.

There they tried to fortify their positions using mattresses and furniture to secure doors and windows, but the volley of gunfire from the federal troops and police was too much for them. Byrnes, along with several other police officers, stormed one barricaded house only to discover the rioter inside had taken his own life rather than be taken prisoner. Slowly, one by one, the rioters surrendered, coming out of the houses with their arms raised.

The battle on Thirty-first Street, and the rounding up of the rioters, was the final significant melee in the ravaged city. There were skirmishes during the weeks that followed, but for the most part, the mob's back had been broken and the city began to lick its wounds.

THE DRAFT AND THE RIOTS

There is no doubt that the riot was a cause of great rejoicing to our enemies, whether in our midst, or at the South, or abroad. Coming as it did, right in the midst of the news of Gettysburgh, Vicksburgh, Port Hudson, and Charlestown, they all clutched at it most eagerly to save their drowning hopes. They affected to believe, perhaps did believe, that this was the commencement of a movement which should put a stop to the draft everywhere. The London *Times* stated, as rejoicing as it could, in the midst of such disasters, that if the draft was suspended in this City, it would be 'hopeless to enforce it.'—whatever that may mean, and added: 'If MR LINCOLN can only recruit his armies by conscription, and the conscription fails, his Government will have collapsed at the very crisis of its policy. The hopelessness of the enterprise is never more evident than at a time when it seems most promising.' The *Times* was mistaken, of course. The suspension of the draft here did not involve the slightest delay in it throughout the country. The President and the people, as it will find, had and have no idea of allowing the Government 'to collapse at the crisis of its policy,' and the [London] *Times* will have again to eat its own words and make lame excuses for false prophecies. . . . Within a month after its occurrence fifteen or twenty of the rioters were already undergoing the sentence of the law by imprisonment for periods up to fifteen years, and that about a hundred more were under indictment. . . . The [London] *Times* will be prepared for the announcement that the draft has been carried out in New York without disturbance. . . .

New York Times
August 15, 1863

———

Draft rioters had killed eighteen men, a dozen of whom were black. Four police officers were reported to have been slain, including one who was accidentally killed by federal troops while trying to quell the riots. Approximately twelve hundred of the rioters had been killed or injured. Altogether, more than eight thousand innocent New York citizens were injured, and countless others were reported missing, either dead or having fled the city.

More than fifty buildings were burned, including the Orphan Asylum for Colored Children and two police stations. Countless stores and businesses had been ransacked and looted. Close to $3 million in damages and losses were reported. Only twenty rioters were brought to justice despite a hundred more being placed under indictment. Nineteen of the twenty rioters charged were convicted and imprisoned. None of the nineteen were ever charged with the lynching of the twelve black men. The average sentence for the convicted men was five years.

New York City mayor George Opdyke issued a proclamation praising the police action and hailing the end to the vicious rioting that had gripped the city for five tumultuous days.

"The riotous assemblages have been dispersed, business is running in its usual channels. The various lines of omnibuses, railway, and telegraph have resumed their ordinary operations. Few signs of turmoil remained, except in a small district in the eastern part of the city, comprising a part of the Eighteenth and Twenty-first Wards. The police is everywhere alert. A sufficient military force is now here to suppress any illegal movement, however formidable," Opdyke said.

"Be assured that the public authorities have the ability and the will to protect you from those who have conspired alike against your peace, against the government of your choice, and against the laws which your representatives have enacted," he concluded.

Draft riots like the one that took place in New York City had happened in cities throughout the North, but New York's riots were the most brutal and the most widely publicized. The popular Democratic governor of the state, Horatio Seymour, who had openly reviled President Lincoln's policies and the war, expressed his deep concern in the aftermath of the rioting, but even then he refused to give Lincoln's federal troops credit for ending the riots.

"Let all citizens stand firmly by the constituted authorities, sustaining law and order in the city, and ready to answer any such demands as circumstances may render necessary for me to make upon their services, and they may rely upon a rigid enforcement of the laws of this State against all who violate them. . . . In the sad and humiliating history of this event, it is gratifying that the citizens of New York, without important aid from the State or Nation, were able of themselves to put down this dangerous insurrection," Governor Seymour said.

Before the riots, the city's black population was more than twelve thousand. The numbers fell below ten thousand immediately following the incident, as black residents fled the city in droves. Of those who remained, many were now without homes or jobs, and lived in temporary and makeshift housing, including staying at police stations throughout the city. Some white landlords and business owners drove blacks out of their homes and jobs, frightened that they would become targets of reprisals by other whites. Even in the year following the riots, white businesses and landlords refused to rent to or hire blacks.

Attempts to rebuild the former Orphan Asylum for Colored Children at its original site were stopped because abutting businesses feared their property would be targeted for arson. The orphanage that police patrolman Thomas Byrnes had tried to defend was forced to rebuild at 143rd Street in Harlem, which later became New York's predominantly black neighborhood.

All in all, Byrnes had handled himself admirably during the riots. His keen sense of observation and his dedication to duty did not go unnoticed. After joining the police force as a patrolman in 1863, Byrnes rose through the ranks; he became a sergeant in 1869 and was promoted to captain in July 1870. He was just twenty-eight years old.

Even with his promotion to the rank of captain, Byrnes was still living at home with his mother in the same run-down tenement apartment in Five Points. Although his salary had increased from $1,200 a year as patrolman to $1,600 as sergeant and then to $2,000 as captain, it still was not enough for Byrnes to support himself and his elderly mother in a nicer section of the city. Both his sisters, Kate and Molly, were married and settled and did not require any assistance from him. Still, as the head of the family, with his father long since gone, Byrnes kept a watchful eye on his sisters and their well-being. A devoted Catholic, Byrnes remained a faithful parishioner at St. Patrick's Cathedral on Prince Street and attended Mass there daily, often bringing his mother when the sickly old woman felt up to it.

Unlike many of his contemporaries in the police force, Byrnes did not seek out or take bribes from saloon owners, houses of prostitution, politicians, or criminals, to look the other way. He remained an anomaly—an honest cop—during this period in the city's history. New York was a veritable nest of political corruption, graft, bribes, and payoffs at all levels of city government, including the police ranks.

William Marcy "Boss" Tweed and his political cronies ran New York City from the early 1860s until November 1872, when he was finally convicted of 204 charges of fraud and sentenced to twelve years in prison. Tweed and his "Tammany Hall Ring" of political hacks and insiders stole an estimated $30 million to $200 million from the city coffers during their reign of greed and corruption. Tweed is still considered one of the most notorious politicians in U.S. history.

———

Focusing on the saloon, the brothel, and the gambling den, [Lincoln] Steffens soon discovered that the police were involved in a ring of corruption. But he drew distinctions. Although the average policeman participated in the corruption they were, to Steffens, not responsible for it. The evil resided, instead, in the "system" and those who controlled it. The police "protected" illegal activities and received a percentage of the illicit profit from vice, prostitution, and gambling as a reward. This was the "price" criminals paid for police corruption. But beyond the police force were the political machine and its political allies in both the Democratic and Republican parties. These political leaders and their legions of followers dealt in the spoils of office, and the profits of vice and were responsible for the corruption of the city, its politics, and its police.

—FROM *AMERICAN REFORMERS: 1870–1920: PROGRESSIVES IN WORD AND DEED* BY STEVEN L. PIOTT

One of the most notable examples of police corruption during the 1870s was found in New York City's "Tenderloin District." Under the command of the much-decorated Captain Alexander S. Williams, the Twenty-ninth Precinct, with its station house at 137 and 139 West Thirtieth Street, encompassed Seventh Avenue, Forty-second Street, Park Avenue, Fourth Avenue, Union Square, and Fourteenth Street. Within the district were the most exclusive and expensive hotels, restaurants, theaters, clubs, gambling parlors, stores, and other amusements that made up the city's glittering nightlife—all of them paying a substantial financial tribute to their police protectors and to Boss Tweed's political machine.

When Captain Williams was given command of the district, no one knew how involved he was in police corruption. Williams had joined the police force at the same time as Byrnes, and the two men had become close friends over the years. Williams earned the nickname "Clubber" because of his ruthless tactics when dealing with street thugs. "Clubber" Williams once beat up two street thugs singlehandedly with his billy club and tossed the culprits through a plate-glass window. Later when Byrnes was appointed chief inspector of the Detective Bureau, he frequently called upon his friend's talents to elicit information from criminal suspects.

In 1894, during hearings held by a select committee investigating New York City police corruption, the Lexow Committee, Williams denied any involvement in the flagrant extortion and bribes uncovered within the Twenty-ninth Precinct, despite corroboration from other officers that Williams had received hush money from various gambling houses and brothels. The committee questioned Williams about how he managed to acquire a luxurious home in a fashionable Connecticut neighborhood and a yacht, all on a police captain's paltry salary of $2,500 a year. Williams smugly told the committee he had made some investments in Japan that had paid off handsomely.

During questioning Williams did admit that he had coined the term *Tenderloin District* to describe the Twenty-ninth Precinct. According to Williams, "When I was transferred from the Fourth Precinct to the Twenty-ninth, I told a newspaper reporter that I had been eating rump steak down in the Fourth Precinct and that I would have a chance now to eat some of the tenderloin." Williams would now be able to solicit bribes from more and much wealthier businesses.

When asked what he meant by his statement, Williams claimed he was only referring to the better class of hotels and restaurants located within the district. Following the investigation by the Lexow Committee, Williams was forced to resign his police commission rather than face trial on charges of corruption.

Williams wore a gold police badge with the inscription: PRESENTED TO CAPTAIN ALEXANDER S. WILLIAMS, IN ACKNOWLEDGMENT OF HIS VALUABLE AID IN SUPPRESSING THE ROUGHS AND DEFENDING HIS OFFICERS IN THE DISCHARGE OF THEIR DUTIES. NEW YORK, SEPTEMBER 16, 1872.

———•◦•———

The taint of corruption that permeated the New York City Police Department did not reach Captain Thomas Byrnes, despite increasing pressures for him to let it. It was difficult to support his sickly mother and himself on a captain's $2,000-a-year salary, and he was surrounded by fellow officers who freely accepted bribes from legitimate businesses for protection, as well as from criminals wishing to operate unencumbered by police presence. Byrnes managed to maintain his integrity, at least during his early years on the force.

Byrnes was a constant fixture at the Fifteenth Precinct. Tall and broad-shouldered, with a drooping mustache, and a burning cigar ever present in his mouth, Byrnes reported to work early and left late. He was an impeccable dresser and kept his uniform in immaculate condition. Like all captains on the force, Byrnes was issued one uniform, which included a dark blue, wool, double-breasted frock coat with a stand-up collar and two rows of eight gold buttons down the front. The collar and cuffs were made of dark blue velvet. Pinned to his chest on the left side of the coat and at a precise distance from the row of gold buttons was his gold badge, with his rank and precinct embossed onto it.

Beneath the frock coat, he wore a starched white shirt and a single-breasted, dark blue wool vest, plain black trousers, and white gloves. Byrnes's uniform was topped off with a navy blue cap with gold wreath braiding above the visor and along the sides. Inside the wreath in the center of the cap were embroidered in gold, CAPTAIN, and below it, also in gold, FIFTEENTH PRECINCT. Byrnes never showed up at work without his pants expertly creased, his black boots shined, and his frock coat pressed. He was an icon of police style and decorum.

Author Julian Hawthorne, the son of Nathaniel Hawthorne, described Byrnes as ". . . a handsome man, large and powerful in every sense of the word. His head is well-shaped, with a compact forehead, strong nose, and resolute mouth and chin, shaded with a heavy mustache. His figure is erect, his step light, his bearing easy and alert. His eyes are his most remarkable feature. They are set rather close together in his head, increasing the concentration of his gaze. . . . His voice is melodious and agreeable, but he often seems to speak between his teeth, and when aroused his utterance acquires an impressive energy. His good humor and temper make him attractive, but when need is he can be as severe and unrelenting as Rhadamanthus himself."

In Greek mythology, Rhadamanthus was the son of Zeus and Europa. Rhadamanthus became so superior in his judgment of law that he served as one of the three judges in the underworld. Ironically,

Julian Hawthorne would write several popular detective books with Thomas Byrnes as the main character before running afoul of the law himself in 1913 when, as the president of Hawthorne Silver and Iron Mines, he and three other men were charged with defrauding the public and misuse of the United States Postal Service. According to the charges, Hawthorne and the other men secured funds from false mining shares, grossing more than $3.5 million. Found guilty, Hawthorne served a year in prison.

————

CONVICT THREE MEN IN HAWTHORNE CASE

Jury Finds Son of Novelist, Dr. W.
J. Morton, and Albert Freeman
Guilty of Mining Frauds
Acquits Ex-Mayor Quincy
Hawthorne and Morton Sentenced to
A year and a Day from Nov. 25,
1912—Five Years for Freeman.

Julian Hawthorne, son of the novelist, who has attained prominence as a writer himself; Dr. William J. Morton, son of the discoverer of ether, and a nerve specialist, and Albert Freeman, a promoter, were found guilty in the Federal District Court of having used the mails to defraud in connection with mines in Canada. Josiah Quincy, twice Mayor of Boston, and Assistant Secretary of State under President Cleveland, who was tried with them, was acquitted. . . .

Some surprise was expressed that Quincy was acquitted, and Hawthorne said:

"I was willing to take a fighting chance and to stand or fall with my associates. It seems to me the indictments should have been interlocking and we should have been all found guilty or all acquitted. . . ."

Meanwhile Dr. Morton talked rapidly and nervously of what he called the "anesthesia curse."

"I am not surprised," he said. "All my life I have expected some terrible misfortune, and after the way the American people treated my father, it is not strange that something terrible should happen to his son. The American nation allowed my father to die penniless at 48, and I had to take care of his family."

—*New York Times*
March 15, 1913

Following his release from prison, Hawthorne published a blistering attack on the American judicial system called *The Subterranean Brotherhood*.

Byrnes's swift ascension through the ranks was propelled by his hard work, vigilance, and his incredible attention to detail, all of which boded well for him in solving a slew of cases. During his rise to captain, Byrnes had put together an impressive record of arrests of shoplifters, fences, pickpockets, murderers, and any other assortment of thugs and lowlifes.

Perhaps his most astounding police work came in 1874 when he tracked down and arrested murderer William Jones in Philadelphia. Jones was a small-time assassin for hire, and for the paltry sum of six cents was hired to murder an unidentified stranger at The Crown flophouse along the waterfront. Although Jones had left no clues at the murder scene, Byrnes's interrogation of several known criminals staying at The Crown revealed his identity and the fact that Jones was known to hire out as a fisherman. He had been drunkenly boasting about a job he had coming up on an oyster boat. Byrnes knew that the New York waterfront, although swarming with fishing boats, was not particularly invested in oyster fishing. In the early part of the century, oyster beds flourished in and along the city's waterways. For the most part oysters were cheap and mostly eaten by the lower classes. It wasn't until the oyster beds began to dry up and the demand for them grew that they were considered a delicacy. Byrnes interrogated several fishermen along the waterfront, and none of them knew of any oyster-fishing vessels leaving the port. He knew through his reading (Byrnes had two addictions—cigars and reading—he was an avid reader of anything and everything) that the Delaware Bay oyster was a prized delicacy in and around Philadelphia.

Taking a train to Philadelphia, Byrnes scoured the waterfront, pretending to look for someone who might want to make a few dollars to "rough someone up" for him. He was immediately directed to one of the fishing boats, an oyster boat, still in port, where he was introduced to William Jones. Jones boasted to Byrnes that he would do more than just "rough someone up" if Byrnes so desired. Byrnes said he wasn't sure he could trust Jones, and the prideful Jones told him outright that he'd just killed someone in New York City and had gotten clean away with it. Not clean away, Byrnes told him, handcuffing the startled Jones. Jones was brought back to New York, stood trial, was found guilty, and was sentenced to life in prison. The running joke around the Fifteenth Precinct after Jones's arrest was that Captain Thomas Byrnes sure knew his oysters.

———————

The Fifteenth Precinct station house was at 251 and 253 Mercer Street. It had once been a residence but was transformed into a police station. The precinct included the Bowery, Broadway, Fourth and Sixth Avenues, and Bleecker, Carmine, Fourteenth, Hancock, and Houston Streets. Eighty-one police officers, including patrolmen and officers like Byrnes, were assigned to the precinct.

The precinct was made up of every walk of life from the poor and destitute to the entitled rich—the respectable to the despicable. It had an array of boardinghouses, saloons, banks, hotels, theaters, brothels, high-end stores, libraries, and churches. By 1870, when Byrnes was promoted to captain at the Fifteenth Precinct, the population of New York City had soared to approximately one million people. Accordingly, at the time an estimated two thousand police officers were assigned throughout the metropolitan area. The ratio of police to population was 1:470.

Before being permanently assigned to the Fifteenth Precinct, Byrnes did brief stints at the Twenty-first and Twenty-third Precincts. He was assigned to the Fifteenth Precinct until he was promoted to the position of detective in 1880.

One of the city's most luxurious hotels, the Grand Central Hotel, was located within the Fifteenth Precinct. The largest retail store in the world, A. T. Stewart's, was also in the precinct. And one of the wealthiest banks, the Manhattan Savings Institution, was there as well. All three places would play a role in Byrnes's rise to power within the New York City Police Department.

In January 1872, Ned Stokes shot and killed James Fisk Jr., one of the wealthiest and most flamboyant Wall Street investors, in broad daylight at the Grand Central Hotel on Broadway. Stokes was a business partner of Fisk's. Captain Byrnes tackled the case.

Alexander Turney Stewart was one of the wealthiest retail merchants in the world when he died in 1876. In 1878, grave robbers broke into Stewart's grave, stole his body, and held it for ransom, demanding $200,000 from Stewart's widow, Cornelia. Captain Byrnes investigated the gruesome crime.

Also in 1878, the Manhattan Savings Institution was robbed of approximately $3 million during one of the city's most sensational capers. Byrnes would set off in search of the bank robbers.

The New York City Police Department was created in 1844 with the passage of the Municipal Police Act. A police force of an estimated eight hundred men began to patrol the city's streets under the leadership of the first chief of police, George W. Matsell. Officers wore copper stars pinned on their coats that were inscribed with the seal of the city.

The force was organized along the hierarchy of a military command, including patrolmen, sergeants, captains, and detectives, with the head of the force being the chief. The chief of police was answerable to the city's police commissioners, who comprised the mayor of the city, the city recorder, and an appointed judge.

In 1857 the New York legislature passed the Metropolitan Police Act to reorganize the force. In 1870, a new city charter abolished the Metropolitan Police and established the New York City Municipal Police Department. In 1873 the New York City Police Department was once again reorganized. Byrnes was the chief inspector for the detective bureau from 1880 until 1883. At that time New York City detectives were not centralized and worked out of various precincts. It wasn't until 1882 that a centralized New York City Detective Bureau was created, and in May 1883, all the detectives previously assigned to individual precincts throughout the city were consolidated under one roof at 300 Mulberry Street. Byrnes was then placed in charge of this newly reorganized bureau. He was named as the chief detective and was in charge of all New York City detectives.

The first civil service rules for the police force were enacted in 1884, and a civil service board was established to make appointments to the police department and promotions purportedly based solely on ability and merit. Even this failed miserably, since Tammany Hall insiders appointed the members of the civil service board, making the appointees obligated to Tammany politicians. Because the police department had been organized along the lines of the city's political wards, it had been the aldermen from each ward who appointed men to the police force. Many appointments to the police force were controlled at first by Boss Tweed and his Tammany Hall gang, but even after Tweed and many of his cronies were ousted and sent to jail, the abuse of power within the police department continued. Those wishing an appointment to the police department were forced to pay tribute to their Tammany Hall benefactors, and even after appointed to the force, police officers were forced to pay for their personal advancement.

Even as late as 1894, when Republican state senator Clarence Lexow was named chairman of the seven-member committee studying crime and corruption in the city (the Lexow Committee), New York City police commissioner James J. Martin reported to the committee that 85 percent of appointments and promotions within the police department were still made on Tammany's recommendations.

The Lexow Committee interviewed nearly seven hundred witnesses and recorded more than ten thousand pages of testimony. More than nine thousand of these pages were devoted to testimony about corruption in the police department. Commissioner Martin told the committee that he had promoted only two men based on merit alone. He did not identify who they were. According to testimony received by the committee, it cost $2,500 for a patrolman to be promoted to sergeant, and anywhere from $10,000 to $15,000 to be promoted to the rank of captain. At the time, a New York City police captain's salary was a mere $2,750. To be promoted to inspector, the committee was told that it would cost $12,000 to $20,000 in bribe money. According to the findings of the Lexow Committee, the police corruption involving payoffs for promotions within the department totaled approximately $7 million a year.

Once appointed to the police department, officers at every level were assured of making their money back on their appointment or promotion investment tenfold, based on payoffs. Legitimate businesses within a police officer's precinct could be induced to pay protection money to keep their establishments free from criminal activity. If criminals had broken into or robbed the establishment, the protection money was paid to police for the return of any stolen goods. Often these establishments paid bribes to the police to obtain necessary police permits, or in case certain city ordinances were violated. Conversely, criminals of all walks were forced to pay off the police to avoid arrest and prosecution. Police officers received bribes from every saloon, house of prostitution, thief, pickpocket, prostitute, con artist, and even murderers within their precinct. It was an all-around lucrative business for any enterprising police officer in New York City. There was never any evidence that Byrnes ever participated in the "pay-for-promotion" scheme.

. . . each precinct at the mercy of its captain, who, more often than not, ran it as an extortion ring for his personal benefit . . .
—FROM LOW LIFE: LURES AND SNARES OF
OLD NEW YORK (1991), BY LUC SANTE

———•·•·•———

The official motto of the New York City Police Department is "Faithful Unto Death." The motto first appeared in 1872 on the New York City Flag of Honor commemorating the police department's role in preserving the peace during the infamous Civil War draft riots of 1863. That flag was on prominent display in the Fifteenth Precinct station house in 1872 when Thomas Byrnes served as a police captain there.

AMERICAN ALMANAC, 1872

For Thomas Byrnes, as well as the rest of the country, 1872 proved to be an extraordinary year, especially in terms of presidential politics.

Ulysses S. Grant was reelected president despite his scandal-plagued first term. Grant, the Republican candidate, received more than 3.5 million votes. Horace Greeley, the editor of the *New York Daily Tribune* and the Democratic candidate that year, received more than 2.8 million votes.

Susan B. Anthony tested the Fourteenth Amendment by leading a group of women to cast ballots in the presidential election. She was arrested, found guilty, and fined $100, which she refused to pay and never did.

Victoria Claflin Woodhull became the first woman to run for president of the United States in 1872. Women did not have the right to vote at the time. Her name did not appear on the ballot. Out of the more than six million votes cast in the presidential election, two thousand uncategorized votes were cast. It is not known if these votes went to Woodhull. She was the first female Wall Street broker, a newspaper editor, a clairvoyant, and an advocate for sexual freedom.

"Boss" Tweed's powerful and absolute dynasty of political corruption ended when members of his inner circle at the infamous Tammany Hall provided evidence of Tweed's massive corruption schemes to the *New York Times*. From July through December 1871, the *Times* ran a series of articles exposing Tweed. He was ultimately arrested and charged, and in November of 1872 he was convicted of 204 of the 220 charges brought against him. He was sentenced to twelve years in prison.

The Montgomery Ward & Company Catalog House, which was founded in Chicago, aimed at selling goods directly to customers through mail orders, and so the retail mail-order business began. Its slogan, "Satisfaction Guaranteed or Your Money Back," which appeared on all its catalogs, is the oldest and most frequently used slogan in retail advertising.

Luther Burbank developed the new, disease-resistant Burbank potato in Lunenburg, Massachusetts, in 1872. In 1875, Burbank sold his newly developed potato variety for $150 to J. H. Gregory of Marblehead, Massachusetts. Gregory named the new potato "the Burbank" and made a fortune from it. Luther Burbank continued his horticultural research in California.

In New York City and elsewhere, music took a more-conservative Christian bent with the popularity of songs like "Onward Christian Soldiers," which became a staple in various religious communities in America in 1872, and "You Never Miss the Water Till the Well Runs Dry," another popular music-house favorite.

Onward, Christian soldiers,
marching as to war,
with the cross of Jesus going on before.

Christ, the royal Master,
leads against the foe;
forward into battle see his banners go.

Onward, Christian soldiers,
marching as to war,
with the cross of Jesus going on before.
—Words by Sabine Baring-Gould. Music by Sir Arthur Sullivan. Published as a supplement to the *Musical Times*, London, 1871.

You Never Miss the Water Till the Well Runs Dry
When a child I liv'd at Lincoln with my parents at the farm,
The lessons that my mother taught to me were quite a charm;
She would often take me on her knee, when tir'd of childish play,
And as she press'd me to her breast, I've heard my mother say:

> Waste not, want not, is a maxim I would teach,
> Let your watchword be, despatch, and practice what you preach,
> Do not let your chances like sunbeams pass you by,
> For you never miss the water till the well runs dry.
>
> As years roll'd on I grew to be a mischief making boy!
> Destruction seem'd my only sport, it was my only joy;
> And well do I remember, when ofttimes well chastis'd,
> How father sat beside me then, and thus has me advis'd:
>
> Waste not, want not, is a maxim I would teach,
> Let your watchword be, despatch, and practice what you preach,
> Do not let your chances like sunbeams pass you by,
> For you never miss the water till the well runs dry.
> —WORDS BY HARRY LINN. MUSIC BY ROLLIN HOWARD. FROM *COMIC SONGS
> AND DANCES*, 1872

QUIPS AND QUOTES

Cautious, careful people, always casting about to preserve their reputations . . . can never effect a reform.
> —SUSAN B. ANTHONY

When woman rises from sexual slavery to sexual freedom, into the ownership and control of her sexual organs, and man is obliged to respect this freedom . . .
> —VICTORIA CLAFLIN WOODHULL

It was my fortune, or misfortune, to be called to the office of Chief Executive without any previous political training.
> —ULYSSES S. GRANT

I know only two tunes: One of them is "Yankee Doodle," and the other isn't.
—ULYSSES S. GRANT

Flowers always make people better, happier, and more helpful; they are sunshine, food, and medicine for the soul.
—LUTHER BURBANK

Satisfaction Guaranteed or Your Money Back
—MONTGOMERY WARD & COMPANY

The way to have power is to take it.
—WILLIAM MARCY "BOSS" TWEED

Honesty is worth two in the bush.
—JAMES FISK JR.

4

THE MURDER
OF JUBILEE JIM

*In which the notorious and flamboyant Wall Street speculator James
Fisk Jr.—known as "Jubilee Jim"—is shot and killed by a jealous former
business partner. While investigating the highly publicized case, Captain
Byrnes is introduced to Jay Gould, one of the richest men on Wall Street.*

The murder of Jubilee Jim was Byrnes's first introduction to the rich
and powerful Wall Street players to whom he would later attach himself. During the course of the Fisk murder investigation, he would
meet New York financier Jay Gould, one of the wealthiest men on
Wall Street. Their relationship would last nearly a lifetime. Gould
ultimately became Byrnes's personal financial consultant, leading
the lawman to acquire between $300,000 to $350,000 in personal
wealth on a lowly salary of $5,000 a year. Or at least that's how Byrnes
explained how he came by his vast fortune during the 1894 Lexow
Committee hearings on police corruption. But in January 1872, those
days were a long way off.

On Saturday, January 6, 1872, a former business associate of Jim Fisk
Jr.'s left the Yorkville Police Courthouse during an adjournment and
drove by carriage across the city to Delmonico's restaurant for dinner.
The man had only one thing on his mind, and it wasn't the famous
Delmonico's oysters on the menu.

Edward Stokes, who was born in 1841 in Philadelphia, came from
one of that city's most prominent and wealthy families. A prep school
graduate, Stokes was described as dashingly handsome, athletic, and
well liked, by women especially, if not a bit eccentric. Beneath the
veneer of his good looks, education, and proper manners, Stokes
masked a severe gambling addiction, which most were more than
willing to write off as his simply being a "sporting man."

After coming to New York City in the early 1860s, Stokes invested his money on Wall Street and amassed a substantial fortune. He managed to lose more than he earned at the racetrack and playing cards. Yet, regardless of how much he lost, he was always able to turn to his family to support him. Ultimately, he became the owner of the Brooklyn Oil Refining Company. In 1864, Stokes met the notoriously successful Wall Street speculator, James Fisk Jr., known as "Jubilee Jim" because of his outrageous behavior and his penchant for lavish spending on wine, women, and song. Fisk was a partner of another of the country's most successful Wall Street speculators, Jay Gould, at the infamous Erie Railway Company. In 1868, Fisk and Gould worked together using stock fraud and bribery to keep Cornelius Vanderbilt from taking control of the Erie Railway. Between the two of them, the flamboyant Fisk and the dour Gould had all but brought the country to economic collapse on September 24, 1869, when they tried to corner the gold market on the New York Exchange. Known as Black Friday, or the Fisk/Gould Scandal, it caused a national financial panic that ruined many investors—except, of course, Fisk and Gould, who profited from the elaborate scheme.

Black Friday occurred when President Ulysses S. Grant attempted to rally the American economy, which was still reeling because of the Civil War, by reducing the supply of paper money, buying back the "greenbacks" that were in circulation, and replacing them with currency that was backed by gold. Fisk and Gould used a go-between, Abel Corbin, a financier who was married to Grant's sister, to keep the government from selling its gold, at least long enough for Fisk and Gould to corner the gold market. They also bribed one of Grant's former generals, Daniel Butterfield, who served as the United States assistant treasurer. Butterfield was responsible for the sale of government gold on Wall Street, and he agreed to provide Fisk and Gould with information on when the government was going to release gold into the marketplace. In the meantime, Fisk and Gould bought up as much of the precious metal as possible. Ultimately, the scheme was uncovered, and President Grant ordered the sale of approximately $4 million in government gold.

As Fisk and Gould had figured, the price of gold had gone through the roof, increasing more than $30 an ounce. When the government gold hit the streets, the price plummeted. But by then, having been tipped off by Butterfield, Fisk and Gould had sold off their gold holdings at their highest price and made a fortune, while other investors, who had borrowed extensively to buy up gold when the price was rising, raced to unload their holdings in gold. But it was too late. Without capital to pay back the money they had borrowed to purchase the gold, many financiers went bankrupt and were ruined forever. It took years to recover from the Black Friday panic; meanwhile, the financial careers of Fisk and Gould flourished.

THE GOLD EXCITEMENT
The Panic in the Gold Room
Yesterday Culmination of the Great Bull Movement
The Rise and Fall of Thirty Per Cent
Dismay of All Parties
The Scenes and Incidents In and Around Wall-street
The Action of the Secretary of the
Treasury

The tremendous struggle of the bulls and bears in gold culminated before noon yesterday amid scenes of frantic excitement, which, it is not too much to say, were never paralleled even in the Gold Room.

Neither the fluctuations of the two previous days nor their frenzy—violent though both of these were—bore any comparison to those of yesterday when operators seemed to lose their five wits, and, when the price of gold shot up and down ten, twenty, thirty per cent, in the course of a few minutes . . . Taken altogether, the day was one of wild excitement in the Gold Room, and the wonder is that more failures were not reported.

To-day, when the accounts have been settled, the financial world will know where it stands.

It is said that the Adjutant-General of the State ordered that two Brooklyn regiments be kept in readiness to move on Wall-street in case of a riot.

—*New York Times*
September 25, 1869

THE GOLD RING
Complete Exposure of the
Great Plot
How and by Whom It Was
Worked Up
Causes of Its Failure
The Persistent Efforts to Entrap
The President
How Circumstantial Evidence was
Manufactured
The Part Played by Tammany
Defeat of the Ring at Every Point

With all the cunning and adroit manipulation of circumstantial evidences with which the King spirits of the Gold Ring have undertaken to relieve themselves of universal public odium, how singularly and completely they have failed may be comprehended by the exposition of the plot which follows. Not that Generals GRANT and BUTTERFIELD need a defense personally to wholly clear themselves of each and all the base allegations of complicity with the Gold Pool managers, but because the Democracy, through Tammany instigation, is employing these allegations for the purposes of making political capital do we take the time and space to exhibit the Ring and its true standing. . . .

—*New York Times*
October 18, 1869

The President and the Gold Ring

Undismayed by previous discomfitures the organs of the Gold Ring have renewed their attempts to identify the President with the recent transactions of FISK and GOULD. . . . In no way, has General GRANT, or Mrs. GRANT, had the remotest interest in any speculative transaction whether relating to gold or bonds. Neither with Corbin nor FISK, neither with BUTTERFIELD nor GOULD, have they held any correspondence touching the late gold conspiracy. And any allegation to the contrary is unqualifiedly false. . . .

—*New York Times*
October 22, 1869

Fisk and Gould were the kind of men Edward Stokes wanted to be associated with. For Jubilee Jim Fisk, the feeling was mutual, and the two men became business partners and fast friends. Their relationship was profitable for both of them and probably would have extended for years if it had not been for Josephine Mansfield, a stunningly beautiful former showgirl who was Jubilee Jim's mistress. Although Fisk was married, his wife, Lucy, was ensconced in their home in Boston, Massachusetts, leaving the flamboyant and jovial Fisk to carry on his elaborate affair with Mansfield. He went so far as to buy Mansfield a brownstone on West Twenty-third Street, practically next door to the Grand Opera House that Fisk had bought and refurbished, and which housed on the top floors the business offices of Fisk and Gould's Erie Railway operations. Mansfield became privy to almost all of Fisk's disreputable financial endeavors.

She and Jubilee Jim entertained their many friends and business associates at this extravagantly furnished home, where she earned the nickname "The Cleopatra of Twenty-third Street." Among the multitude of guests who attended their lavish dinners was Edward Stokes. Despite his vast wealth and gregarious personality, the short, rotund, physically unappealing Jubilee Jim was no match for the astonishingly attractive Edward Stokes. Stokes was classically handsome. He had jet black hair and mustache and was a fabulous fashion plate. It was rumored that he often spent several hours grooming and dressing before he ventured out. Tall, lean, and always immaculately dressed, he was three years younger than Fisk, educated, refined, and an obsessed social climber. He had married Helen Southwick, the daughter of a wealthy furniture magnate, and had one child, a daughter. His own father was a prosperous produce wholesaler. Despite filing for bankruptcy when his oil refinery business went bust and his gambling debts piled up, Stokes was able to live a life of luxury by borrowing heavily from his parents and in-laws.

Besides being short and portly, Jubilee Jim had a larger than usual head and wide-set bulging eyes. His reddish hair was parted down the middle and ended in two tiny spit curls waxed to his forehead. He had a full, drooping red mustache that he kept waxed to a point on both ends, and he often wore bright and fancy tailored suits, or elaborate and gaudy personally designed military uniforms. He also sported a silk low-cut vest so as to show off his peach-pit-sized diamond shirt stickpin.

Soon Josie Mansfield and Stokes became secret lovers, right under the rather bulbous nose of Jubilee Jim Fisk. They often carried on their illicit love affair in her Twenty-third Street home while Fisk worked close by on the top floors of the nearby Opera House. Together, Mansfield and Stokes, who was not remotely as wealthy as Fisk, plotted to swindle money out of their unsuspecting benefactor. Their plans didn't work.

Stokes left his wife, and in short order, Mansfield told Fisk they were through. Lucky in money, Fisk was unlucky in love, and although he vainly pleaded with Mansfield not to leave him, Mansfield refused. At first she threatened to blackmail Fisk, and then she sued him in court for money she claimed he had been holding for her in a fiduciary capacity.

Betrayed by Mansfield and Stokes, Fisk lashed out at both of them. He published affidavits written by two of Mansfield's servants (whose salaries Fisk had paid while they were in service to Mansfield) that claimed they had overheard Mansfield and Stokes planning to blackmail Fisk. It only got worse from there.

THE FISK-STOKES CASE
A Stay of Proceedings Granted by Judge Pratt— Tammany Fears the Publication of the Letters—Miss Mansfield Sues Fisk for $50,000

. . . The Fisk injunction is regarded as nothing less than a political move in the interests of Tammany. The papers sought to be suppressed would have, if published, it is thought, a damaging effect upon the November elections, and hence the anxiety evinced by FISK and certain Tammany politicians to suppress their publication. . . . In connection with this case, few are aware that a suit was instituted on Friday last, in Superior Court, on behalf of Miss MANSFIELD, and papers served on FISK for the recovery of $50,000, which she loaned to FISK to speculate with in stocks as her agent, and which sum she claims FISK has not repaid. . . .

—*New York Times*
October 22, 1871

FISK AND MANSFIELD
The Case Yesterday Before Justice Bixby—A crowded Court-Room and Outbursts of Applause—The Examination Postponed

At 10 o'clock yesterday morning JAMES FISK, JR., appeared before Justice BIXBY at the Yorkville Police Court to answer the charge of libel preferred by Mrs. HELEN JOSEPHINE MANSFIELD. The appearance of the distinguished "commodore" and "Colonel" of the famous Ninth Regiment in the character of a defendant to a criminal prosecution would undoubtedly have attracted considerable attention at any time, but . . . the nature of the litigation and the spicy developments which have already resulted in its prosecution created an unusually strong feeling of interest in the proceedings. . . . FISK was rather tardy in putting in an appearance. He did not arrive until long after the appointed hour, evidently with a view to create a sensation. He was attired in naval uniform, and a host of Erie retainers, who were present, greeted him with suppressed applause. . . .

—*New York Times*
November 19, 1871

FISK AND STOKES
The Effort to Prevent the Publication
of the Letters

The proceedings instituted by JAMES FISK, Jr., to restrain EDWARD H. STOKES and others from publishing certain letters written to and affidavits made by Miss HELEN JOSEPHINE MANSFIELD, came up before Judge BRADY in the Supreme Court Chambers. . . . It really seemed that while Mr. FISK'S interests were protected by keen, shrewd, sagacious lawyers, Mr. STOKES was left without protection. Not a human being pointed out how or where this publication was threatened. . . .

—*New York Times*
December 2, 1871

As Mansfield sued Fisk for libel, a sensational trial was played out in the New York City newspapers. Fisk then had Stokes arrested for embezzlement, charging that he stole $65,000 from the oil refinery business in which he and Stokes were partners. The charge against Stokes didn't stick, and a court-appointed arbitrator found that the only liability owed between the two men regarding the oil refinery business was that Fisk was required to pay Stokes $10,000 as compensation for his imprisonment on the wrongly filed embezzlement charge. Fisk paid the money, and Stokes signed a letter agreeing to the conditions.

Stokes later had a change of heart and sued Fisk on the grounds that Fisk had defrauded him. During these hearings, Stokes attempted to have the love letters that Fisk had sent to Mansfield published as part of the testimony. Fisk fought to keep the controversial letters out of public view. The judge ruled in favor of Fisk, and the letters were kept secret. The city's newspapers, however, had a field day speculating on the contents of the reported love letters. On January 6, 1872, before the court adjourned for the day, Fisk obtained an indictment in another court against Stokes, charging him with blackmail. Following the adjournment Fisk went back to his offices at the Opera House to freshen up, and Stokes took a carriage to Delmonico's downtown restaurant.

———

Two great forces met yesterday. . . . These two colliding forces were Marc Antony Fisk Jr., who has offered up an entire railroad . . . and an opera house, together with a fleet of Sound steamboats at the feet of a woman . . . Cleopatra Helen Josephine Mansfield, the beautiful and gorgeous heroine . . . owner of the palace in Twenty-third Street . . .

—*New York Herald*
November 25, 1871

———

His moustache bristled ferociously . . . and a big diamond pin shone out of his fat chest . . .

—*New York Herald*
November 25, 1871

———

The exquisite Stokes was all glorious in a new Alexis overcoat of a dull cream color. An elegant diamond ring glowed on his little finger . . . and a cane swung carelessly to and fro between his manly legs. Stokes looked so handsome that Mrs. Mansfield found it quite impossible to take her eyes off his face while she directed only withering glances of contempt at the agonized Fisk.

—*New York Herald*
November 25, 1871

———

Mrs. Mansfield looked so lovely that she created quite a flutter. . . . She is much above the medium height, having pearly white skin, dark and very large lustrous eyes. . . . Her delicate white hands were encased in faultless lavender kid gloves, and over her magnificent . . . dark hair was perched a jaunty little Alpine hat, with a dainty green feather. . . . At her snowy throat the only article of jewelry on her person, a small gold pin, glistened and heightened the effect.

—*New York Herald*
November 25, 1871

———

Fisk, Jr. has robbed the woman whom he seduced . . .

—*New York Tribune*
December 12, 1871

———

Colonel Stokes was, as usual, fashionably attired wearing an elegant overcoat of Ulster frieze, with light pants and an immaculately polished pair of boots . . .

—*New York Herald*
January 6, 1872

———

The voluptuous charms of Mrs. Mansfield were splendidly set off by a dress of black silk, velvet jacket, jockey hat, and illusion veil . . .

—*New York Herald*
January 6, 1872

Following the court adjournment on January 6, 1872, Edward Stokes borrowed Josie Mansfield's carriage, a magnificent brougham that Fisk had bought for his mistress, and rode to Delmonico's restaurant in the company of his attorney John McKeon and assistant district attorney John Fellows. The three men sat down in the fashionable restaurant and dined on oysters and beer. Mansfield was taken back to her Twenty-third Street home in a separate carriage. While the three men were enjoying their meal, Judge George Barnard joined them. Barnard had some news to share. He explained that the grand jury had just returned an indictment against Stokes and Mansfield on charges of blackmail. The one man who had the most to lose concerning the news, Stokes, had gone to the bar just as Barnard came to their table. It is unknown whether he heard the news or was told about it on his return. In any case Stokes abruptly excused himself from the table and left. Stokes took a carriage to Mansfield's home. He joined his love in the parlor, where they talked briefly before someone knocked at the front door. A servant let in the man, a friend of Mansfield's, who rushed into the parlor and blurted out that Stokes and Mansfield had been indicted for blackmail and that an arrest warrant had been issued for Stokes. Stokes sprang from his seat, wild-eyed and cursing loudly. Mansfield tried to calm him, but Stokes would have none of it. He grabbed his hat and coat and raced out of the house, leaving the front door wide open. Mansfield ordered the servant to close the door behind him.

Stokes had the carriage driver take him just a short way up the street to the Grand Opera House, where he imagined Fisk was. When he was told Fisk was no longer there, Stokes demanded to know his whereabouts. He was told that Fisk had gone to the Grand Central Hotel to visit friends from Boston. Stokes stormed out of the Opera House, jumped into his carriage, and told the driver to take him directly to the Grand Central Hotel on Broadway and Amity Street, one of the city's fashionable five-star hotels. Stokes grew impatient with the ride and ordered the driver to let him out a half-block or so from the Grand Central. He raced the rest of the way on foot, his topcoat flapping in the wind behind him, clutching his top hat and cane under his arm.

Like a man possessed, Stokes ran down the sidewalk, bumping into several people out casually strolling and nearly knocking one young woman over. He never stopped to apologize or help the young woman or any of the others. Instead, he dashed into a side entrance to the hotel on Broadway, generally used as an entrance for ladies. A hotel porter, John Redmond, who was high up on a ladder cleaning several gaslights, saw Stokes dart in, but he could not climb down off his ladder fast enough to catch Stokes, who proceeded up the stairs to the hotel's upper lobby. There, a visibly agitated Stokes paced back and forth, mumbling incoherently to himself. Stokes was finally able to compose himself enough to search for Fisk in several adjoining hotel waiting rooms, though without any luck. He decided to go back downstairs, and as he descended the staircase, he ran into Fisk.

Jubilee Jim Fisk had left the Yorkville Police Courthouse earlier that day feeling vindicated. He knew he was well on his way to defeating his ruthless and traitorous adversaries. He went from the courthouse directly to his Erie Railway office on the top floor of the Opera House, where he freshened up and had a glass of lemonade. He changed his clothes, putting on one of the many ornate military uniforms he had especially created, slipped into his long cape, and donned his top hat. He had an appointment at the Grand Central Hotel with family friends who were visiting from Boston. He climbed into his elaborately decorated carriage, which he had specially designed to his own gaudy specifications, and told the driver to take him to the Grand Central, the long way. Fisk wanted time to think about the recent turn of events and his next move. The driver took him across the city and across Madison Square to the hotel. Fisk asked the driver to let him off at the side entrance on Broadway, the same entrance that Stokes had used earlier. Hotel porter John Redmond was done cleaning the gaslights and was busy putting away the seven-foot ladder when Fisk came through the ladies' side entrance. Fisk wasn't supposed to use this entrance either, but Redmond wasn't about to stop Jubilee Jim Fisk, of all people. Fisk tipped Redmond; he was renowned for being a big tipper and one who would tip for the slightest reason. Both men were standing in front of one of the many huge plate-glass windows that adorned the magnificent hotel with an unobstructed view of the blue skies overhead outside.

Fisk asked Redmond if he knew whether the Morse family from Boston was in the hotel. Redmond told Fisk that Mrs. Morse and one of her daughters had gone out, but that another daughter was still upstairs in her room with her grandmother. Fisk thanked him and ambled up the stairs toward one of the many second-floor waiting rooms. Redmond followed along behind him.

Fisk was about halfway up the staircase when he saw Stokes coming down the stairs. He had a gun in his hand.

According to court testimony later given by Stokes, both men glared at each other, and he saw Fisk reach beneath his ornate military cape and produce a revolver.

Stokes testified that Fisk aimed the pistol at him, and believing that Fisk was going to shoot and kill him, he drew his own pistol and shot Fisk twice, hitting him in the arm and the stomach. Nothing could have been further from the truth, according to eyewitness accounts.

Thomas Hart, a bellboy at the hotel, happened to be standing at the top of the stairs and saw Stokes brandishing a revolver. Hart later testified in court that he heard Stokes call out, "I've got you now."

Redmond, the hotel porter who had accompanied Fisk up the stairs, testified that Stokes quickly fired twice. The shots were fired at point-blank range, the two men, standing less than a half-dozen steps apart. Given the girth of the ample Jubilee Jim, it would have been impossible for Stokes not to hit him.

Fisk fell onto the stairs and cried out for help.

"For God's sake, will anybody save me?" he reportedly shrieked.

Redmond testified that when he looked up to see where the shots had come from, he saw Stokes on the stairs ahead of Fisk with a revolver in his hand. The first shot penetrated Fisk's abdomen and sent him reeling. He cried out and staggered but clung to the railing for support. Stokes shot him again, and this time the bullet hit Fisk in the arm. Fisk fell, his body sliding like a pile of old laundry down to the bottom of the stairs. Still he managed to get back on his feet. By then Stokes had bolted back up the stairs and disappeared into the hotel lobby, where a crowd who had heard the shots began to gather. Dozens of hotel employees and guests ran to the bottom of the stairs where Fisk stood, hanging onto the staircase railing, blood pouring from his stomach. Several men helped Fisk into a vacant room. The hotel doctor, Dr. Tripler, was summoned. He found Fisk still standing with blood dripping from his arm and his stomach soaked in it. He ordered Fisk to lie down on a sofa and brought him a glass of brandy and water. The hotel doctor treated and bandaged Fisk's arm. The shot had entered his left arm just above the elbow. It passed through the bone and out the back of his arm.

Dr. Tripler had Fisk remove his shirt so he could examine the wound in his abdomen. The bullet had entered Fisk's stomach just above his navel. The stomach wound was more severe. Tripler probed for the bullet but could not locate it. The bullet had apparently gone deep into Fisk's bowels.

Fisk was transferred to the bed and made as comfortable as possible. Fisk's private physicians were summoned to the hotel.

JIM FISK MURDERED
He is Deliberately Shot Down in the Grand Hotel
Edward S. Stokes the Author of The Desperate Deed
Fisk Twice Wounded and Reported As Dying
His Ante-Mortem Statement Taken by The Coroner
The Murderer Promptly Arrested On the Spot
Exciting Scenes in and About The Hotel

The startling intelligence that EDWARD S. STOKES had shot and mortally wounded JAMES FISK JR., flew like lightning through the City yesterday afternoon about 4 o'clock, unenviable notoriety of both persons imparting unusual agility to the seven-leagued boots of busy rumor. For some time past the respectable dwellers in our City have been shocked and disgusted with the unavoidable publicity of their licentious amours; unavoidable because they have been discussed in the Police and Law courts. No sympathy with plaintiff or defendants was possible. It was a mere loathsome exhibition of depravity and cupidity such as, thank Heaven, does not often bring a blush to pure maiden faces or cause the ears of pruriency to tingle with its filthy recitals.

The sequel has come. The natural consequence of a vicious life has happened. A man lies dying—murdered; and his enemy—his murderer—is now discussing with himself the folly of his crime in a prison cell. . . . The injury to the arm was found to be merely a flesh wound, but the first shot had taken a more deadly course. They saw its orifice five inches above the umbilicus and two inches to the right of the medium line. From its appearance, they were of the opinion it was mortal. . . . After firing the second shot, STOKES paused for a single instant, as if to look upon his work, then turned and walked leisurely away. Reaching the door of the ladies' parlor, a few paces distant from the head of the stairs, he stepped insides and threw his still smoking and blackened Derringer pistol upon the sofa. He instantly stepped back into the corridor, and, walking more hurriedly, passed to and down the grand stairway, which leads up from the main hall and office of the hotel. . . . Just as he had reached the entrance to the barbershop of the house and when he was only a few steps distant from the door opening into Mercer-street, STOKES slipped and fell. Before he could regain his feet he was seized by some of the men attached to the hotel who were in pursuit of him. . . . He was carefully guarded by his captors until the arrival of the Police. . . . He was then, by order of Capt. BYRNES, taken back and locked up in an ordinary cell where he was soon afterward visited by his counsel. . . . Capt. BYRNES, having been informed by the attending Surgeons that Mr. FISK was in dying condition, at nonce dispatched an officer to summon Coroner YOUNG to attend for the purpose of taking the antemortem statement of the wounded Colonel. . . .

—*New York Times*

January 7, 1872

This afternoon at about 4 o'clock I rode up to the Grand Central Hotel. I entered by the private entrance, and, when I entered the first door I met the boy, of whom I inquired if Mrs. Morse was in. He told me that Mrs. Morse and her youngest daughter had gone out, but he thought the other daughter was in her grandmother's room. I asked him to go up and tell the daughter that I was there. I came through the other door, and was going upstairs and had gone up about two steps, and on looking up I saw Edward S. Stokes at the head of the stairs. As soon as I saw him I noticed that he had something in his hand, and a second after I saw the flash, heard the report, and felt the ball enter my abdomen on the right side. A second after I heard another shot, and the bullet entered my left arm. When I received the first shot I staggered and ran toward the door, but noticing a crowd gathering in front, I ran back on the stairs again. I was then brought upstairs in the hotel. I saw nothing more of Stokes until he was brought before me by an officer for identification. I fully identified Edward S. Stokes as the person who shot me.

—ANTEMORTEM TESTIMONY OF JAMES FISK JR.,
JANUARY 6, 1872

Captain Byrnes didn't have to resort to a full-scale manhunt for Fisk's killer nor did he have to employ his usual third degree. Edward Stokes was handed to Byrnes on a silver platter. Still, Byrnes managed to take full credit for his apprehension.

After the shooting, Stokes reportedly threw his pistol under a sofa in the women's parlor and sat down to rest for a few minutes. Stokes then thought better of it and tried to make his escape. Moving quickly but not running, Stokes tried to leave through the Mercer Street exit. As he made his way through the crowd that had begun to gather, Stokes reportedly shouted out that a man had just been shot upstairs. What he didn't expect was that the bellboy, Thomas Hart, who had witnessed the whole event on the staircase, had taken off after Stokes and had followed him. When Stokes called out about the shooting upstairs, no doubt trying to throw people off his track, Hart called out, "Yes, and you are the man that did it." Stokes looked back over his shoulder but could not see anyone. He headed for the exit that was near the hotel barbershop. By then, H. L. Powers, the manager of the Grand Central Hotel, and a small contingent of employees and hotel patrons were in hot pursuit of the killer. Stokes might have made it to the exit if he hadn't lost his footing, slipped, and fell. Powers and the others caught up with Stokes and grabbed him, holding him until the police arrived. It didn't take very long.

Word had already reached the Fifteenth Precinct headquarters, where Captain Byrnes was on duty. Not knowing at first who had been shot, only that a shooting had occurred at the Grand Central and that the shooter was being held, Byrnes dispatched one of his patrolmen, Officer Henry McCadden, to apprehend the suspect. It was McCadden who arrested Stokes. He found no weapon on the suspect, and Stokes put up no resistance. By the time McCadden had Stokes in custody, Byrnes had received word at the station house that it had been Fisk who had been shot by his nemesis, Edward Stokes. Byrnes grabbed his derby, topcoat, and a pocketful of cigars and raced out of the station. If anyone was going to take credit for arresting Stokes, it was going to be him.

Byrnes caught up with McCadden and his prisoner inside the hotel. Stokes was in handcuffs and Byrnes relieved McCadden of his duty, taking over the arrest of Stokes himself.

Byrnes led Stokes through the mob now surrounding the two. Byrnes told Stokes that he had several questions. Stokes shrugged nonchalantly, expressing irritation at the minor inconvenience that was being imposed on him. Byrnes asked if he had anything he wished to say about the shooting. Stokes said that he had nothing to say and would say nothing, at least not until he had his lawyer present. Byrnes asked his home address, and Stokes refused to answer.

"What did you do with the pistol?" Byrnes asked.

Stokes simply laughed.

Byrnes later discovered the gun, a Colt four-shot derringer, beneath a sofa in the women's parlor at the hotel, where Stokes had thrown it after the shooting. Two bullets had been fired from the gun, and the bullet that had hit and passed through Fisk's arm was found on the staircase. The bullet fragment matched the bullet from the Colt revolver Stokes had tossed beneath the sofa. Stokes was then taken to the Tombs to be held. His lawyer was sent for.

On the way to the Tombs, Stokes reportedly asked Byrnes if they could stop somewhere along the way for a drink. It was an astonishing request, even for Captain Byrnes, who thought he had heard everything. Byrnes shook his head and continued with his prisoner to the Tombs. When he was finally locked in his cell, Stokes asked that a box of his favorite cigars be brought to him. Unable to grant his request outright, Byrnes reached into the pocket of his topcoat and handed Stokes a handful of his own favorite cigars. Stokes began smoking one cigar after another, barely finishing one before he asked to have another lit for him. He paced the small cell, muttering to himself, shrouded in a cloud of cigar smoke. Despite his circumstances, Stokes retained his haughty demeanor, requesting that a plate of oysters from Delmonico's be brought to him along with some cold beer. His requests were refused. Finally he asked, "What do you think, is the man seriously injured?" Fisk was more than seriously injured. He was dying.

Byrnes later escorted Stokes to the room at the Grand Central Hotel where Fisk lay dying. A team of physicians had probed the wound in Fisk's stomach several times, but the bullet had gone deep into his bowels and could not be retracted. Fisk was still conscious and alert when Byrnes brought Stokes in to be identified. Although bandaged and lying in bed, Fisk gave no impression that he was in any pain.

Stokes continued to look and act as a man who had been inadvertently put upon and at any moment matters would be all cleared up and he would be on his way. His face was expressionless, and he seemed more intent on touching up his hair and mustache than listening to the proceedings. He even asked one of the doctors in the room if he might have a comb or brush.

Fisk's room was filled not only with doctors, seven in all, but many of Fisk's closest associates, including Jay Gould and Boss Tweed, and his brother-in-law. His wife, Lucy, who was in Boston, had been sent for.

"Colonel Fisk, you see this man? Was it he who shot you?" Byrnes asked, holding Stokes at arm's length.

"Yes, that's the man who shot me. That's Stokes," Fisk said. After the identification of Stokes by Fisk, the prisoner was taken away. Byrnes stayed to take Fisk's final statement.

Boss Tweed, who had recently been indicted, jailed, and subsequently released on $1 million bail, which Jay Gould had paid, stayed at Fisk's bedside.

Taking Byrnes aside, Gould warned Byrnes that Stokes's life was in jeopardy, that Byrnes should assign a special contingent of guards around the Tombs where Stokes was being held, and that officers should be sent to Josie Mansfield's home to protect her from possible mob violence. Downstairs in the lobby of the Grand Central, hundreds of Erie Railway employees and soldiers from the city's Ninth Regiment, the regiment that Fisk commanded, had gathered and were openly making threats against the lives of Stokes and Mansfield. There was talk of storming the Tombs and lynching Stokes. Byrnes notified police superintendent James Kelso, who ordered 250 officers to the city prison to protect Stokes. Another smaller contingent was sent to protect Mansfield at her Twenty-third Street home.

By the time the police arrived at Mansfield's brownstone, she had heard the news about Fisk's shooting and Stokes's arrest.

When questioned about the events by a New York City newspaper reporter, Mansfield replied that Stokes must have been out of his mind and that she had nothing to do with the shooting.

"I have only my reputation to maintain," the one-time showgirl and mistress of both Fisk and Stokes said.

Jubilee Jim Fisk, the flamboyant Wall Street speculator who had been born in Vermont, worked as a door-to-door salesman and circus barker, and risen to become one of the richest and most-talked-about personalities in New York City—who owned a fleet of luxurious steamships, the Fall River Line, and had awarded himself the title of commodore. He had bought the city's Ninth Military Regiment, paid top dollar for new uniforms, horses, and weapons, and bestowed the rank of colonel on himself. Fisk, the consummate showman, died at 11 o'clock on Sunday morning, January 7, 1872. His wife, Lucy, Jay Gould, Boss Tweed, and a host of family, friends, and associates were at his side.

The New York City press, the longtime nemesis of Jubilee Jim Fisk, now went to every extent to pay homage to Manhattan's most colorful rogue.

"There was a grandeur . . . about [Fisk's] rascalities which helps lift him above the vulgar herd of scoundrels," an editor of the *New York Times* wrote.

Speaking at his funeral, Boss Tweed said Fisk was "a man of broad soul and kindly heart. . . . He has done more good turns for the worthy but embarrassed men than all the clergymen in New York."

A funeral procession for Fisk began at the Opera House where he laid in state. More than twenty thousand people gathered in the streets to pay their respects. These included officers from his steamship company in full dress regalia, employees from the Erie Railway, six platoons of National Guard officers, and the Ninth Regiment's marching band. Nearly a quarter-mile of carriages carrying distinguished mourners followed the casket through the city.

". . . No more striking phenomenon of human nature has been seen in our time," the *New York Herald* proclaimed.

Fisk's body was taken by train for burial in his hometown of Brattleboro, Vermont.

Stokes remained jailed in the Tombs but was made more comfortable with a plush carpet installed in his cell, along with a rocking chair, his favorite books, and meals brought to him directly from Delmonico's rather than from the prison kitchen.

His normal prison garb had been exchanged for attire he was far more comfortable in: a frilly diamond-studded shirt, lavender pants, a velvet dressing jacket, silk stockings, and embroidered slippers. All the comforts of home, except for the bars and bedbugs.

Captain Byrnes, who was now receiving much praise in the newspapers and among many of Wall Street's finest, including Jay Gould, testified at Stokes's first trial, which began on June 19, 1872. Byrnes testified that he had first heard of the Fisk shooting about ten minutes after four o'clock.

"I was going up the stoop of the station house. I was told by one of my sergeants," Byrnes testified.

Byrnes told the jury that he went to the room at the Grand Central Hotel where James Fisk was being cared for.

"I was given a ball [a bullet] at the Grand Central Hotel," Byrnes testified.

He explained that a hotel employee had given him the bullet and that it had been found at the foot of the staircase where Fisk had been shot. Byrnes testified that a woman also handed him a pistol that she said she had found hidden in a sofa. According to Byrnes, the ball came from the pistol the woman had discovered. Byrnes then told the jury that he personally searched the barbershop, the reading room, and the writing room in the hotel.

"I was not present when Mr. Stokes was arrested." Byrnes truthfully testified.

"I have not heard of any reports of a pistol being found in 217, where Mr. Fisk was taken," Byrnes said, disputing Stokes's self-defense claim that Fisk had drawn a pistol and threatened to shoot him.

After getting the case on July 13, the jury deliberated for forty hours and could not come to a unanimous verdict. The jurors were discharged, and Stokes's second trial began on December 18, 1872. This time the jury found him guilty of murder. On January 6, 1873, the anniversary of the murder of Fisk, Stokes was sentenced to be hanged. A date was set for February, and Stokes was taken to the Tombs and placed on death row. Stokes's attorneys appealed the verdict. Six months later, in June 1873, a mistrial was declared by the Court of Appeals, and Stokes was granted a new trial.

During this third and final trial, new witnesses were presented who claimed that Fisk did have a gun on him the day he was shot. In addition, John Moore, who worked at the Grand Central Hotel, claimed that when he asked Fisk what had happened to him after the shooting, Fisk replied, "He was too quick for me this time."

Patrick Logan, a former police officer, testified that the two eyewitnesses to the shooting, hotel porter John Redmond and bellboy Thomas Hart, had been promised $500 each if they testified that Stokes shot Fisk outright. Despite the new testimony, Stokes was found guilty of manslaughter in October 1873. He was sentenced to four years in the state prison. Stokes spent most of that time in the prison's hospital ward.

Stokes was discharged from the state prison in October 1876, released early for good behavior and time served. He entered the hotel business and became the proprietor of the Hoffman House in New York City. Following years of costly litigation with his cousin over another business enterprise, The Postal Telegraph Company, he sold his interest in the hotel and retired from public view. For the last few years of his life, Stokes was a haunted man, afraid that an assassin would kill him for what he had done to Jubilee Jim Fisk. Stokes died in November 1901 at his sister's home, where he had been living for a few years.

Ballistics, the science of how ammunition operates, plays a vital role in today's law enforcement investigations. It is a highly complex, sophisticated, and widely accepted science. More and more forensic scientists are engaged in firearm and bullet identification and trajectory. But, before the early 1900s, police officers like Thomas Byrnes did not have the multitude of sophisticated apparatus now used in criminal detection. They had to rely on simple observation, the physical matching of a bullet to a firearm, and the caliber determination based solely on the examination of the size and shape of a bullet. Although the New York City Police Department was not equipped with a ballistics department, Byrnes knew as far back as 1872 the importance that matching a bullet to a firearm played in a criminal investigation. Byrnes developed a rudimentary knowledge of firearm trajectory and bullet size and markings, a technique he applied in the Jubilee Jim Fisk murder investigation and one he improved upon throughout the years.

The Fisk murder case also gave Byrnes entrée into the Wall Street world of high finance, by establishing a friendship with financier Jay

Gould, Fisk's former partner. Byrnes reportedly benefited financially through this relationship, as Gould provided him with investment advice throughout the years. Byrnes was reciprocal in his relationship. One of his first directives when appointed to the Detective Bureau was to establish an office on Wall Street to protect the holdings of wealthy friends like Gould.

THE MURDER OF MAUDE MERRILL

In which Captain Byrnes tracks down the murderer of the beautiful, young prostitute, Maude Merrill. Using love letters found in her possession, he discovers the shocking identity of the killer.

———

The murder of the young prostitute, Maude Merrill, was one of the most sordid cases that Byrnes ever investigated. Twenty-year-old Maude Merrill was murdered in her room at an infamous house of prostitution at 10 Neilson Place on Mercer Street on Tuesday, December 10, 1872.

Most of the murders, robberies, assaults, and petty larcenies Byrnes had seen were committed by dangerous career criminals and thugs. Byrnes had long ago steeled himself from any emotional attachment to these cases. The men and women he arrested and sent off to prison were the scum of the earth, and deserved to be there as far as Byrnes was concerned. But the case of Maude Merrill was different. The victim was a young Irish girl, and what was worse, she was killed by someone she should have been able to trust to help pull her out of the depths of deprivation she had fallen to. If there was one tenet Byrnes adhered to throughout his life, it was loyalty to family and friends. It was the role of the man of the house, which Byrnes had taken on at an early age, to take care of the family in whatever ways he could. Byrnes had taken care of his own widowed mother for years before her death, and was always a stalwart defender and guardian of his two older sisters, despite their having their own husbands and families. It was a man's job to take care of his family. Byrnes saw it no other way, which is why the case of Maude Merrill affected him so much.

———

No Clue to the Murderer or the Motive for the Deed-Intense Excitement in a Noted Uptown Brothel.

A very remarkable and mysterious murder was perpetrated last evening in the fashionable house of ill-fame, at No. 10 Neilson-place, Mercer-street, of which Emma Cozzens, a notorious woman, is the proprietress. The victim is Martha Smith, a young courtesan, known in the house as Maude Merrill, and the assassin is a man who passed as her uncle, but who had been visiting her at intervals for seven or eight months past, and who is supposed to have been either her "lover" or her husband. The murderer made his escape, and, as he is still at large, nothing definite about him, or the motive for the murder, could be ascertained last night. . . .

Who the murderer is, is a problem yet to be solved. Capt. Byrnes professes to have obtained a clue to the identity of this man, but refused to give the reporters any information in regard to the affair. The Police have instituted an active search throughout the City, and it is to be hoped that he will be captured.

—*New York Times*
December 11, 1872

Merrill was shot and killed and her body was discovered by Mary Ann Allison, a housekeeper at the brothel where Merrill plied her trade. The house, located at 10 Neilson Place on Mercer Street, was well known to the police. Its proprietress, Emma Cozzens, was also well known to officers. Her weekly payments to the police kept her operations from being closed down or her patrons and girls from being harassed or rounded up. The housekeeper had identified Merrill's murderer as thirty-six-year-old Robert Bleakley, a man who had been passing himself off as Merrill's uncle. But according to Allison, Cozzens, and others familiar with the goings-on at the house, Bleakley had been visiting Merrill in her room on a regular basis during the six months prior to the murder. He was thought to be a paying customer of the young prostitute.

According to testimony given by Allison, Bleakley arrived at the Neilson Place address around four o'clock in the afternoon on that Tuesday, asking for Merrill by name. Allison recognized him as a frequent visitor, and although he was adamant about introducing himself as Merrill's uncle, Allison suspected otherwise. She allowed Bleakley to go upstairs to Merrill's room on the third floor and continued on with her housecleaning chores. She reported to police that later that afternoon, when she happened to pass by Merrill's room, she had heard loud voices and then what sounded like someone being slapped or hit. Then she heard a loud thud, and the wall to the room shook as if someone had been thrown against it. Allison claimed that she stayed outside the door to the room, listening for a few minutes more, and that the voices and sounds coming from inside the room had stopped. Thinking nothing more of it, Allison went about her business.

Less than a half-hour later, as she was making her way back down the hallway toward the staircase heading to the first floor, she ran into Bleakley as he was coming out of Merrill's room. He appeared calm and collected, and there was nothing about him, according to Allison, that made her think anything was wrong, until he spoke.

"I have just killed my niece, and I am going to give myself up," Bleakley said nonchalantly. He shrugged and shoved his hands deep into his pants pockets before turning and heading downstairs. Allison said she could distinctly hear him whistling as he sauntered down the staircase.

Shocked, Allison stared wide-eyed at Bleakley as he strode off. After he had left, Allison came to her senses and rushed to Merrill's room. She knocked loudly at the door. No one answered. She tried the door. It was unlocked, but she couldn't open it. It was jammed. She could feel something pushed up against it. Allison put her shoulder to the door and managed to shove it open. Lying on the floor, facedown, with her head resting against the door, was the body of Maude Merrill. The nightclothes she was wearing were smeared with blood, and there was a pool of blood on the carpet beside where she had fallen. Mary Ann Allison screamed. Dozens of young girls came running from their rooms to see what was wrong, only to begin crying and screaming when they entered Merrill's room and saw her dead body on the floor. They swooned and one young girl fainted. Many of the girls had known Merrill. Customers, several of them well-known businessmen or local politicians, fled the building. Other less-scrupulous customers lingered. The known criminals and waterfront thugs in the crowd sought to dispel their involvement in the murder by claiming loudly that they had been in the company of another girl and could prove it. Emma Cozzens knew that no amount of bribes to the police department could cover up this tragedy. She immediately sent for the police. Captain Byrnes was the first to arrive. Seeing the partially naked girl lying on the floor, he asked for a sheet to cover her up. Once he had cleared the room, Byrnes checked the girl's body for a pulse. She was dead. He carefully checked her for wounds and discovered she had been shot. The shot had entered from the back and pierced her lungs. Byrnes checked the door and four walls, taking note of what appeared to be two bullet holes in the wall beside the door. Byrnes went to the girl's desk and nightstand, where he found a batch of letters and other papers. He took the letters and other material, knowing that scrutinizing them could help turn up some clue as to the motive behind the girl's murder.

By the time other police officers had arrived, Byrnes was questioning Mary Ann Allison. According to Allison, the man, Bleakley, who had confessed that he had murdered Maude Merrill, appeared to be about forty years old, approximately five feet, ten inches tall, not very stout, broad-shouldered with a dark complexion, black hair and a drooping mustache, and dark eyes. He was wearing a topcoat that looked expensive and a silk top hat. The description of the man was sent to every police precinct and station throughout the city and Brooklyn. Bleakley was reportd to be armed and dangerous.

The coroner arrived at the murder scene several hours later and examined the body. He found a bullet wound in Merrill's back immediately under her left shoulder. He probed the wound and determined that the bullet had taken an inward and downward path after entering her back and then passing through her lungs. He concluded that Merrill had died from internal hemorrhaging. He noted that there were some slight abrasions on the girl's nose and face, and there was a scratch on her left breast that the coroner determined she must have received during a struggle with her murderer. He ordered the girl's body be removed to the undertaker's on the corner of Bedford and Carmine Streets, where he would perform a postmortem examination.

Based on his examination of the girl's room and what Mary Ann Allison had told him about the loud noises she had heard outside the door, Captain Byrnes determined that a desperate struggle had taken place between Merrill and her murderer. The girl had broken free from her killer's grip and had been running for the door when she was shot in the back. The murderer fired three shots. The first two appeared to have missed her, hitting the wall near the door instead. The third shot hit its mark, killing the girl. She fell against the door, her body draped in sheer nightclothes, her head hitting the threshold to the bedroom door. Her killer must have shoved her aside just enough to open the door, since the door opened inward, stepped over her dead body, and let himself out. Byrnes's ability to stitch together the events at a crime scene never ceased to amaze his peers at the Fifteenth Precinct station house. While others were scouring the city for Merrill's killer, Byrnes busied himself with putting together what had happened inside the girl's bedroom and then, laying out her letters on his desk at the station, he began to read them in an attempt to determine why she might have been killed.

Very little was known about Maude Merrill's background. Just twenty years old and a native of Ireland, she was a beautiful young girl with a light complexion, raven hair, and blue eyes, small, and with a pear-shaped body, but very well developed. She must have been pouring a bath for herself before her killer arrived, as her tub was filled with lukewarm water when Byrnes arrived at the crime scene. Merrill was wearing a sheer bathrobe with a loose bed jacket over it. According to testimony from Emma Cozzens, Merrill had been engaged in prostitution for approximately the past two years and had been plying her trade for about eight months at a house on West Twenty-sixth Street, before coming to Cozzens's establishment.

Byrnes found an article from a November 23, 1872, newspaper in Merrill's room. A section had been underlined in pencil:

". . . an inquest was held in Cork, upon the body of Charlotte Smith, the wife of Richard Smith, a hair-dresser, of Gillabey-street, who committed suicide the previous day. The deceased was stated to have been addicted to drink. She opened an artery in her arm with a razor and bled herself to death. The jury found the stereotyped verdict of temporary insanity. Deceased had been only a week out of prison where she had been confined for a month for stabbing her husband and attempting to take his life."

Byrnes had a hunch that Charlotte Smith must have been the girl's mother and the man, Richard, mentioned in the article, her father. As it turned out, he was exactly right. It was later revealed that Maude Merrill's real name was Mary Ann Smith, and that her mother was Charlotte Smith. Robert Bleakley, the man who murdered her, was her mother's brother. Mary Ann Smith, aka Maude Merrill, had a sister named after their mother who was just seventeen years old and living on her own in New York City. It was Charlotte "Lottie" Smith, the younger sister, who identified and claimed the body.

MAUD MERRILL
Latest Developments Concerning Murdered Magdalene And Her Slayer
The Record Of Both Lives
Interviews with Bleakley's Landlord And Maud's Employer

The case of the murdered Magdalene, Mary Ann Smith, alias Maud Merrill, who was shot at No. 10 Neilson place, New York, on Tuesday night, grows at once more interesting and mysterious the more it is looked into. From all that is at present known, the murderer and the murdered girl stand to each other in the relationship of uncle and niece.

—*Broolyn Daily Eagle*
December 12, 1872

———

Mary Ann Smith was born in Cork County, Ireland, in 1852, and came to New York City in 1870 as a ward of her uncle, Robert Bleakley. She was briefly married to Thomas Foley, a reputable businessman, but the marriage lasted only a few months. Foley discovered her infidelities, and despite his pleadings for her to give up a series of lovers, she refused. Crushed by this revelation, Foley abandoned her and, not desiring to face the ridicule of being a cuckold, moved to Texas to be as far away as he could from his errant wife and the shame she had caused him. Although her uncle, Bleakley, offered to take her in, Mary Ann refused and instead entered into an open life of prostitution. A young, pretty, shapely girl, she had no trouble selling her wares. She first entered into an arrangement at a brothel at 116 West Twenty-sixth Street, where she quickly became a favorite of the clientele who visited the place. Smith contracted pneumonia and was taken to Bellevue Hospital to convalesce. She remained confined at Bellevue for approximately eight months. Following her long recovery, Smith applied for room and board at Emma Cozzens's Neilson Place brothel, where she resumed her life of shame and degradation. During this period, Lottie Smith, her younger sister, often visited her. Bleakley was also a frequent visitor. Lottie was living with Bleakley. Both Lottie and Bleakley tried to persuade Mary Ann to leave behind her life of prostitution and rejoin her husband in Texas, but Mary Ann refused. She claimed that she was making an incredible amount of money and was able to live in an extravagant manner that her former husband could never have afforded.

Among the papers Captain Byrnes found in her room was a copy of the *Irish American* newspaper that ran the story of the suicide of her mother, Charlotte Smith. According to Lottie Smith, she had brought a copy of the newspaper account to her sister only a few days before the murder, and Mary Ann had broken down in tears after reading of her mother's suicide. Lottie told Byrnes that their mother had been severely abused by their father, and that his abuse was the cause of her drinking, her subsequent attack on her husband, and ultimately, her suicide.

Byrnes interviewed a series of people who knew the dead girl, including Mary Hall, who had hired Mary Ann as a domestic servant when Smith first arrived in the country. According to Hall, Mary Ann did earn an honest living for a brief time, working for her.

Hall said that, aside from being attractive, she found Smith, whom she knew as Maude Smith, to be polite and modest. Hall told Byrnes that while Maude was working for her, a man who claimed to be Maude's uncle visited her at Hall's house on the corner of Johnson and Pearl Streets. The man in question turned out to be Bleakley. A reporter from the *Brooklyn Daily Eagle* later interviewed Hall.

Reporter: Did anyone know that he was her uncle when he called?

Mrs. Hall: Not that I know of.

Reporter: Was there no one who knew beside you of his having called?

Mrs. Hall: Yes, the servant Ellen.

Whereupon Ellen was (at the request of the reporter) called, and made the following statement:

Ellen: I am a cook in the house of Mrs. Hall; I remember who has been shot, and who gave her name to me as Maude Smith, came to do housework in the place where I am now employed as a cook.

Reporter: What was she like?

Ellen: She was rather a good-looking girl.

Reporter: Did appearances lead you to suppose that she was inclined to be immoral?

Ellen: Well, I don't like to say; she was smart.

Reporter: Was she what is called too smart? You know what I mean.

Ellen: I think she was.

Reporter: Did you know anyone come to see her?

Ellen: No one but a man she called Waggoner, but his real name was Griffith.

Reporter: Did you notice anything improper pass while they were in each other's company?

Ellen: No, but I had my suspicions.

Reporter: Did you ever see her uncle, who has been reported to have shot her?

Ellen: Yes, once.

—From an interview appearing in the *Brooklyn Daily Eagle*,
December 13, 1872

Byrnes questioned Ellen Layaden, a young girl who worked at Hall's home as a cook. She claimed to have known Smith while they were both employed there. Layaden told Byrnes that a man fitting the description of Robert Bleakley came to the house, asking to speak with Maude. She told Byrnes that on that occasion Maude came downstairs, greeted the man, and took him back upstairs to her room. They weren't gone long when, according to Layaden, Maude came back downstairs looking scared. One side of her face was reddened. She told Layaden that the man had slapped her across the face. Layaden asked who had slapped her, and Smith told her it was her uncle. When she heard her uncle coming down the stairs, Smith hid in another room. When Layaden confronted Bleakley, he asked where Maude had gone. "Who are you looking for?" Layaden asked.

"That dumb whore!" Bleakley bellowed.

Maude later confided in Layaden that her uncle was drunk and that he showed her a pistol and threatened to shoot her for what he claimed was "improper behavior."

Layaden told Bleakley to wait in the dining room, adding that he had no right to say such awful things in Mrs. Hall's home. She went and informed Mrs. Hall, who came and met with Bleakley. Smith remained in hiding. When Byrnes questioned Hall, she told him that she met with Bleakley, who informed her that she was keeping an improper character in her house.

According to Hall, Bleakley told her that he was a married man with two young children. He told her that Smith had ruined him and his family and that he had lost both his job and his residency at a boardinghouse because of Smith. He did not elaborate on any of the circumstances, but demanded that Hall fire Smith immediately. He threatened he would come back as often as it took until Hall fired the girl.

Finally Hall demanded that Bleakley leave her home, which he did. She said that she could smell alcohol on his breath and that he appeared to be staggering. After he had left, Hall confronted Smith and told her she was fired. Smith packed her bags and left. Later that day, Bleakley returned to the house and apologized to Hall for his earlier behavior. Before leaving, Smith had told Hall that Bleakley had threatened to shoot her and even showed her a pistol he had with him. Hall confronted Bleakley about the gun. Bleakley admitted that he did carry a revolver, but only for his personal protection, and that he had never threatened Smith with the gun. "There is no danger," Bleakley told her. When he learned that Hall had discharged Smith, Bleakley left.

———————

From the various letters found in Smith's room, Byrnes was able to verify that the dead girl's uncle was Robert Bleakley and that he lived in Brooklyn. Byrnes sent two police officers to Bleakley's last known address on Gold Street, a seedy boardinghouse. The officers were told that Bleakley had left earlier that evening and hadn't returned. Inside the small room where Bleakley lived, the two officers found Lottie Smith. One of the officers escorted her back to the station house.

The other officer questioned several people living at the boardinghouse, including Ernest Timmons, who told the officer that he was supposed to meet Bleakley later that evening at a bar along the navy shipyard. The officer was afraid that, despite Timmons's willingness to help in the capture of Bleakley, he might have a change of heart and decide to warn Bleakley. So he had Timmons arrested as a material witness and taken to the Fifteenth Precinct station house, where he was jailed for the time being.

At the station house, Captain Byrnes told Lottie Smith what had happened to her older sister. The girl broke down weeping. Byrnes did his best to console her. It was not in his nature to show empathy for criminals or victims, but he made an exception in this case. The dead girl was so young and Lottie even younger. Byrnes opened the desk drawer and took out a bottle of Irish whiskey. Not a drinker himself, he kept a bottle handy in case he needed it to cajole a suspect or bribe a criminal to squeal on one of his cronies. Byrnes had long ago seen the horrible impact of drink on many of his friends and had sworn off any type of alcohol.

He poured the distraught girl a small glass of whiskey and told her to take several sips to calm herself. Lottie Smith did as she was told. The whiskey made her gag. She claimed she had never had a drink before. Byrnes poured her a glass of water. He reached into his desk, grabbed one of the already-rolled cigarettes he kept there, lit it, and offered it to the girl. She refused, saying she didn't smoke either. Byrnes's little test proved enlightening. Lottie Smith seemed pure as the driven snow, at least on the surface. She never once swore, didn't drink or smoke, and appeared to be an upstanding Catholic girl. Byrnes felt he could trust her to help in the investigation.

Lottie told Byrnes that her uncle had made plans to leave for California. Byrnes checked the Brooklyn harbor and found that the steamship *Henry S. Chauncey* was scheduled to leave for San Francisco the next day. He personally made the trip down to the steamship and had it searched from stern to bow, but there was no sign of Bleakley. Byrnes returned to the Fifteenth Precinct. When he arrived, a telegram was waiting for him from the Brooklyn police. Robert Bleakley had turned himself in.

Walking into the Brooklyn police station, Bleakley had surrendered himself to Captain John Smith. "Captain, I want to give myself up. I am the man who shot that girl in New York yesterday," Bleakley confessed. He was locked up immediately, and Captain Byrnes was contacted.

The case of Maude Merrill took a surprising turn following Bleakley's surrender to police, which no one, not even the self-assured Captain Thomas Byrnes, could have suspected. After his surrender in Brooklyn, Bleakley was transferred to the Fifteenth Precinct station house on Mercer Street. There, Mary Ann Allison, the Neilson Place housekeeper, positively identified him as the man who had confessed to her the day Smith was shot to death in her room. He was then positively identified by Lottie Smith, the dead girl's sister, as her uncle.

"Is this man your sister's uncle?" Byrnes asked the distraught young girl.

"Yes, he is my mother's brother," Lottie Smith said.

Byrnes questioned Bleakley at length about the day of the murder. Bleakley answered all of Byrnes's questions and then some.

"Mr. Bleakley, this is a sad affair. How many shots did you fire at her?" Byrnes asked.

"I'm blamed if I know, Captain," Bleakley said calmly. In Byrnes's eyes, he did not appear in any way shaken by the events.

"The first one I fired when I was standing near the grate. Then I ran over to the door and fired again and again," Bleakley said.

"Was she lying down when you fired at her near the door?" Byrnes asked.

"I don't think she was, but she was bent over," Bleakley said.

The police found the six-shot National revolver Bleakley used to kill the girl in the pocket of his topcoat. It appeared to most to be an open-and-shut case against Bleakley; still, Byrnes was both intrigued and appalled by what he construed as the motive in the case. Having read the letters sent between Bleakley and the dead girl, Byrnes let it slip to reporters that the contents of some of the letters were not the kind of things any decent man would write to his niece. The reporters demanded to see the letters but Byrnes refused. Although the killer was in custody, Byrnes's refusal to release the contents of the letters only fed into the sensationalism of the case. The question had to be asked: Was Bleakley Mary Ann Smith's lover as well as her uncle? For the time being it remained sordid speculation. While Byrnes had his suspicions, only Bleakley himself knew the truth.

The testimony of Lottie Smith was very damaging to Bleakley. She told Byrnes that her older sister never lost touch with her and wrote to her often. Lottie told Byrnes that she visited her older sister often, and that Mary Ann had stated on more than one occasion that she was planning on leaving behind her life of shame and degradation just as soon as she had saved enough money to support the both of them. According to Lottie Smith, she had received a letter from her sister on the day of her murder, asking her to visit her that afternoon around three o'clock. When she was leaving the boardinghouse where she lived with her uncle, she ran into him. He asked where she was going, and when she told him, he forced her back into the house, telling her that he was going to see Mary Ann himself. According to Lottie, her uncle appeared drunk and grew angrier as he spoke. He locked Lottie in their room and left. Lottie said she feared the worse, but there was nothing she could do.

<hr />

My name is Robert P. Bleakley. I am thirty-six years of age and a block-maker by trade, and my residence is at No. 365 Gold-street, Brooklyn. I am the uncle of the girl that is dead; her mother was my sister. The causes of what ended last night go back a good many years. . . . In 1866 I received news that my sister, Mrs. Smith, the mother of this girl, was being abused by her husband. She had sixteen children. The quarrel between them was a religious one. She being a Protestant and he being a Catholic, one half of their children were reared one way and the remainder brought up the other way. She wrote to me, asking me to go to Ireland and bring her to this country. I went to Ireland in 1866 and found her sick and unable to come with me, so I came back to this country without her. From 1866 to 1869 I received many letters from her, all complaining of bad treatment. I went to Ireland in 1869. She was ill and unable to come, having been badly beaten by her husband. She asked me to take her younger daughter Charlotte (or Lottie) to this country, and I did. . . . I sent $12 to my sister to pay her pas-

sage to this country, but instead of coming herself, she sent her eldest daughter, the girl that is dead. . . . Both had procured situations and Mary Anne was living in the house of the Rev. Mr. Williams, pastor of the Episcopal Church in High-street. One day she came to my boardinghouse, Mrs. Beebe's, in Clinton Street near Flushing Avenue, and said she had left her situation, as the minister had attempted to take improper liberties with her. She had only been in Mr. Williams's house two weeks, and so I was loath to believe in the charge she made, so I thought I would try and find what way she had behaved herself in the houses where she had been at service before living in Mr. Williams's house. A friend of mine, Mr. William Wallace, gave her a room in his house until his wife could find her a situation. While there she behaved so badly that Mrs. Wallace refused to procure a situation for her. She then got a place in the house of Mrs. Hall, in Pearl-street, Brooklyn pretending she had just arrived from Ireland, as she had no letters of recommendation. In the meantime, I had written about her to Rev. Mr. Myers, of Montague-street, Brooklyn, in whose service she had been before entering the household of Mr. Williams. He wrote in reply that she needed close watching, as from her behavior she was likely to disgrace her family. I wrote to Ireland informing her mother of her conduct, and when she asked me a few days after if I was going to prosecute Rev. Mr. Williams, I told her I would not, as her character would not stand the test. She told me that I, her mother, and the remainder of the family were a pack of fools, and I slapped her across the face. She left the house and left her place of work. I recollect that I had seen her in company with a young man named Griffiths, who lives in Sands-street. I dogged him from his place of business to a house of ill-fame in Twenty-sixth-street. I did not go into the house that night, but came over the next Sunday and they did not let me into the house. She told the persons I was not her uncle, but was only a fellow who wanted to be her lover. . . . She told me she didn't want to see me or any of her relatives anymore. She denied having made any remarks about my being a lover, and it was well for her at the time that she had not. . . . I asked her to give up her mode of life and respect her mother's ashes, for I had heard of her mother's death in Ireland. She answered me in a way that gave me hope. I saw her once again and she promised to amend. . . . Three weeks ago her sister Lottie told me that Mary Anne had bought a pistol to shoot me with, saying if she did not do it, she had a friend who would. So I went there prepared. I was determined to see her if it cost me my life. In return for going to her I was greeted with the abuse and slang common among her class. . . .

—STATEMENT OF ROBERT BLEAKLEY TO THE *NEW YORK TIMES,*
DECEMBER 12, 1872

. . . A short time since, the girl, Mary Anne Smith was brought to me by an old lady, a communicant in my church who kept the boardinghouse where Mr. Bleakley boarded. The old lady said the girl had been at her house for several days and wanted to get a situation. I wanted the girl to show me a recommendation. She said she had none, but said she would get one in a day or two. . . . I allowed her to come to work in the house. She behaved well enough while she was in the house as far as I knew, but when she was in the house two weeks she came to me one day and asked me for her wages; I told her I would give her a portion of her wages; that her month was not up yet; she would not take a portion, but wanted the whole which I refused to give her. On that evening Mr. Bleakley came to my house partially under the influence of liquor and said his niece had informed him that I had taken improper liberties with her. I indignantly scouted the charge, when he began to talk about bringing the matter before the public. It occurred to me that this was a case of blackmailing, and I told him so, and said if he intended to try this on me, he had the wrong man to deal

with; that I had never done anything to his niece while she was in my house, and that I was willing that everyone should know all that happened while she was in my house; that my other servant was in the house all the time she was here, and further, that if his object was to make money he might spare himself the trouble, for I had none. I then called Mary Smith up, paid her what wages were due her, and told her to leave my house, which she did, and that was the last I saw of her. A few days afterwards Bleakley came to me and told me he had made inquiries about his niece and found that she was a very bad girl indeed. He penitently and humbly begged my pardon for what he had done, which I gave him, of course. I understood afterward that he went down on his knees to Mrs. Beebee and begged her pardon for having introduced the girl into the house. This is all I know about the matter.

—Statement of the Rev. Mr. Williams,

pastor of the High Street Episcopal Church

to the *Brooklyn Daily Eagle*,

December 13, 1872

An inquest into the murder of Mary Ann Smith, aka "Maude Merrill," was held by the coroner. Among those present was Emma Cozzens, the proprietress of the 10 Neilson Place brothel, and Lottie Smith, Maude's younger sister. Following the murder of her older sister and the arrest of Robert Bleakley, the young girl was destitute and was forced to enter a purported "poorhouse," the Home for the Friendless. A handcuffed Bleakley was brought into the courtroom where the inquest was held, escorted by Captain Byrnes and several other police officers. Bleakley showed little emotion as the charges against him were read to the jury. Lottie Smith testified first.

"Mary Anne Foley, alias Maude Merrill, was my sister. I last saw her at 10 Neilson Place on Friday. I called there by myself. . . . I had conversations with her regarding Bleakley, her uncle. I told her for her own sake not to see him, as I was afraid something would happen. I have heard him threaten her. . . . She was very sad and talked affectionately to me. She was always so good to me and I loved her. I have been three years in this country, my uncle brought me here. He went to California and left me in Brooklyn without making any provisions for me," she told the jury.

Bleakley jumped to his feet after hearing Lottie's testimony and asked if he could ask a question. The coroner refused his request.

"I have no counsel, and I desire to make some notes of some objections," Bleakley said.

He was told to sit down and that he would be able to ask questions later.

Mary Anderson, who knew Mary Ann Smith when she lived at the brothel on West Twenty-sixth Street, told the court that Mary Ann confided in her that she was afraid of her uncle. On one occasion when Bleakley came to the house, Anderson also testified, he demanded $50 from Mary Ann. Anderson told him that he could not possibly expect the girl to have that kind of money, and Bleakley answered that she better get it.

Captain Byrnes detailed Bleakley's confession and introduced as evidence the letters he had found in Smith's room on the day of the murder, including an affectionate letter written to Mary Ann from her former husband in Texas, and an equally affectionate letter written back to him. Byrnes then introduced a letter written by Smith to Bleakley. In it she wrote: "I am not satisfied with the tenor of your letter. It looks as if you were wanting to cast suspicion on my sister Lottie. Perhaps you want to drive her to ruin too, by persecution. She is a good, pure girl . . ."

In a letter to a friend, the dead girl wrote: "I really don't know what to say about this business with my uncle. He has plagued the life out of me. He brought Lottie to spend the evening with three people, and never spoke a word to me. People told him it was a shame for him to treat me so. He told them he would never speak to me again, so I have told him good-bye for the last time. . . ."

Byrnes then introduced a series of letters written by Bleakley and sent to the dead girl.

"I hope you will excuse me if I trespass on your feelings in this matter. I simply want to tell you that I do not in any way want to intrude on your time by calling on you, and if you will only be so kind as to let me know by note when I can have an opportunity of seeing you uninterrupted, I will be happy to do so and transact any little business we may have. . . . I shall be happy and willing at any time to see you, for you know I always liked you, notwithstanding your old trouble, and anything I can do for you I will do as cheerfully as ever. . . . It gives me great pain to go to see you such a long distance and have to come away like I did the other night."

It was signed, "Your affectionate uncle."

Byrnes told the jury that in his confession, Bleakley said, "I shot her and I am glad that I killed her. She is the only one who has brought disgrace on my family, and I would do the same thing over again."

The housekeeper, Mary Ann Allison, Emma Cozzens, and several other witnesses testified. They all reiterated the testimony they had given during prior questioning by Captain Byrnes, naming Bleakley as the man who had come to the Neilson Place house and shot and killed Mary Ann Smith without remorse.

Another witness, Annie Weaver, who testified that she had known the dead girl while they were both living at her former West Twenty-sixth Street address, told the jury that Smith had confided in her that her uncle had been "very intimate" with her. According to Weaver, Bleakley called on her frequently, asking Smith for money. He told Weaver that Smith owed him $50, and that he would take it in "any way he could get it." According to Weaver, Mary Ann would lock herself in her room whenever Bleakley came to call on her.

"She was afraid of him," Weaver told the jury. "She said he was jealous of her, but would not say why."

Following the introduction of all the evidence and the testimony by witnesses, the coroner ruled that there was sufficient evidence before the jury and declared the matter closed. The jury retired, and after ten minutes of deliberations, returned a verdict of guilty.

The verdict read: "That deceased came to her death from a pistol shot wound at the hands of Robert Bleakley."

Bleakley sat emotionless as the verdict was read. The police took him to the Tombs to await the action of the grand jury.

———•••••———

Bleakley's trial was set to begin on April 23, 1873. Before the trial could get under way, Bleakley cut his wrists with a razor while being held in jail. He was tended to by a prison doctor. He had written and left behind several letters addressed to those who had testified against him, including a long, rambling letter addressed to Lottie Smith, in which he swore he had never lived off the money Mary Ann Smith had earned as a prostitute. His trial began in earnest on April 28, 1873. Bleakley appeared in court with his wrists bandaged.

———•••••———

MAUD MERRILL'S MURDER
Trial of Robert P. Bleakley—Two Jurors Obtained

The trial of Robert P. Bleakley for the murder of his niece Mary Ann Foley, known as Maud Merrill, was commended this morning in the Court of Oyer and Terminer, Judge Brady presiding. Bleakley was very pale and appeared quite feeble, being apparently barely able to walk. Instead of sitting beside his counsel as is customary, at their request he was conducted by the Sheriff's officers to a remote corner of the room. Bleakley was constantly making irrelevant suggestions, which his counsel desired in this way to avoid. District Attorney Phelps conducted the prosecution, and ex-mayor Hall and Mr. Howe represented the defense.

The first juror called was Joseph Ewing. His sympathies, he said, were generally on the side of the accused and his impression of Bleakley from looking at him was that he was weak minded. This opinion gave great umbrage to the prisoner who vehemently uttered displeasure and characterized the proceedings as a farce. . . .

—*Brooklyn Daily Eagle*
April 28, 1873

SENTENCED FOR LIFE

End of the Bleakley Trial—A remarkable Verdict—He is
Found Guilty of Murder in the second Degree

At the opening of the Court of Oyer and Terminer yesterday
morning, Mr. Hall continued his summing up for the prisoner
Bleakley, the court-room being crowded to its utmost capacity.
Counsel criticized the evidence of Mary Weaver, and claimed
that by her own statements she entertained a dislike to the
prisoner, and her testimony was prejudiced against him. He
traced at length the events of the ten days preceding the prisoner's crime, and the accumulating troubles against which he
struggled, his discharge from the Navy-yard, his sister's suicide, and his niece's shameful life, in which she was sinking
lower and lower. . . . The prisoner's life was in their hands; he
was a poor, broken, unfortunate wretch, in whom there was
not much life; he appealed to them to let mercy decide which
way the scale should go. . . .

District Attorney Phelps began his summing up. He said
the prisoner had treated his murdered niece with violence
and was uncontradicted, and who was to say that it was
not his brutality which had driven her from her place as
an honest domestic to a house of ill-fame. He asserted that
the evidence of her sister Lottie and of the prisoner himself
had shown his bad treatment and that the murdered girl
repeatedly expressed her fear of him, and her determination
not to see him. . . . He refuted the imputations of the other
side upon the testimony of Mary Weaver, who had testified
that Bleakley had persistently demanded money from his
niece and asked what reason there was for not believing her
testimony. . . .

Judge Brady, then, at a little after 4 o'clock, charged the
jury. . . .

After the charge of Judge Brady the jury returned to the
court at 7:10. On being asked by the Clerk if they had agreed
on a verdict the foreman rose and said: "We have. We do not

find the prisoner guilty of murder in the first degree, but we do find him guilty of murder in the second degree. . . ."

—*New York Times*
May 9, 1873

———

Robert Bleakley was sentenced to life in prison. After the trial, one juror told a *Times* reporter that the jury did not believe that Bleakley's crime was premeditated, and that the panel felt it was the result of "a sudden impulse consequent upon finding that all his exertions to save her from a life which he abhorred had proved unavailing."

———

To a Common Prostitute

Be composed—be at ease with me—I am Walt Whitman, liberal and lusty as Nature,
Not till the sun excludes you do I exclude you,
Not till the waters refuse to glisten for you and the leaves to rustle for you, do my words refuse to glisten and rustle for you.

My girl I appoint with you an appointment, and I charge you that you
make preparation to be worthy to meet me,
And I charge you that you be patient and perfect till I come.

Till then I salute you with a significant look that you do not forget me.

—WALT WHITMAN
LEAVES OF GRASS, 1867

———

Prostitution flourished in New York City from the very wealthiest neighborhoods to the poorest. The business of prostitution was conducted openly. Brothels engaged in their business overtly, protected by police who received kickbacks. Common streetwalkers gamely subjugated many of the city's major thoroughfares, including Broadway, Fifth Avenue, and the waterfront.

Mary Ann Smith's murder was not unique. It was, in fact, commonplace. In 1871 the Reverend Dr. Henry W. Bellows, a Methodist minister, estimated that more than 20,000 prostitutes were working in New York City. Police reports on the number of prostitutes in the city were much lower, for obvious reasons: to show that the police department was doing its job in eradicating the prostitution problem, and to conceal what was a lucrative source of bribery for everyone from politicians to judges, and, of course, the police themselves. Bribes paid to the police from houses of prostitution accounted for a large percentage of the graft and corruption that permeated the department. Police reports issued during the 1860s estimated that there were as few as 2,100 prostitutes in the city and approximately 600 brothels.

Religious leaders like Bellows and other reformers had been launching full-fledged assaults on the prostitution problem for decades. In 1831, the Reverend John R. McDowall, a Presbyterian minister, founded the New York Magdalen Society. The biblically named society was a group of social reformers dedicated to teaching morality to prostitutes so they might follow the example of Mary Magdalene, who, according to some Christian teachings, had been a prostitute before becoming a follower of Jesus Christ. The society also opened a home for prostitutes wishing to reform their shameful lives. McDowall's Magdalen Society wanted to abolish prostitution, not just control it. A host of organizations were founded over the next twenty years to rid the city of prostitution, but none of them worked. Organizations like the American Society for Promoting Observance of the Seventh Commandment (*Thou shalt not commit adultery*) and the New York Society of Public Morals sprang up. The Catholic Church created the Sisters of Mercy to discourage Irish girls from falling into a life of degradation and shame, and the Sisters of the Good Shepherd, a refuge for those many Irish girls who had fallen into a life of prostitution to find safety and support as they redeemed themselves.

Irish girls like the young Maude Merrill (Mary Ann Smith) made up the largest number of the immigrant population that turned to prostitution as a means of survival. According to a study published in 1858 by Dr. William Sanger, resident physician at Blackwell's Island Hospital in the city, Irish girls accounted for 35 percent of the prostitutes in New York City. Sanger had been charged with examining the scope of venereal disease among the poor, but expanded his study to include an examination of prostitution citywide and the resulting spread of disease.

Sanger's study found that, although prostitutes came from every age group and every walk of life, the majority were poor, uneducated immigrants. The one characteristic that New York City prostitutes had most in common was their youth. According to Sanger's report, the vast majority of prostitutes were twenty-five years old or younger. Sadly, the Sanger study discovered that some of the youngest prostitutes were fourteen and fifteen years old. There were other incidents of children well below this age engaged in prostitution, including several girls reported to be eight years old.

———◦••◦———

Prostitution was a major moral and social crisis in New York City during the Gilded Age. Despite good-hearted efforts to rid the city of this social ill and moral quandary, overall public sympathy for most young women who engaged in this sordid occupation was nearly undetectable. Men who paid for the services of prostitutes were not readily condemned by society. Women held a lower social status than men in the nineteenth century, most assuredly when it came to the issue of prostitution. An example of this moral duality and hierarchy between the men who purchased the services of prostitutes and the prostitutes themselves was never more clearly illustrated than by the author Charles Loring Brace, who wrote in his study published in 1872, entitled *The Dangerous Classes of New York; and Twenty Years' Work Among Them*, ". . . there is no reality in the sentimental assertion that the sexual sins of the lad are as degrading as those of the girl. The instinct of the female is more toward the preservation of purity, and therefore her fall is deeper."

The Gilded Age, an era whose name was coined by American humorist and author Mark Twain, along with his coauthor, Charles Dudley Warner, in their 1873 book, *The Gilded Age: A Tale of Today*, was a time of colossal economic division in the country, and this division between rich and poor was nowhere more visible than in New York City. Businessmen, who became known as America's robber barons—like Andrew Carnegie, John D. Rockefeller, and Cornelius Vanderbilt—amassed extravagant wealth and lived lives of lavish excess and luxury, while most New Yorkers during this period, a vast immigrant population numbering over one million people, lived in dire poverty and squalor, huddled in unsanitary tenement housing, their pitiful lives shrouded in violent crime. Although this period was marked by unparalleled industrial growth and invention for some, it was also a time of massive immigration, poverty, crime, and unemployment. According to national economic indicators, a mere 1 percent of the population owned 99 percent of the wealth. Many poor, young immigrant girls saw prostitution as a way of earning a living.

But these prostitutes did not just ply their trade along the dangerous waterfront and in the slum districts. According to *New York by Gaslight*, a survey of prostitution written in 1882 by *Evening Sun* reporter James McCabe, West Twenty-third Street and Sixth Avenue housed more than one hundred brothels. According to McCabe, every form of sexual encounter with any type of prostitute—young, old, women, men, girls, and boys—could be purchased at one or all of these houses of prostitution. An even more enlightening observation noted by McCabe was that men from all walks of life and every strata of society purchased these sexual services. According to McCabe, ". . . men who at home are models of propriety seem to lose all sense of restraint when they come to New York."

Prostitutes often had as many as twenty customers per night and were forced to work sixteen hours a day, seven days a week, earning as little as 50 cents per customer. Half of their earnings typically went to the brothel's madam.

Young immigrant women and girls arrived in the country with hardly any money, no benefactor to care for them, nowhere to live, no real employment skills, and little ability to speak English. They were easy pickings for criminals (pimps) who preyed on them, often selling them into prostitution as a source of income for themselves.

The dichotomy between the rich and poor was even evident in their sexual vices. The brothels frequented by the privileged and wealthy men of means and high repute—judges, politicians, doctors, lawyers, businessmen, and even some ministers—were known as "silk-hat parlors," not by their common name, whorehouses. These parlors thrived just outside the upscale brownstones and luxurious hotels and restaurants that were the stomping grounds for the social elite. They were refined and stylish enclaves that employed beautiful, cultured young ladies who catered to the often-perverse sexual desires of society's leading and upstanding citizenry.

The lower classes had to be content with visiting the seedier whorehouses located along the waterfront—hotels like the East River Hotel, where Carrie Brown was brutally murdered, or brothels like the one where Maude Merrill had plied her trade before her murder. These whorehouses were second-rate in everything, including their lowlife clientele. Some of New York City's rougher trade frequented these houses of ill repute. Women found in these environs were often more desperate and many times sick with venereal or other diseases. Many of them were alcoholics or drug-addled from their frequent use of opium.

The doom of the fallen woman is sure. Once entered upon a career of shame, the whole world sets its face against her.
—JAMES McCABE
NEW YORK BY GASLIGHT, 1882

By the mid- to late 1870s, the New York City political machine took over the prostitution business in the city. For decades there had been a debate regarding everything from the reform-minded efforts to eradicate it from New York society, to legalizing and regulating it. Efforts to legalize prostitution failed to materialize, as did the good-intentioned efforts by religious groups to reform wayward girls. Finally, the prostitution problem was left in the hands of Tammany Hall, where it was incorporated into the political bosses' overall scheme of greed, graft, and corruption. If people were going to purchase the services of prostitutes, then there was no reason that a portion of the profits, like a portion from every other business concern in the city, shouldn't end up in the pockets of the bosses of the political machine.

Before the takeover of the prostitution business by New York City's political machine, most brothels were owned and operated by women. But then all that changed. Police were still under orders to arrest known prostitutes, but payoffs to the police by the more-established brothels and wealthier prostitutes, especially those in the "silk-hat" parlors frequented by men of means, kept the focus of their crackdowns on prostitution by common streetwalkers.

Outraged citizens and reformers clamored that prostitution was allowed to exist and even flourish, often right under the noses of the police because they were being paid off to protect the prostitutes and brothels. One known house was located next door to the Fifth Ward police station. In 1887, former New York City police chief George Walling stated that it was a common practice for the police to blackmail poor hookers. Walling did not comment on how widespread and systematic this practice was.

And if kickbacks to the police did not come in the form of money, they came in the form of providing the police with tips as informants. Since prostitutes were constantly in touch with the criminal element as well as reputable citizens, they came by information that the police could use in more-important investigations. In many instances the police did not perceive prostitution as a crime, and if it was, it was a victimless one. However, being allowed to operate without harassment might cost a house madam or a hooker a tip about who might have been involved in a recent burglary, or the whereabouts of some stolen merchandise.

And now a word or two upon a subject, distasteful to all, but at the same time one which must be considered in connection with the proper government of a large city like New York. I refer to the "social evil," so called . . . Not that the number of prostitutes is smaller, but the existence of the evil is less apparent to a stranger, who does not find himself accosted on the street in broad daylight, as would be the case were he walking on certain streets in London. But for all that, some stringent regulations are required in order to deal properly with this important problem. . . . Under no consideration whatever should a woman be allowed to approach or solicit men on the street. Such a system would undoubtedly prevent wholesale blackmailing to which I have every reason to believe the poor degraded women who sell their bodies for gain are forced to submit at the hands of unprincipled police officials . . . because while it is a moral certainty this blackmailing exists, it is almost impossible to obtain the evidence of a third party as to the payment of money in such instances. . . .

—GEORGE W. WALLING,

RECOLLECTIONS OF A NEW YORK CHIEF OF POLICE, 1887

The highly publicized Merrill case brought Captain Thomas Byrnes's name to the forefront of New York City newspapers. A young—he was only thirty years old in 1872—and dashing man, he looked as if he'd been sent straight from central casting. Although he did not cultivate relations with reporters, he remained accessible to them throughout the Merrill case. And although he refused to divulge the contents of the letters written by Bleakley to the murdered girl, he did so, or at least it appeared to most, for the most noble of reasons—to protect the reputations of the victim and the suspect. The Merrill case also pointed out Byrnes's energetic doggedness when it came to the pursuit of criminals, a trait he never lost throughout his long career. Perhaps more importantly, it was the Merrill case that pinpointed Byrnes's unorthodox and pioneering investigative technique. Any other police officer might have readily disregarded the stack of newspaper clippings and letters found in Merrill's room, thinking them to be junk. But not Byrnes. He was already developing the keen understanding that would become his trademark—that everything at a crime scene, even old letters, could serve as evidence in a case.

AMERICAN ALMANAC, 1878

In 1878, the icon of political fraud, William Marcy "Boss" Tweed, died. It would be nice to say that New York then entered into an era of enlightenment, but that was not the case. Political kickbacks, bribery, and fraud at all levels of municipal government continued. Although Thomas Byrnes's name was never associated with any corruption within the police force, the department itself was riddled with it. If not an era of political enlightenment, New Yorkers were on the cusp of a different type of enlightenment when the inventor Thomas Edison opened his electric light company in Manhattan.

Boss Tweed, the infamously corrupt New York City political boss and head of the Tammany Hall Ring, died in debtors prison at age fifty-five. He was buried in Brooklyn's Green-Wood Cemetery. His trial on corruption charges in 1872 resulted in a twelve-year prison term. The sentence was reduced to one year after an appeal to a higher court. Tweed was subsequently arrested based on a $6 million civil suit filed against him by the State of New York. Bail was set at $3 million, and he was thrown in debtors prison until he could make bail. In 1875 he escaped from prison and fled to Cuba and then to Spain. He was extradited to New York in 1876 and returned to prison.

There was Tweed;
Under his rule the ballot-box was freed!
Six times as big a vote he could record
As there were people living in the ward!
—SONG LYRICS BY W. A. CROFFUT

Thomas Edison established the first electric light company, Edison Electric Light Company, to market his incandescent lamp and other inventions. The company was located on Fifth Avenue. Edison helped finance the company with investor J. P. Morgan. In 1892 Edison's company became General Electric.

Despite the crime, corruption, and poverty that pervaded New York in 1878, the city was also home to one of America's most popular song styles, "The Cakewalk."

The Cakewalk became a popular song style in America. Its popularity began with a song, "Walking for Dat Cake," which was performed by the New York City musical team of Harrigan and Hart. The song style mimicked plantation songs sung by slaves. The Cakewalk later evolved into the American musical style called "ragtime."

> *'Twas down at Auntie Jackson's,*
> *Dar was a big reception, of high-toned colored people.*
> *So full of sweet affection,*
> *Such singing and such dancing,*
> *We made the ceiling shake.*
> *The cream of all de evening was,*
> *A walking for dat cake.*
> *So gently on de toe we darkies step out so,*
> *Easy and so gracefully around de room we go,*
> *De wenches captivate, we all perambulate,*
> *High-toned colored people dar a walking for dat cake.*
> —"WALKING FOR DAT CAKE"
> MUSIC BY DAVID BRAHAM
> LYRICS BY EDWARD HARRIGAN

New York City was not the only mecca of crime. In California, Charles Bolton made a name for himself as a stagecoach robber. Considering all the many types of criminal activities Thomas Byrnes had seen during his career, he never had to deal with stagecoach robbers.

Black Bart robbed a Wells Fargo stagecoach in California, getting away with a mere $400. Wearing a mask to hide his identity, Bart left behind a taunting poem at the scene of his crime, which became a trademark of his criminal career. His next stagecoach robbery netted him nearly $5,000. Pinkerton detectives tracked down Bart in 1888.

He was identified as an elderly gentleman, Charles Bolton, who lived in San Francisco.

> *Here I lay me down to sleep*
> *to wait the coming morrow,*
> *Perhaps success, perhaps defeat*
> *And everlasting sorrow,*
> *Yet come what will, I'll try it once,*
> *My conditions can't be worse,*
> *And if there's money in that box,*
> *'Tis money in my purse.*
> —POEM BY BLACK BART

QUIPS AND QUOTES

> *H-A double R I-G-A-N spells Harrigan.*
> *Proud of all the Irish blood that's in me.*
> *Divel a man that says a word agin me.*
> *H-A double R I-G-A-N you see,*
> *It's a name that a shame never has been connected with*
> *HARRIGAN, That's me!*
> —GEORGE M. COHAN, "HARRIGAN"

Anything that won't sell, I don't want to invent. Its sale is proof of utility, and utility is success.
—THOMAS EDISON

If you have to ask how much it costs, you can't afford it.
—J. P. MORGAN

I'm a gentleman.
—BLACK BART (CHARLES BOLTON),
WHEN ARRESTED BY PINKERTON DETECTIVES
WHO CHARGED HIM WITH BEING AN OUTLAW

6
THE GREATEST BANK ROBBERY
IN AMERICA

In which Captain Byrnes, using his unique methods of detection, uncovers the identities of the mysterious robbers of the Manhattan Savings Institution, whose heist is considered one of the most sensational bank robberies in the country.

The career of Thomas Byrnes had always been on the rise, but nothing propelled him upward as fast and as far as solving the Manhattan Savings Institution robbery in October 1878. It was considered the greatest bank robbery in the history of New York City, if not the world. The amount stolen during the weekend burglary amounted to nearly $3 million, approximately $50 million by today's monetary standard. Most of what was stolen, close to $2.8 million, was in registered and coupon bonds that were nonnegotiable. The rest, a paltry sum of approximately $11,000, was in cash.

In 1878, Byrnes was still serving as captain of the Fifteenth Precinct. During the six years since the Fisk case, he had made a name for himself as a capable and inventive police investigator. He had been instrumental in closing down more than a dozen illegal gambling houses and pool halls, testifying before the Legislative Committee on Crime in New York in 1875 that while he was serving as captain of the Fifteenth Precinct, he had shut down gambling operations on Broadway, Bleeker, Amity, Fourth, and Twelfth Streets. "There is no difficulty in closing houses of gambling," Byrnes told the committee. He regaled committee members with the names, dates, and fines of more than two dozen men involved in the gambling operations. As an example, Byrnes told the committee, "I arrested for gambling Samuel Watson, No. 653 Broadway; he was held in $500 bail by Judge Cox . . . George Woods, No. 609 Broadway, held in $1,000 bail by Judge Cox; no trial; William Cutter, No. 702 Broadway, discharged by Judge Cox . . ." and so on.

Byrnes's name cropped up almost weekly in newspaper crime reports. He was involved in everything from cases of petty larceny, the sale of stolen bonds, assaults, murder, and burglary. In 1874, Byrnes apprehended notorious burglar Albert Wilson and his coconspirator, William "Big Doc" Dougherty, after the two broke in and robbed $2,000 from a dry-goods store on Broadway. Byrnes had seen Wilson and Dougherty on the street, and knowing them to be hardened criminals, put a tail on both men. When the dry-goods store was robbed, Byrnes immediately apprehended Wilson and Dougherty. The two men still had the stolen loot in their possession. It was yet another example of Byrnes's innovative recordkeeping. He had kept a file on Wilson and knew his modus operandi.

Byrnes suffered one embarrassing incident during the intervening years—he had his badge stolen.

In May 1874, a gold badge that was to be presented to New York City's top crime fighter, Captain Thomas Byrnes, was stolen from the jeweler who had made it. The badge, made out of solid gold with two diamonds in it, was to be given to Byrnes for his many charitable works throughout the city, and was valued at approximately $1,200.

It was made by W. M. Lindemark Jewelers. The day before the gold shield was to be presented to Byrnes at a lavish ceremony honoring him, it was reported stolen. The jeweler told police that he had left the badge on his desk in his office and that a peddler had come in and briefly engaged him in conversation. The peddler then left abruptly. After he was gone, the jeweler noticed that the gold badge was gone as well, and he told police he suspected that the peddler had taken it.

Although a gold badge was ultimately presented to Byrnes, a rumor made the rounds among the criminal underground that the gold badge had been stolen by one of its own most daring robbers. That man was reportedly a well-known criminal named Jimmy Hope. Coincidentally, Hope would play a pivotal role in the Manhattan Savings Institution robbery.

On the morning of Sunday, October 27, 1878, Louis Werckle, the custodian at the Manhattan Bank Building on Bleecker Street that housed the fortress-like Manhattan Savings Institution—a repository of money, jewels, bonds, and other valuables belonging to the city's most wealthy—burst into a barbershop in the basement of the building and breathlessly blurted, "The bank's been robbed!"

Werckle was barefoot, barely dressed, a pair of handcuffs dangling from one of his wrists. The startled customers in the barbershop could hardly believe their ears. The Manhattan Savings Institution, a labyrinth of massive vaults, thick metal doors, and complex bolts and locks, was thought to be impenetrable. How could anyone have broken into it without being discovered? Someone surely would have heard the dynamite blast that the burglars used to open the secured vault and safe. How else could they have done it? But no explosions or anything else suspicious had been reported; the robbers had broken in and gotten away with the largest heist in New York City history.

Since the bank was in the Fifteenth Precinct, the investigation fell under the auspices of Captain Byrnes. Byrnes was mortified that such a daring robbery had taken place right under his nose. Although he had no money of his own in the bank, Byrnes took the robbery personally, and vowed to devote his every waking breath to tracking down the burglars.

Byrnes had been attending church when word of the bank robbery reached him. He raced out of the cathedral to survey the damage at the bank, and then headed to the barbershop to interview the barely coherent Louis Werckle. Byrnes was still dressed in his Sunday best: a neat, dark cutaway coat and dark trousers, vest, tie, and derby. From his demeanor, which exuded self-confidence and power, Byrnes might have been easily mistaken for one of the bank's presidents, or one of its wealthy patrons who had come to assess the situation. Only the lit cigar clenched between his teeth, hovering just below his flowing mustache, gave anything away about who he was or what might have been on his mind. Byrnes chomped down hard on his cigar, making the end of it glow in a red ember followed by a cloud of smoke. As he spoke, the cigar bobbed in his mouth like a conductor's baton, orchestrating his every word.

The Manhattan Savings Institution was six stories tall. The bank was on the first floor and had approximately one hundred feet of frontage on Bleecker Street, and another fifty feet of frontage on Broadway. Next door was the St. Charles Hotel. The bank had huge plate-glass windows on both the Bleecker Street and Broadway sides. The basement included the barbershop, a bathhouse, and the apartment where Werckle, his ailing wife, and his elderly mother-in-law all lived.

Werckle told Byrnes that, as was the usual custom, the bank's night watchman, Dan Kelly, had awakened him at 6 a.m. that Sunday morning, when Kelly's shift had ended. While he began to dress, Werckle said, several masked men broke into his apartment and took him, his wife, and his mother-in-law hostage. His wife began to scream, but the men pulled out guns and threatened to kill them all if she didn't stop. They took the women into another room and tied them up. They then threatened to kill Werckle if he didn't tell them the combination to the safe. Werckle had no other choice but to comply. The robbers left one of their men behind to guard the family while the others went to break into the safe.

Byrnes discovered that the robbers had left their many intricate and expensive tools and devices scattered on the floor of the vault. They were, by Byrnes's estimation, some of the finest burglary tools he had ever seen. Byrnes, who himself had a substantial collection of some of the finest burglary tools ever used in the city, had never seen such craftsmanship. Based on the workmanship and materials, Byrnes estimated that the tools had to have been worth at least $3,000—an awful lot of expensive equipment to leave behind, but small potatoes compared to the $3 million the thieves had managed to steal.

THE RESPONSIBILITY FOR YESTERDAY'S BANK ROBBERY

The daring robbery of the Manhattan Savings Institution, situated at the corner of Bleecker Street and Broadway, N.Y., yesterday morning, will probably be remembered as the most sensational in the history of bank robberies in this country. The sum of money represented by the securities stolen, namely $73,000 in negotiable and $2,506,700 in registered securities, together with $11,000 cash, makes this haul the largest yet recorded . . .

—*Brooklyn Daily Eagle*
October 28, 1878

The robbers had forced the main door of the vault open and then systematically broken into the various safety-deposit boxes in the huge safe. They made so much noise busting open the metal compartments within the safe that Werckle told Byrnes he could hear them all the way upstairs. It was a wonder, he confided to Byrnes, that no one else had heard the noise, including the watchman who had taken over that morning, or the police officer who was on duty. Byrnes couldn't agree more that someone else should have heard the noise if what Werckle said was true. Byrnes ordered one of his men to find out the name of the officer on duty that morning and obtained the name of the bank watchman who was supposed to come on duty after the night watchman. Byrnes was told that police officer John Nugent was working that morning, and that Patrick Shevlin had come on duty as watchman for the bank. Byrnes gave orders to shadow the two men, but under no circumstances were they to be questioned about the robbery. If anyone was going to question them, Byrnes decided he would. He wasn't about to let this pivotal case slip through his fingers.

Byrnes was often quoted using the old cliché that there was no honor among thieves. According to Byrnes, "I never met a thief in my life, provided he could benefit by peaching on his confederates, from whom I could not find out anything I was desirous to know."

Since neither Shevlin nor Nugent were professional criminals, and since the bank job had been carried out by a sophisticated bunch of criminals, Byrnes was sure that one of the two men would be the first to crack under questioning if, in fact, they were involved. Byrnes found no signs of forced entry into the bank building, or to any of the doors or windows leading to Werckle's apartment. Therefore, Byrnes concluded that someone either let the robbers inside or they had a pass key of some sort. In either case, Byrnes suspected that it must have been an inside job—someone connected to the bank was involved. The only two people remotely connected to the bank who might be implicated were Shevlin and Nugent, but Byrnes did not want to tip his hand at this point. Byrnes knew that, if they were involved, one or both of them would sooner or later lead him to the real robbers. Byrnes was sure that surveillance of the two men was the key to breaking open the case.

It had only taken the robbers about three hours to break into the seemingly impenetrable bank vault and clean the place out—an expeditious undertaking. The doors leading to the bank vault and the door to the vault's safe were made of thick steel, and the entire foundation of the vault was encased in cement. The twenty-five safety-deposit boxes inside the safe were also made of thick, hard metal. For some reason the robbers only managed to break open and steal the contents from fifteen of them, leaving behind another ten, and nearly $250,000 more in cash and securities. Something must have scared them off, Byrnes determined; otherwise, why not break open all the safety-deposit boxes? Still, from the looks of it, this was not a job done by amateurs by any stretch of the imagination.

A more extraordinary burglary than this one in this respect has seldom been committed.

—*New York Times*
October 28, 1878

There were twenty-five of these boxes in the safe, of which fifteen were opened and ten remained in tact.

—*Brooklyn Daily Eagle*
October 28, 1878

Werckle, the janitor, who was frightened, and besides saw those who bound, gagged and imprisoned him . . .

—*New York Times*
December 14, 1878

A false alarm caused the burglars to abandon one of the compartments of a safe which contained about a quarter million dollars in money and negotiable securities.

— *New York Times*
October 6, 1879

The burglary of the Manhattan Bank was the most audacious and successful that was ever committed in this country.

—*New York Times*
February 12, 1879

Byrnes was more than familiar with the cream of the crop of New York City bank robbers and quickly surmised that the Manhattan Savings Institution robbery could have only been pulled off by one of the city's top gangs. He had three possible gangs in mind: the Miles Gang, the Patchen Avenue Gang out of Brooklyn, and the Leslie Gang. Each gang had the wherewithal and professional sophistication to pull off a job of this magnitude and precision. And each gang was led by intelligent career criminals. Among his top suspects were the notorious Max Shinburn, who was part of the Miles Gang; a murderous thug named Johnny Irving and his partner Billy Porter, who led the Patchen Avenue Gang; or the most likely suspect, George Leonidas Leslie, known as the "king of the bank robbers." The Manhattan bank job had the imprimatur of Leslie.

There was only one problem: George Leslie was dead by the time the Manhattan Savings Institution was robbed. Still, Byrnes had a feeling that Leslie had somehow been involved in the robbery, and his instincts were right.

Although Leslie had been murdered by one of his own gang members in May 1878, he had been planning the heist for three years before it was carried out. He had put together a gang of some of the city's top bank robbers, including Jimmy Hope, Jimmy Brady, Abe Coakley, Red Leary, Shang Draper, Johnny Dobbs, Worcester Sam Perris, and Banjo Pete Emerson. He obtained financing for the robbery from the city's number-one criminal fence, Fredericka "Marm" Mandelbaum and "Traveling Mike" Grady.

Leslie was not the typical New York criminal. He was the son of a wealthy Cincinnati brewery owner and had graduated from college with a degree in architecture. For a short time he had his own architectural firm in Cincinnati, but he gave it up to head to New York City, where he entered into a life of crime—bank robberies in particular. A well-dressed, handsome, and intelligent dandy and man about town, Leslie lived a duplicitous life, hobnobbing with some of the city's most wealthy elite while becoming famous within the criminal world as a premier bank robber. Because of his mechanical engineering abilities and his knowledge of architectural drawing, Leslie was able to put his considerable talents to work planning and carrying out some of the most successful bank heists in the country. According to some police reports, Leslie was credited with having a hand in 80 percent of the bank robberies in America during a near-decade-long period (1869–1878). He was never arrested, and he never spent a day in jail. Leslie went on some of the bank robberies he planned himself, while for others, he was simply paid a fee to plan the robbery. The Manhattan Savings Institution heist was intended to be his masterpiece. He never lived to see it through.

Leslie's plans for robbing the Manhattan Savings Institution were precise and intricate, using split-second timing. He knew he couldn't use dynamite to blow open the vault and get to the safe inside because the noise would attract attention; shattering plate-glass windows at the bank would alert the police. He had other plans. First he made contact with Patrick Shevlin, the watchman. He bribed Shevlin with a promise of $10,000 from the proceeds. Shevlin agreed to let Leslie into the bank after it closed so Leslie could determine what tools he needed and could also practice manipulating the lock on the safe. After Leslie determined the type of combination lock on the safe, he bought a safe of the same make and style so that he could experiment with the combination. By drilling a small hole beneath the combination knob and then using a contraption of his own making, called "the Little Joker," Leslie was able to determine how to open the safe without using any explosives. "The Little Joker" was simply a flat piece of metal with a wire attached to it; it was placed inside the knob on the safe to record where the tumblers of the combination stopped.

With Shevlin's help, Leslie was able to bore a hole in the bank safe, insert his "Little Joker," and find out the safe's combination. Leslie meticulously put the combination lock back together, adjusted the tumblers, and left. The next day, bank officials could not open the vault using the old combination. They were not aware that Leslie had tampered with the safe the night before. The bank had a new lock and combination installed. This threw Leslie's intricate plans into a tailspin. He had to have Shevlin let him back into the bank to experiment again with the new lock. The whole process was time-consuming and nerve-racking. Leslie didn't want to leave any detail to chance, so he enlisted the help of a crooked beat cop, John Nugent, who was also to be cut in on a share of the profits from the heist. Nugent kept watch outside the bank while Leslie was inside trying to determine the combination. Leslie now had an inside man in Shevlin and an outside man in Nugent.

In May 1878, less than six months before the bank job, Leslie disappeared from sight. No one seemed to know what happened to him or where he might have gone. In June police found the decomposing body of a man hidden in the brush at Tramp's Rock in Brooklyn. He had been shot twice, once in the head and once in the heart. A pearl-handled revolver was found next to the body. The death was reported as a suicide, and the identity of the man unknown. But it was neither a suicide nor would the dead man's identity remain unknown. It was George Leonidas Leslie, and he had been murdered. Marm Mandelbaum was the one who identified the body and later paid Leslie's funeral expenses. The murder was never solved, but rumor had it that Leslie, who was always a ladies' man, had been having an affair with the wife of one of his gang members—Shang Draper—and that Draper killed Leslie in a fit of rage and dumped his body at Tramp's Rock. The woman in question, Babe Draper, was later found dead.

With its mastermind gone, the Manhattan Savings Institution robbery was at a standstill, but Mandelbaum and Traveling Mike Grady had invested too much money in the plan to see it fall through. Jimmy Hope, a member of the original gang and a close associate of Leslie's, took over the operation. They set late October as a date to hit the bank.

GEO L. HOWARD [LESLIE]
How the Bank Burglar is Said to Have Been Killed
A Series of Clues that Seems to Lead to the Belief that Shang Draper, Billy Porter, Johnny Irving, and Others were Implicated

An alleged history of the circumstances leading to the tragic death of George L. Howard [Leslie], the noted bank burglar, who was murdered on the night of May 29, 1878, has been given to the public. If the alleged clues are true, it would seem that Shang Draper, Billy Porter, Johnny Irving, John Dobbs, and a burglar named Perris are all implicated in his death, although it is not stated which one of them, if any, fired the fatal shot. . . .

—*Brooklyn Daily Eagle*
March 10, 1879

With George Leslie dead, Jimmy Hope became the titular leader of the Leslie Gang, although Mandelbaum and Grady gave the orders. Like Leslie, Hope did not come to a life of crime in the usual way, nor was he the typical New York City criminal lowlife. And much like Leslie, Hope was one of the country's most successful bank robbers. His robberies were always marked by boldness and sagacity.

In 1869, Hope rented office space in the basement of a building housing the Ocean Bank, located at the corner of Fulton and Greenwich Streets. He and his gang proceeded to bore a hole through the stone ceiling, cutting directly into the bank vault, where they stole nearly $1 million in cash, bonds, and securities.

In 1870, Hope robbed the Smith's Bank in Perry, New York, but was captured and sentenced to serve five years in Auburn State Prison. Three months into his sentence, he escaped.

During the robbery of the Kennsington National Bank in Philadelphia in 1871, Hope reportedly entered the bank dressed as a police officer, claiming he was sent to guard the bank against a suspected robbery. After being left in the bank to guard it, Hope let two of his gang members in, overpowered the janitor, and made off with more than $100,000.

In 1873, Hope and others planned to rob the First National Bank in Wilmington, Delaware. They kidnapped one of the bank cashiers and his entire family and tried to force the cashier to open the bank vault for them—the same modus operandi used in the Manhattan Savings Institution robbery. According to police reports, a servant in the cashier's house managed to escape and alert the police. Hope and the others were arrested and sentenced to ten years in prison. Within a year, Hope escaped.

———

Although Jimmy Hope now led the Leslie Gang, it was Marm Mandelbaum who called the shots. Mandelbaum was known as the "Queen of the Fences." Born in Germany, the stout, pug-faced 250-pound Mandelbaum came to New York City, where she and her husband opened a dry-goods store and haberdashery at 79 Clinton Street. Situated in a three-story building, the first-floor business looked respectable and unassuming. The shelves of the store were stocked with the usual dry goods. The rear of the building, however, was a different story. Here the rooms were lavishly furnished with the finest antiques: chairs, tables, and couches of the most accomplished workmanship, expensive paintings, rich Persian carpeting, glittering chandeliers, luxurious silk drapes, and expensive, ornate silver and glassware. It was considered one of the most sumptuously decorated homes in all of New York City—furnished entirely with stolen merchandise that Mandelbaum had fenced for her criminal clientele.

Mandelbaum entertained many of the city's wealthiest and most powerful citizens, including judges, politicians, and even police. Along with these upstanding representatives of the social elite, Mandelbaum also entertained many of her criminal cohorts; often, criminals mixed freely with police and judges during one of the many dinner parties she held in her luxurious second-floor home. Mandelbaum was smart enough to know that to keep her fencing operation in business, she had to pay off city officials. She gladly did so. According to police reports, Mandelbaum handled nearly $10 million in stolen merchandise during her reign as "Queen of the Fences." She also maintained her reputation within the criminal underworld by paying the robbers a fair price for the goods they stole and providing them with legal assistance if they were caught by law enforcement. She reportedly kept one of the finest criminal defense firms, Howe & Hummel, on retainer. If and when one of her many criminal colleagues needed bail money or legal services, Mandelbaum was quick to offer it. In this way, Mandelbaum kept her associates out on the streets doing what they did best—stealing—and then selling the stolen merchandise to her at a far-reduced price. She paid in cash and on time, and did, on occasion—as in the case of the Manhattan Savings Institution robbery—advance money needed to pull off certain potentially lucrative heists. Nearly every criminal, thief, and bank robber in New York was in her debt or service.

Over the years she was in business, Mandelbaum kept a citywide array of warehouses containing a wide assortment of the plunder that passed through her hands. Although she seldom dealt in stolen bonds or securities, she arranged with Traveling Mike Grady to handle that part of the Manhattan Savings Institution robbery.

———————

The third among the unholy trinity that oversaw the sensational Manhattan Savings Institution robbery was John D. Grady, known as "Traveling Mike."

Grady was also known as the "banker of the burglars," having financed most of the major bank robberies in the country. A short, fat, rumpled man who dressed in shabby clothes, Grady liked to appear as a beggar, but was a diamond merchant by profession who had found his role in criminal society a much more lucrative occupation. He was known to carry a worn, old satchel in which he reportedly kept stolen merchandise and money. He is said to have kept nearly $150,000 in cash and valuables, including stolen jewelry and diamonds, in the bag. The satchel was his office, and the seedy streets of New York City were where he plied his trade. Grady was a close business associate to most of the city's top criminals, including George Leonidas Leslie. He lent them money to front their operations, whatever they might be, from robbing banks to cleaning out estates. From them he received stolen securities, cash, and property, much of which he would sell at a higher price to other nefarious individuals.

———————

Police Captain Thomas Byrnes was ready to move heaven and earth to find the Manhattan Savings Institution robbers, but he discovered that he didn't have to venture into the celestial realm in order to crack the case. Slowly, but surely, the mysterious case began to unravel.

The bank robbers stole as much as they could that Sunday morning after taking Werckle, his wife, and his mother-in-law hostage and forcing Werckle to divulge the combination to the vault's huge door. From what Byrnes could surmise, the robbers loaded the stolen cash, bonds, and securities into suitcases and left the bank undetected in broad daylight. Still, it bothered Byrnes that, given the otherwise thoroughness of the thieves, they had left behind ten unopened safety-deposit boxes. They must have known they contained more cash and securities. The only logical explanation Byrnes could come up with was that the gang of robbers must have been somehow surprised by someone or something and decided to make a sudden getaway. What had interfered with them remained a mystery until Byrnes was approached by one of his own men. Officer John Van Orden, of the Fifteenth Precinct, was on duty that morning and had looked into the bank's front plateglass windows. He told Byrnes it was just something he instinctively did while making his rounds. Van Orden said that he had seen someone inside the bank. He did not recognize the man, but whoever it was had his shirtsleeves rolled up and appeared busy, dusting the counters and desks. He nonchalantly waved at Van Orden as if he knew him and continued with his work. Van Orden admitted that he mistook the unidentified man for a janitor cleaning up the place. Van Orden waved back and continued on his rounds, never thinking the bank was being robbed. That, Byrnes guessed, was what had surprised the robbers and made them flee the bank before looting it entirely.

Less than an hour after Werckle went running into the barbershop to alert everyone that the bank had been robbed, every officer from the Fifteenth Precinct and then some were on the case. Superintendent of police George Walling put every resource he had toward the investigation.

"The detectives assigned to the case all agreed that never before was such a safe-wreck seen. No such 'ripping out' had occurred in any bank burglary that had come under their notice," Superintendent Walling would later write. "For a while the case was a complete mystery, and the public came to the conclusion, when some time passed and no arrests were made, that we had given up a perhaps hopeless search. But we had not."

The bank directors closed the bank on Monday as the investigation continued.

Everyone knew that the Manhattan Savings Institution was one of the wealthiest banks in New York City, the place where many of the city's richest, most prominent, and most powerful people kept their

omas Byrnes epitomized law and order a century before there was *Law & Order*. His
rce of will and strength of character forever changed the New York City detective
reau. Aside from being credited as the father of modern detective work, Byrnes was
strumental in solving some of the most sensational cases in the city during the latter
rt of the nineteenth century (1863–1894).

86 PROFESSIONAL CRIMINALS OF AMERICA BY INSPECTOR THOMAS BYRNES

THE RIOTS IN NEW YORK: DESTRUCTION OF THE COLOURED ORPHAN ASYLUM.

Thomas Byrnes distinguished himself as a heroic law enforcement officer during the New York City draft riots in the summer of 1863, when an angry mob caused nearly $3 million of property damage, killed four police officers, and lynched a dozen African Americans in the streets. Trying to protect the Colored Orphan Asylum during the riot was among his earliest duties.

...he Rogues' Gallery at police headquarters. Byrnes was instrumental in detective bureaus'
...corporation of intelligence gathering as a vital part of police work and initiated the
...ractice of photographing criminals when they were arrested, creating the first "Rogues'
...allery," a photographic lineup of suspected criminals.

FRANK LESLIE'S ILLUSTRATED NEWSPAPER

No. 851—Vol. XXXIII.]   NEW YORK, JANUARY 20, 1872.   [Price, 10 Cents. $4 00 Yearly. 13 Weeks, $1 00.

NEW YORK CITY.—ASSASSINATION OF COLONEL JAMES FISK, JR., BY EDWARD S. STOKES, AT THE GRAND CENTRAL HOTEL—THE SCENE OF THE TRAGEDY.—See Page 207.

A cover illustration from the January 20, 1872, issue of *Frank Leslie's Illustrated* depicting the murder of James Fisk, Jr., by Edward Stokes. Byrnes was introduced to Jay Gould, one of the richest men on Wall Street, during his investigation into the murder of the notorious and flamboyant speculator James Fisk, Jr.— known as "Jubilee Jim." Over the years, Byrnes cultivated his relationship with Gould and other wealthy and influential citizens of New York City.

se five photographs are among the many that Byrnes's men took of arrested individuals ing his career in the New York Police Department. A selection of the photographs, includ- these five, were published by Byrnes in his landmark book on criminals, *Professional minals of America*.

mas Leary was a career inal, arrested by Byrnes ing his investigation into infamous Manhattan ings Institution robbery, sidered the largest bank t in American history. ry was never charged in crime.

Pete Emerson, alias Banjo Pete, was part of the New York City underworld. He had a successful career as a bank robber and jewelry thief throughout the late 1870s and early 1880s.

Johnny Hope went on trial for complicity in the Manhattan Savings Institution robbery in June 1879. Hope and his confed- erates, including his father, Jimmy, had planned and car- ried out the sensational rob- bery. Hope was found guilty and sentenced to twenty years of hard labor in the state prison.

Gustave Kindt was one of New York City's most notori- ous and cleverest safe crackers. He often boasted that he could open any safe ever made. He was no match for Byrnes, however, who threatened to throw Kindt's only child, his daughter, in prison, if Kindt did not confess his various crimes to authorities. Kindt confessed.

lthough credited by Byrnes ith being the leader of the gang burglars who broke into the anhattan Savings Institution, mmy Hope never spent a day of s life in prison for his involve- ent. Byrnes pursued Jimmy ope with a vengeance, to the int of having him extradited om California, where Hope as already serving time for bungled bank robbery in San ancisco in 1880, but Hope did t stand trial for his complicity the bank robbery.

PHOTOS FROM 1886 PROFESSIONAL CRIMINALS OF AMERICA BY INSPECTOR THOMAS BYRNES

Alexander Turney Stewart was one of the wealthiest retail merchants in the world when he died in 1876. In 1878, grave robbers broke into Stewart's grave, stole his body, and held it for ransom, demanding $200,000 from Stewart's widow, Cornelia. Captain Byrnes investigated the gruesome crime.
LIBRARY OF CONGRESS

Alexander Turney Stewart died on April 10, 1876, at seventy-two years of age in his palatial home, dubbed the "Marble Mansion," located on the corner of Fifth Avenue and Thirty-fourth street in the heart of New York City. Stewart was one of the wealthiest men in America when he died, leaving behind a fortune estimated at $40 million. In 1878, when thieves broke into Stewart's grave and stole his body, Byrnes managed to arrest and charge two men with the crime a little more than a week after the theft, once again putting the City of New York in awe of his incredible investigative skills.
LIBRARY OF CONGRESS

In 1892, the Reverend Dr. Charles H. Parkhurst of the Presbyterian Church in Madison Square began his campaign against vice and police corruption. From his pulpit, Parkhurst indicted New York City politicians and police alike for getting rich on the city's vast network of debauchery and vice. He became an ardent foe of then Superintendent of Police Thomas Byrnes.
LIBRARY OF CONGRESS

An 1892 illustration by the famous muckraking cartoonist Thomas Nast depicting the bulldog NYPD getting fat on corruption. In March 1894, the Lexow Committee began hearings into crime and police corruption and in January 1895, the committee issued a scathing report on the New York City police. Though not one bit of evidence connected Superintendent Thomas to any of it, Byrnes officially tendered his resignation in May 1895 when then New York City Police Commissioner Theodore Roosevelt called into question how Byrnes could be worth approximately $300,000 based on his meager municipal earnings as a police officer.
LIBRARY OF CONGRESS

detectives the rank of detective-sergeant and the same salary as regular police sergeants— $1,600 a year. A contingent fund was created to be drawn upon for legitimate expenses.

INSPECTOR THOMAS F. BYRNES.

Over four years have now elapsed since Inspector Byrnes was placed in command, and a few days ago he made the remark that the Detective Bureau was the "greatest bulwark against crime in this or any other country."
.... orney Olney decided to arrest

Whatever his flaws or human foibles, whether his tactics were abusive or his behavior self-serving, one thing clearly remains: Byrnes's legacy as the father of modern American detective work cannot be disputed. His use of mug shots, police line-ups, early forensic methods, interrogation tactics, and crime-scene investigation remains as the foundation of law enforcement procedures all over the world.

valuables. It was also well known throughout the city in both legitimate and illegitimate circles that it was thought to be impregnable. Robbing it was a criminal feat like no other in the city's history. Someone, Byrnes thought, had to want to take credit for the daring robbery. The heist had all the markings of a George Leslie caper, but Byrnes knew Leslie was dead. If Leslie didn't do it, then who did? And how did they come by the expensive burglary tools left behind, and how did they know seemingly every inch of the bank, inside and out? That had always been a trademark of Leslie's—knowing every detail about the banks he robbed. This was not a catch-as-catch-can operation. Except for being startled by Van Orden, the whole scheme had run like clockwork.

Byrnes had Officer Nugent and bank watchman Shevlin under surveillance. He now knew why the robbers had left in such a hurry. And he knew this caper was pulled off by a gang of top-notch criminals. It wasn't that hard to figure out who had the money and criminal connections necessary to finance such a heist—Marm Mandelbaum and Traveling Mike Grady. Byrnes put them both under surveillance on the chance that some of the stolen securities might come their way.

Just as Captain Byrnes had thought, someone did want to take credit for the robbery, but ironically, it was the least important link in the case. Nugent had no idea he was being watched as a possible suspect in the case. After a period of time, he began to run off at the mouth to various people about the huge amount of money taken during the daring robbery. He even laughed about how the robbery had been carried out right under the noses of the police. Suspiciously, he didn't include himself in this admonition. He even went so far as to tell someone how he had helped carry out a "boodle" of money from the bank that morning.

Although Nugent boasted about the crime, he wasn't the first to crack. That honor went to Shevlin. Byrnes's men reported back that Shevlin had begun spending time at known hangouts of some of the city's most notorious criminals, including the bar owned and operated by Tom "Shang" Draper, who had been in many scrapes with the law. Byrnes decided to take Shevlin in for questioning. The questioning

lasted several days, and Shevlin remained in custody. During his interrogation, Shevlin, who was no criminal mastermind or, for that matter,
had never even been in the slightest trouble with the law, began to
crack. Byrnes had tried every method of the third degree except beating Shevlin with his own hands. Byrnes knew that the investigation
was under the proverbial microscope, watched by every newspaper
in the city, bank officials, and the wealthy patrons who were victims
of the robbery. Shevlin was no big-time criminal. He was only small
potatoes in the larger scheme of things. Byrnes cajoled Shevlin by
offering him immunity if he would confess and reveal who the real
culprits were. The shrewd police captain went so far as to mock Shevlin for being taken advantage of by the robbers, who probably, Byrnes
guessed, gave him next to nothing for his role in the crime.

Byrnes tried another tactic. He arrested two suspects in early
December 1878, John "Red" Leary and John "Butch" McCarthy, and
charged both men with being accomplices in the robbery. Leary and
McCarthy were career criminals, and both had long records involving
attempted bank robberies. When asked what he was basing his arrest
on, Byrnes told reporters, "I believe as firmly as I believe anything that
at least one of the prisoners was engaged in the crime."

Byrnes was bluffing. He had no evidence either man was involved in
the robbery, but their arrest solved two problems for Byrnes. The police
department had been stymied in its investigation, and the public was
clamoring for results. Leary and McCarthy were clear signs of results.
Getting Shevlin to confess was his other problem, but with Leary and
McCarthy in custody, he was able to use the carrot and the stick with
Shevlin. The stick was that Byrnes told Shevlin one of the two men was
willing to confess to the robbery and expose the other members of the
gang. Byrnes said that he would be willing to give whoever confessed
first immunity from prosecution, but that once someone did confess,
no one else would get immunity, including Shevlin. He wouldn't need
Shevlin's confession after that, and Shevlin would face the same stiff
charges as the rest of the gang. The carrot was that if Shevlin decided to
confess first, he wouldn't be prosecuted. Shevlin decided to take a big
bite out of the carrot Byrnes dangled before him, before it was too late.

Byrnes expertly used the arrest of Leary and McCarthy to plant the seed of doubt in Shevlin's mind, and it worked.

"Some people seem to have doubts as to whether Leary and McCarthy were arrested as two of the Manhattan Bank burglars. They were arrested for nothing else," Byrnes later told reporters.

"The evidence upon which I undertook to arrest the prisoners and other men whom I have not yet found was furnished by reliable people, who said they were sure they could identify these men as some of the robbers," Byrnes said.

At the time Leary and McCarthy were arrested, Byrnes had no eyewitnesses and hardly a clue as to who had pulled off the bank job, although he had his suspicions. But it would take more than suspicions to solve the case and apprehend those responsible. He needed someone to snitch on the others, and Shevlin was the likely choice.

"Of course, whether I can legally convict or not is another thing, but whether or not, my certainty will not be shaken," he told reporters.

"Some believe that it will be impossible to secure any convictions in the case unless there be a dead give-a-way, by some of the gang, of others," he said.

Worrying that either Leary or McCarthy might implicate him in the robbery, Shevlin finally confessed, hoping to cut a deal with Byrnes for his testimony against the others. He admitted to Byrnes that he had given in to the overtures of the gang; that he had given the gang duplicate keys to get into the bank; and that he had provided the robbers with as much information as they needed about the place. And yes, he admitted to Byrnes, he had been given very little for his role in the robbery, especially considering the huge take in the close-to-$3-million heist. The gang, Shevlin said, was headed by Jimmy Hope. Once he had his confession from Shevlin, Leary and McCarthy were released. Byrnes had no real evidence to hold them.

Shevlin admitted that Hope had managed to gain his confidence and that he had assured him that no one would ever suspect him of being involved in such a high-level caper. Besides, Hope had told him he would get a fair share of the loot. Shevlin said he made very little money as a watchman, and Hope had said he would make Shevlin a very wealthy man if he agreed to help in the robbery. Shevlin admitted to letting George Leslie into the bank to experiment on the safe's combination. He told Byrnes that after Leslie had twice been let into the bank at night, he didn't have any further dealings with Leslie, and that after Leslie's disappearance, Jimmy Hope became his main contact with the gang. According to Shevlin, Hope and his gang came together for final preparations on October 25, the Friday night before the robbery. On Sunday, when Shevlin was working at the bank, they struck.

It didn't take Byrnes long after he had secured a confession from Shevlin to act. In February 1879 he arrested Johnny Hope, the son of reported gang leader Jimmy Hope. In a police lineup, Officer Van Orden identified Johnny Hope as the man he had seen in the bank and mistook for a janitor. Ultimately a dozen other men, some of whom had scattered to the four corners of the country, were arrested on charges of taking part in the Manhattan Savings Institution robbery. Among those apprehended were: Bill Kelley, Jimmy Hope, Johnny Dobbs, Sam Perris, Abe Coakley, Pete Ellis, Pete Emerson, Ed Goodrich, Patrick Ryan, Jim Brady, John Leary, and Tom "Shang" Draper.

The trial of Johnny Hope for complicity in the Manhattan Savings Institution robbery began in June 1879. The trial took place at the New York City General Sessions Court with Judge Rufus B. Cowing presiding. The courtroom was a three-ring circus with a standing-room-only crowd of newspaper reporters, police, bank officials, curiosity seekers, and even a few criminals.

The assistant district attorney related in detail to the judge and jury the circumstances surrounding the bank robbery on the early morning of October 27, 1878. He told the court that he would prove beyond a shadow of a doubt that Johnny Hope and his confederates, including his father, Jimmy, had planned and carried out the sensational robbery. The assistant district attorney said he would show that

Johnny Hope was seen in and around the bank on the days leading up to the robbery. He would produce four witnesses who would attest to seeing Hope, including a police officer, John Van Orden, who had mistaken Hope for a bank janitor on the morning of the robbery. The assistant district attorney said he would also use the confession of the bank watchman, Patrick Shevlin, to show that Johnny Hope and his father were among those who took part in the bank heist.

Byrnes had arrested Johnny Hope in February 1879 as he was leaving a Broadway theater. Byrnes told newspaper reporters that the robbery had been solved and that the arrest of Hope would lead to other arrests shortly. According to Byrnes, the identities of all the men who had taken part in the robbery were known to police and were being pursued.

The *New York Times* had called the robbery ". . . the most audacious and successful that was ever committed in this country."

This rankled Byrnes in more ways than one. First, the robbery had taken place in his precinct, and second, the newspapers seemed intent on portraying the robbers as criminal geniuses. Although it had taken Byrnes and the police department nearly five months to apprehend the first of the suspects, Byrnes assured the public that he and his men had known the identities of the culprits within twenty-four hours of the robbery, and that these men were all being tracked down and would be brought to justice. Byrnes said that during the intervening period he had gathered every bit of evidence he could and had carefully analyzed it all. He told the press that his initial suspicions about the men who had carried out the robbery had been confirmed.

Byrnes had carefully studied all of the few clues that the robbers had left behind, the way the robbery had been carried out, and the precision with which the robbers had made off with the money and securities. He concluded that only a handful of criminals were capable of engineering such a sophisticated and daring robbery. After sifting through all the available evidence, Byrnes decided that only Jimmy Hope, one of the country's most notorious and successful bank robbers, had the wherewithal to pull off such a daring heist. After Van Orden identified Johnny Hope as one of the robbers, it was easy enough to put two and two together. Johnny Hope was not experienced or daring enough to carry out the robbery. His father, Jimmy, had to be the mastermind behind the heist.

At the time of the robbery, Jimmy Hope was on the lam, having escaped from Sing Sing prison. Hope had been serving time for another bank robbery but escaped by jumping off a bridge while on a prison work detail. Despite being shackled to several other men, Hope had jumped off the bridge, taking the other prisoners with him, and landed on a Hudson Railway train. Although authorities pursued Hope after his daring escape, he managed to elude them. He then joined up with the gang plotting to rob the Manhattan Savings Institution and ultimately became its ringleader.

———

While sitting in the courtroom during Johnny Hope's trial, Byrnes took note of a red-faced man with a long black mustache. The man was following the case intensely, hanging on every word the prosecutor and defense had to say. The man was John Nugent, and although he was dressed in civilian clothes, Byrnes recognized him. He seldom forgot a face.

During his interrogation of Shevlin, Byrnes had learned that one of the burglars was a police officer. Shevlin had seen the man in uniform, standing guard outside the bank when it was being robbed. He said he later saw the same man carrying away a satchel of stolen securities. He didn't know the man's name, but he described him as having a red face and a black mustache. Byrnes had already singled out Nugent as the man Shevlin was talking about and had put him under surveillance. But now, Nugent had fallen right into Byrnes's lap.

Byrnes asked one of his police officers to approach Nugent and tell him that Captain Byrnes wanted to speak with him in the corridor. Byrnes left the courtroom and asked a court officer to bring Shevlin into the judge's private chambers and hold him there. Nugent followed the uniformed police officer out into the corridor where Byrnes was waiting for him. After asking Nugent his name, rank, and precinct, Byrnes told Nugent that he might have a place for him at his precinct at a higher rank and pay. He asked Nugent to come with him into the judge's chambers so they could talk privately about the matter. Inside the chambers Shevlin sat handcuffed to a chair, guarded by a burly court officer. Seeing him sitting there, Nugent's already red face turned crimson.

"Do you know that man?" Byrnes asked, pointing toward Shevlin.

Nugent turned his back to Shevlin, stammered a few words, and finally told Byrnes he had never seen the man in his life.

Hearing what Nugent had said, Shevlin jumped up from his chair and yelled, "Yes, you do!"

Nugent tried to leave, but Byrnes held him by the arm.

"Yes, you do, and I know you," Shevlin said. "You are the man who told me you carried the stuff away from the bank."

Nugent was arrested on the spot.

———

Superintendent George Walling had handed over the Manhattan Savings Institution case entirely to Captain Byrnes. Although Walling viewed Byrnes as a serial self-promoter and disliked his questionable third-degree tactics, Walling knew that if anyone could solve the case, it would be Byrnes.

Byrnes's relentless questioning of Shevlin had paid off. Shevlin named names and gave him the evidence he needed to prosecute Johnny Hope, as well as another known criminal connected with the case, Bill Kelley. Kelley was charged with complicity in the robbery, and his case was tried in the Court of Oyer and Terminer. The first witness was Shevlin, who testified that Kelley had acted as a go-between between himself and the gang of robbers. He testified that Kelley had told him in great detail how they had robbed the bank and how they had surprised the bank janitor Werckle and his family. He even told him how they had coerced the vault combination out of Werckle by putting a gun to his head. It was Billy Kelley, Shevlin told the court, who paid him $1,639 for his part in the bank robbery. Kelley had assured him that once the securities were disposed of, Shevlin would be getting more money.

———

Louis Werckle testified at Johnny Hope's and Billy Kelley's trials. He was, according to a *New York Times* article, ". . . a little old man of no physical strength, and apparently less courage. . . ." Werckle had worked for the bank for twenty years and was never a suspect in the case. His wife, who lived with him in the small apartment in the basement, had a heart condition and needed constant care. His mother-in-law, who lived in the apartment also, was seventy-three years old, nearly blind, and almost deaf.

Werckle testified that the robbers broke into his apartment, handcuffed him and his wife, and tied his mother-in-law up in a sheet. All the robbers were wearing masks. One robber grabbed a set of keys from him and then held a gun to his head and demanded the vault combination. The man brandishing the gun was later identified as Johnny Hope.

Werckle testified that he told the robbers he didn't have the combination. The robber with the gun grew angry and threatened to kill him.

"You lie," the robber yelled at him. "You open that vault every morning. Give it up or I'll kill you."

Werckle told the robber that even if he gave them the combination to the vault, they wouldn't be able to open the safe.

"You leave that to us," the robber said, and laughed. Werckle testified that he had no other choice but to give them the combination. All but one of the masked robbers left. One stayed behind to guard Werckle and his family.

Over the years Byrnes had familiarized himself with the personalities and methods of many of the city's most hardened and notorious criminals. He kept impeccable records and photographs of them. The police officers under his command were required to do the same. By the time of the Manhattan Savings Institution robbery, Byrnes had files full of information on every known criminal and their activities. His methods of detection were new to the New York City police force. Prior to Byrnes, officers had relied on a hit-and-miss method of apprehending criminals. Byrnes did it methodically based on evidence and information he had gathered on various criminals.

By keeping records, he could easily match the method of the crime to the history of the criminal. He knew what pickpockets worked what part of the city, and he knew which criminals were capable of pulling off bank robberies the likes of the Manhattan Savings Institution. Byrnes let it be known to the criminal underworld that not only did he have files on them and their activities, but he also had them under constant surveillance. He instilled in them a fear and distrust by fostering among them the suspicion that at any given time, any one of their associates might implicate them in some crime in order to save their own skin with Byrnes. Byrnes made criminals afraid of possible snitches in their midst by offering immunity to anyone willing to testify against one of their own. Byrnes often ordered random roundups of known criminals, bringing them in for questioning for no reason other than to harass them. Sometimes during these roundups, someone might slip up and give Byrnes unsolicited information about pending or past crimes committed in the city.

His preemptive strikes kept the city's criminals on edge. They never knew where and when Byrnes might swoop down on them. Byrnes's psychological warfare with criminals had never been used successfully before, and his tactics, including the questionable third degree when all else failed, often produced substantial results, as in the case of the Manhattan Savings Institution robbery. He coerced a confession out of Shevlin by promising him immunity if he would testify against the others involved. He used surveillance and trickery to capture John Nugent. And he tracked down and apprehended Johnny Hope and Billy Kelley based on his evidence gathering and knowledge of the criminal element.

—•••—

In July 1879, Johnny Hope was found guilty and sentenced to twenty years of hard labor in the state prison. In passing sentence, Judge Rufus Cowing said: "John Hope, you have been convicted of the grave crime of robbing in the first degree and should be subjected to the most severe punishment. You did not assist in plundering a rich man or rich corporation of men—the popular idea of a bank—but hundreds of poor men and women. . . . Who can tell how many of these poor depositors have suffered bitterly? If we even begin to measure the extent of your crime in this light, it becomes appalling. It appears also that this crime was not your first. I deem it my duty to impose the heaviest penalty known to the law."

Billy Kelley was convicted and sentenced to ten years.

———

Johnny Dobbs was arrested in connection with the Manhattan bank robbery in Philadelphia in May 1879. Dobbs was called ". . . one of the most noted and desperate criminals in the United States."

Dobbs, whose real last name was Kerrigan, had been a thief and waterfront thug all his life. One of his first crimes was shooting a police officer during an attempted burglary. He was arrested and spent four years in prison for the shooting.

Dobbs was arrested in Philadelphia for trying to cash in five $1,000 bonds that had been stolen in the Manhattan bank robbery. Police in New York City had been looking for Dobbs for several years for other crimes, but he had successfully managed to elude them.

Although Dobbs was apprehended in connection with the Manhattan bank robbery, he was never officially charged and did not stand trial. He was ultimately set free.

———

In April 1880, Peter "Long Pete" Ellis and Abraham "Abe" Coakley were also arrested in Philadelphia and charged with complicity in the robbery. Byrnes narrowly missed getting his hands on the elusive Jimmy Hope and another of the bank robbers, Samuel "Worcester Sam" Perris. Both Ellis and Coakley were arrested by Byrnes, who traveled to Philadelphia to put the cuffs on the two men personally. Ellis and Coakley were arrested while standing on a downtown Philadelphia street corner waiting for two friends. They had no idea that Byrnes and his men were on to them. The two men they were waiting for were Jimmy Hope and Perris. Hope and Perris were a few hundred yards away when Ellis and Coakley were arrested. Seeing this, Hope and Perris made a hasty retreat and escaped capture at the hands of Thomas Byrnes.

Neither Ellis nor Coakley were charged in the robbery, and neither man stood trial for their connection to the case.

———•◦•◦•———

The trial of John Nugent in January 1880 ended in a not-guilty verdict. When the foreman of the jury read the verdict, the prosecutor, police, and even the judge, Rufus Cowing, were dumbfounded. Friends of Nugent who had religiously sat through the trial broke into applause. Nugent was a free man. Rumors circulated that Nugent had managed to bribe one of the jurors, although no one was ever able to prove it.

———•◦•◦•———

I desire to state that during the year in which I have occupied the bench, this is the first time that justice has, in my opinion, miscarried. Nugent, I believe you are a guilty man, and all your patriotism you have shown for your country, all the good deeds claimed for you, can never obliterate what, in my opinion, was a most willful and wicked breach of trust on your part. . . . I believe a police officer, such as Nugent, who commits a breach of trust, ten million times more guilty than either Hope or Kelley, who are now serving terms of imprisonment.

JUDGE RUFUS B. COWING,

AT THE CONCLUSION OF THE TRIAL

OF JOHN NUGENT, JANUARY 1880

———•◦•◦•———

Gentlemen, I return you my heartfelt thanks. I am glad that you saw through the manufactured testimony produced against me in this court. It was nothing but a concocted conspiracy.

JOHN NUGENT, TO THE JURY, AFTER THE NOT-GUILTY VERDICT WAS READ,

JANUARY 1880

———•◦•◦•———

Of all the alleged men who took part in the sensational Manhattan Savings Institution robbery, only Johnny Hope and William "Billy" Kelley were ever convicted and sent to prison. Patrick Shevlin, the bank watchman who had testified against the gang, was granted immunity from prosecution. The infamous Jimmy Hope was never convicted, nor did he serve any time for his involvement in the case, despite Captain Byrnes's best efforts.

Byrnes pursued Jimmy Hope with a vengeance, to the point of having him extradited from California, where Hope was already serving time in prison for a bungled bank robbery in San Francisco in 1880.

Byrnes was confident that Hope would be returned to New York City to stand trial for his complicity in the bank robbery, and that he would be convicted. Jimmy Hope was not returned to New York City to stand trial, and instead completed his term of imprisonment in California. After his release, he was returned to New York to complete a previous term of incarceration at Auburn State Prison. Hope was finally released from Auburn in 1889.

Even then Byrnes attempted to have Hope tried in connection with the robbery, but judicial authorities determined that there was not sufficient evidence to prosecute a decade later. Jimmy Hope was set free, having never spent a day of his life in prison for his involvement in the sensational Manhattan Savings Institution robbery.

Jimmy Hope's luck ran out in 1881 when he tried to rob Sather Bank in San Francisco. Hope rented an apartment in a room above the bank vault. Hope and his accomplices drilled a hole through the floor, but during the day an observant bank cashier noticed that cement had somehow fallen from the ceiling over the vault and called in police. By then, the novelty of breaking into banks by boring either up through the floor or down from the ceiling was old hat, and the police staked out the bank.

That night, as Hope and his gang made their final preparations for breaking into the bank by lowering themselves through the hole that had been drilled, the police swarmed into Hope's rented apartment and the bank downstairs, arresting Hope on the spot. He was sentenced to seven years in jail, and this time he did not escape. He was later sent back to serve out the rest of the time he owed at Auburn State Prison. Jimmy Hope died in a run-down New York City flat in 1905.

JIMMY HOPE DIES;
ROBBED MANY BANKS
His Most Noted Job the Looting of
The Manhattan

James Hope, known much better as Jimmy Hope, who was really a pioneer in the bank safe-cracking business and whom achieved great notoriety by breaking into the Manhattan Bank in 1878 died late Thursday night in the unpretentious flat he occupied with his wife at 693 Columbus Avenue. The name of Pat Sheedy, the well known sporting man was on his lips. . . . Sheedy believes, he says, that Hope wanted to tell him an important secret. . . . The whereabouts of the bonds stolen in the Manhattan Bank robbery has always been a mystery. It may have been this secret that was on Hope's lips. . . . The greatest job which he ever had a hand was the Manhattan Bank Burglary in 1878 which was one of the biggest bank robberies in the criminal records of this country. The thieves got away with $3,000,000 worth of stocks and bonds. Little was ever recovered. . . ."

—*New York Times*
June 3, 1905

Neither Marm Mandelbaum nor John "Traveling Mike" Grady, the financiers of the robbery, was ever charged in the crime.

Mandelbaum's long criminal career came to an end in 1884 after the New York City district attorney, Peter B. Olney, along with Pinkerton agents, caught her red-handed with stolen property—several bolts of expensive silk that had been reportedly stolen and secretly marked by Pinkerton agents.

Even though Mandelbaum called on her usual political and judicial cronies, the reform-minded Olney made the charges stick, and Mandelbaum was arrested and jailed. She was released on high bail and scheduled to stand trial in December 1884. When informed by her legal counsel Abe Hummel that it seemed likely she would be found guilty and face a stiff sentence, Mandelbaum fled to Canada, taking with her an estimated $1 million that would comfortably tide her over in her exile. She lived out the rest of her life in relative luxury and died in February 1894 at the age of seventy-six. Her body was taken back to New York City and buried alongside her husband and daughter.

OLD "MOTHER" MANDELBAUM IS DEAD
She Was a Famous "Fence" Well Known to the Police of This City

HAMILTON, Ontario, Feb. 26—Mrs. Fredericka Mandelbaum, known in New York City as a notorious "fence" and who did a profitable business there in that line for a number of years, died here this morning. She came here about ten years ago when the New York authorities began proceedings against her and her conviction seemed probable. A legal fight ensued for her extradition, but with the assistance of Howe & Hummel, the criminal lawyers of New York, she was enabled to remain in Canada. . . . Her body will be taken to New York tomorrow afternoon for interment there Wednesday morning. . . .

—*New York Times*
February 27, 1894

John "Traveling Mike" Grady died in 1880 of heart failure, complicated by a bout of pneumonia, no doubt contracted from his days on the damp, cold streets of the city dressed only in his raggedy clothes. His list of criminal cohorts reads like a who's who of New York City's criminal elite.

BANKER OF THE BURGLARS
DEATH OF JOHN D. GRADY,
RECEIVER OF STOLEN GOODS

No man was better known to the Police, not only of New York but every large city in the United States, and to criminals of high grade, especially bank burglars, than John D. Grady, whose ostensible calling was that of a diamond broker. . . . Many Police officers asserted—and Grady never denied it—that the diamond broker was not only a receiver of stolen goods, but the banker of many first-class criminals. . . . Grady became useful to the police. He enabled officers to make reputations by giving them information in regard to petty crimes, in betraying men who did not belong to his clique, or with whom he was at enmity, or in recovering stolen watches and other property when Police officials were compelled to exert themselves by men of prominence and power who had been robbed. . . . Grady, Police officials say, arranged the details of the Manhattan Bank burglary, and spent $10,000 on the preliminary attempts. . . .

—*New York Times*
October 4, 1880

Despite the lack of convictions in the Manhattan Savings Institution bank heist, Byrnes had earned a reputation as a relentless crime fighter. The rich and powerful in New York City saw Byrnes as a man willing to do anything to protect their financial interests and savings. And in 1880, Byrnes was appointed to head the New York City Detective Bureau. One of his first acts was to establish a police substation in the heart of Wall Street.

BAG OF BONES

In which ghoulish grave robbers steal the body of retail magnate A. T. Stewart and hold it for ransom. Captain Byrnes arrests two suspects only to have the case thrown out. Mrs. Stewart builds the Cathedral of the Incarnation, a costly memorial to her husband, in Garden City.

Not long after the Manhattan Savings Institution robbery, Captain Thomas Byrnes was faced with another sensational crime. On the morning of November 7, 1878, it was discovered that robbers broke into a cemetery vault at St. Mark's Churchyard in the Bowery and stole the body of Alexander T. Stewart, one of the richest and most success-ful merchants in the country. The thieves demanded $200,000 for the safe return of Stewart's remains.

On the advice of family counsel, Judge Henry Hilton, Stewart's widow, Cornelia, refused to pay the ransom. Hilton was not only a family friend; he was the executor of Alexander Stewart's will. What followed was one of the biggest police investigations in New York City's history and a sensational media frenzy. As usual, Byrnes was in the thick of it.

GRAVE DESECRATORS
TRACING THE ROBBERS OF
MR. STEWART'S GRAVE
THE MANNER OF THEIR ENTRANCE TO AND EXIT FROM THE YARD—ROUTE TAKEN IN REMOVING THE BODY—THE POLICE WORKING ON SEVERAL CLUES— THE SUSPICIONS AGAINST THE SEXTON.

. . . it was apparent that after securing their booty the robbers either wrapped it in a sheet or cloth bag, and carried it across the grass to the side of the church. . . . The supposition now is that the robbers had a casket or box that could readily be made air-tight in a wagon standing conveniently in the street and the body was placed in it after being taken out of the cemetery. . . . A well-dressed man called on Superintendent Walling yesterday morning and obtained an audience on the strength of having important facts to disclose. It turned out that he had a theory that the body was stolen at the instance of a phrenologist for the sake of the head. He suggested it might have been shipped abroad on one of the foreign bound steamers and he wanted the Superintendent to cable abroad to have the cargoes searched on arrival. . . . They claim to have positive evidence that but three men were engaged in the outrage, but refused to tell what it is. . . .

—*New York Times*
November 10, 1878

Frank Parker, the assistant sexton of St. Mark's, was the first person to come upon the desecrated vault. Parker, one of only a handful of people who knew the exact location of Stewart's remains, first saw a pile of freshly dug soil just outside the crypt. A pang of fear and apprehension ran through him. He bolted for the church rectory to inform the chief sexton. Judge Hilton was contacted immediately and went to police headquarters to report the ghoulish crime. At that point, no one knew why Stewart's body had been stolen nor had anyone contacted Mrs. Stewart, Hilton, or the police, demanding a ransom.

Stewart's burial chamber was in the middle of the churchyard cemetery. A ten-foot iron fence ran completely around the graveyard. The 150-square-foot vault was made of brick and was approximately a dozen feet deep. The roof was covered with earth and moss. The entranceway was hidden from view by three marble slabs. Its appearance was entirely anonymous and insignificant. No one, except for the immediate members of Stewart's family, Hilton, and three staff members at St. Mark's Church knew the exact location of the vault. Captain Byrnes's first intuition was that the grave robbery was an inside job.

Someone had told the thieves exactly where Stewart's body was. The question was: Who?

Stewart's coffin wasn't the only one inside the vault. There were four others, including the coffins of two of the Stewarts' infant children. The grave robbers dug a hole into the vault and took the top off what was the newest cedar coffin. Beneath the wooden cover was another one made of lead, which the thieves cut through, finally forcing open the coffin of Alexander Stewart. They ripped the expensive, silver inscription plate off the coffin and absconded with it, along with Stewart's remains, mostly bones. The ghouls left behind a lantern and a shovel that they used to do their dirty work. There were no other clues. Police under the direction of Superintendent George Walling and Captain Byrnes were able to uncover the store where the shovel and the lantern were purchased. Coincidentally, they both came from Stewart's own retail store.

$25,000 Reward!—Whereas, in the early morning of Nov. 7, 1878, the vault of the late Alexander T. Stewart, in St. Mark's Churchyard, in this city, was broken into, and his remains removed from there, the above reward is offered by direction of Mrs. A. T. Stewart, and will be paid for the return of the body and information which will convict the parties who were engaged in the outrage. Or a liberal reward will be paid for information which will lead to either of these results.
—Reward notice issued by Judge Henry Hilton,
New York Times, November 8, 1878

At the time of his death in 1876, Alexander Turney Stewart was one of the richest men in the country. He left his wife, Cornelia, an estate worth more than an estimated $40 million.

Stewart made his vast fortune in the retail sales business. He was known as "The Merchant Prince of Manhattan." An Irish immigrant, he began his career in New York City in 1823 selling Irish linens. By

1862, he had built the largest department store in the world. Known as "The Iron Palace," Stewart's six-story store, located on the corner of Broadway and Ninth Street, had a cast-iron front and a glass dome skylight. The immense store employed more than 2,000 people and had nearly twenty departments, selling everything from fabric to furniture. Stewart later established department stores in different parts of the world, including London and Paris.

Not only was Stewart the most successful retail sales tycoon in America, but he also developed a thriving mail-order business for his merchandise, earning an estimated annual income of $1 million a year from it. Other retail stores, notably Sears, Montgomery Ward, and Spiegel, also established successful mail-order businesses during the same period.

In 1869 Stewart built an ornate mansion on the corner of Fifth Avenue and Thirty-fourth Street. Unlike the other luxurious brownstone mansions located along what was referred to as "Millionaires Row," Stewart's was made entirely out of Italian marble cut exclusively for him in Italy and shipped to the United States. Costing approximately $2 million, it took seven years to build. Constructed in Parisian Empire design, Stewart's mansion had three main floors and an attic with a mansard roof. The elaborate home was separated from the sidewalks by a lighted moat, and the main ballroom ran the full length of its Fifth Avenue frontage. Stewart filled the mansion with expensive furniture, antiques, and a large and valuable art collection. There was no home like it in America.

While Stewart was widely esteemed for his shrewdness and business acumen, he was never well liked by his competitors. They found him to be a callous businessman, ruining many of their companies. His employees viewed him as an unrelenting skinflint. He and his wife seldom went to any of the usual galas hosted by his wealthy neighbors, or entertained them. Stewart had few friends, his closest being Judge Henry Hilton. Stewart's attempt to outdo his multimillionaire neighbors, like William and Caroline Astor, with the construction of his lavish home, did not endear him to New York City's powerful and affluent elite. Stewart and his wife found themselves ostracized by their wealthy neighbors, viewed as millionaire upstarts. Still, the high society snubbing did nothing to damage Stewart's retail empire. Following the death of Cornelia Stewart in 1886, the marble mansion was sold, and in 1901 it was torn down.

Stewart did not spend all of his fortune on himself or his wife, and although he was not known as a philanthropist in the ranks of Andrew Carnegie, he was still very generous to those in need. During the Irish Potato Famine of 1848, Stewart sent a shipload of provisions to his native Lisburn and invited young people to take free passage to America, where he found jobs for them within his vast department store complex. He also sent $50,000 to the victims of the Great Chicago Fire in 1871.

His most lasting philanthropic endeavor was the building of Garden City, New York. In 1869, Stewart bought close to seven thousand acres on the Hempstead Plain on Long Island, where he built one of the first planned communities in the United States for his workers. Garden City included sixteen miles of streets and avenues, a central park, affordable homes, stores, and a hotel. Stewart even built a railroad into the city so his workers could take the train to work at one of his many retail, wholesale, or manufacturing businesses. Stewart also planted nearly thirty thousand trees in his development. Stewart did not sell any of the property to the inhabitants but instead acted as landlord of the community.

Some contemporary sources have indicated that Police Superintendent George Walling made the following disparaging remarks concerning the theft of Stewart's remains: "There is a sort of grim justice in it, and the very irony of greed, that this cruel, avaricious, hard-hearted man, who oppressed his employees, ruined his creditors, drove his poorer competitors to bankruptcy should now have his flesh drop off and his bones rattle in a thieves' bag, while the millions he earned are enjoyed by others."

Although attributed to Walling, he did not say this. According to his own book, *Recollections of a New York Chief of Police,* published in 1887, Walling attributed this comment to an unnamed "semi-anarchist newspaper."

Police investigators discovered a trail of strange liquid leading from Stewart's vault, up a grassy hill across the graveyard to an isolated spot along the westerly side of the cemetery. The ghastly odor of the liquid and its composition led investigators to believe that it was a substance oozing from Stewart's remains. The trail led to a far corner of the cemetery hidden from view, and the substance was discovered along the side and top of the ten-foot iron fence that surrounded St. Mark's graveyard. Police were able to surmise that the grave robbers carried the remains out of the vault wrapped in some sort of porous fabric to the westerly side of the cemetery, where they scaled the iron fence and lifted the body up and over it. A forked tree abutted the fence at this juncture and could have been used to climb over it. Police found traces of the substance on the tree limbs. They also found several cakes of dirt with the impression of a boot heel in them on the tree limbs. Once over the fence, the ghouls must have hidden the body in a casket or box and put it in the back of a wagon that had been waiting for them in a courtyard next door to where they had scaled the fence. Police found evidence of the substance and clay boot marks in the courtyard and the imprint of a set of wagon wheels embedded in the dirt. From this location the grave robbers would have been concealed from prying eyes.

Once the news of the horrendous crime hit the front pages of every newspaper in the city, the police and Judge Hilton began receiving letters from a variety of anonymous sources about the grave robbery.

DEAR SIR:

My opinion is that the Jews have something to do with the affair. It would do no harm to search the large safes in and around Broadway. In one particular office the smell is far from pleasant.

NOVEMBER 15, 1878

Excuse pencil.

Mr. Hilton:
I suppose this will go into the little basket under your desk with the rest, but read it carefully and consider well what I am going to tell you before you destroy it.
To begin with I am a lady, a woman, I suppose some would call me; but if you will meet me at the corner of Thirty-seventh-street and Fifth-avenue, Saturday, between 8 and 9 o'clock P.M., alone, I will tell and show you something, and at the same time save your $25,000, for I do not ask for any reward.

G.T.O.

P.S.—I shall be on the watch, and if I see any shadows all right for you. This is no idle boast.

<hr>

NEW YORK, 14th November, 1878

Mrs. A. T. Stewart:

MADAM: Seeing twice in the Herald *an account of the removal of the remains from the burying ground of the late Amity-Street Baptist Church in 1863, I feel it incumbent on me to deny the statement therein, as I was sexton of the church at that time, and had charge of the removal of the remains and know full well that the late Mr. Stewart had nothing to do with the property until after the removal of the remains and the property was in the market for sale. I delivered the keys of the late Amity-Street Church property personally to your lamented husband, Mr. A. T. Stewart, in presence of Mr. Butler, at his office in Chambers-street and Broadway, and I have got in my possession paragraphs clipped from the papers of the time which will constitute the statements made in the* New York

Herald. . . . *Lots were purchased in Cypress Hill Cemetery, and the remains were removed in a Christian-like manner, which can be fully substantiated by many living witnesses.*

Yours respectfully,

R. BROWNLOW

301 First-avenue

DEAR SIR: One week last night Mr. Stewart's body was taken. Your detectives have been within a block of it within 48 hours, and they may hunt until doomsday, they cannot find it, but for $200,000 and no questions asked it will be delivered. A personal in the Herald *saying you will pay this amount with guaranty, will be answered.*

Yours, XERXES.

(It should be noted that this last letter, signed by "Xerxes," was later determined to have been from the actual robbers, since, when negotiations finally began in earnest for the return of Stewart's body, the amount the thieves asked for was $200,000, and the way they agreed to make contact was through personal ads placed in the *New York Herald.*)

Every police officer in the city who was not working on the recent Manhattan Savings Institution robbery was assigned to the Stewart case. A contingent of Pinkerton detectives came to New York from their Chicago offices to help scour the city in the hopes of turning up some clues. Police and detectives fanned out throughout the Bowery, interviewing hundreds of people and following up on every lead in the case, but they turned up nothing. Not so with the illustrious Captain Thomas Byrnes. While working simultaneously on the Manhattan Savings robbery, Byrnes managed to arrest and charge two men with the crime a little more than a week after the theft of Stewart's body. Once again the city was in awe of Byrnes's incredible investigative skills.

Byrnes arrested Henry Vreeland and William Burke of East Twelfth Street and charged them in the crime. The two men were taken into custody and brought before Judge B. T. Morgan of the Jefferson Market Police Court on November 18, 1878, for a probable-cause hearing.

Burke, who was approximately forty years old, lived at 402 East Twelfth Street with his wife and mother, who accompanied him to police headquarters when he was arrested. He was a short, stout man with a full head of salt-and-pepper hair, a beard, and a mustache.

Vreeland, who was approximately twenty-five years old, was described by the *New York Times* as "well-shaped and decidedly handsome." He was bald, except for a band of blond hair that encircled the back of his head, ending in muttonchop-style sideburns and a thin, barely visible, flaxen-colored mustache. Byrnes and other police officers had arrested Burke at home. Vreeland, who reportedly also lived at the same address as Burke, was not at home when Byrnes and the others swept down on the dwelling to arrest Burke. Byrnes staked out the house for two days, and when Vreeland finally returned, he was immediately arrested by police who had been lying in wait for him.

Both men were assigned attorney Joseph H. Stiner as public counsel. Neither of them was unfamiliar to police or the courts. Burke had spent five years in prison for burglary. Vreeland had served three years in Sing Sing for picking pockets. After his release from prison, Vreeland was again arrested, this time for trying to steal a pair of shoes from, of all places, A. T. Stewart's store in downtown Manhattan. He was sentenced to six more months in jail. Although Byrnes believed that Burke and Vreeland were involved in the Stewart grave robbery, he didn't think they had the brains to come up with the idea. Byrnes maintained that they were likely hired to do the job.

Judge Morgan opened the hearing for the two men at two o'clock. Because of the publicity surrounding the case, Burke and Vreeland had been held at an undisclosed location pending the court date and, as was Byrnes's usual behavior in such situations, he had prohibited any of his officers from discussing the case with the press. He kept tight-lipped about it as well.

The small hearing room was jam-packed with newspaper reporters and police. Burke's wife and mother sat in the front row wearing bonnets, with their faces covered by thick veils. Captain Byrnes was sworn in and testified that he had arrested Burke and Vreeland on suspicion of stealing A. T. Stewart's body. According to Byrnes's testimony, he was tipped off about Burke's involvement in the case by a source, whose identity Byrnes refused to divulge to the court, despite objections from Stiner. Judge Morgan denied Stiner's motion to identify Byrnes's supposed source.

Byrnes's source told him that Burke had tried to coax him into taking part in an unspecified crime and had assured him of two things: There would be a lot of money in it should he decide to take part, and the crime, although neither a bank robbery nor the assassination of some prominent figure, would "astonish the whole country," according to Burke. Although the anonymous source didn't take part in the crime, he surmised that the robbery of Stewart's body was the crime Burke had alluded to after news of it hit the newspapers.

Byrnes said he proceeded to arrest Burke, who initially denied any involvement. Later, Burke confessed to knowing something about the case and told Byrnes ". . . but after it, the body, was stolen, I was to get a percentage for what I did. The man who was with me when I was arrested was the man who put up the money and did the whole job. His name is Hank Vreeland."

Vreeland denied having anything to do with the crime.

Byrnes went on to testify that Burke even offered to take the police to the spot in New Jersey where he thought Vreeland had hidden Stewart's body.

———•••———

Captain Byrnes was an imposing figure. His success at solving crimes was well documented, so much so that even lowlifes like Burke and Vreeland knew his reputation. They both knew they were in a mess, especially considering Byrnes's reputation for applying the third degree. Burke was the first to crack, not because of anything Byrnes had done, but because of the threat of what he might do. Burke confessed his connection to the Stewart grave robbery, claiming he was only supposed to receive a small percentage of the ransom for helping dispose of the remains in a safe hiding place. Vreeland was the brains behind the caper, Burke claimed. To demonstrate his sincerity, and in the hopes of getting some leniency, Burke agreed to show Byrnes where Stewart's remains were buried.

According to Burke, Vreeland had hired a team of horses and a wagon and hauled the body to a secret hiding place close to Chatham, New Jersey, some twenty miles from St. Mark's Cemetery. When informed of Burke's confession, Vreeland said he had never been to Chatham and had no idea what place Burke was talking about.

"I don't know anything about this thing," Vreeland told Byrnes. "I don't know where any body is buried."

When Byrnes informed Vreeland that he would seek leniency in the case if he cooperated, Vreeland also confessed, saying he had only been involved after Stewart's remains had been stolen from the vault. Both men then agreed to lead Byrnes to where they had supposedly hidden the body.

Byrnes took a contingent of men, along with both suspects, to Chatham, where Vreeland told Byrnes that Stewart's body was buried near a mill on the Passaic River. Byrnes and his men searched the area but found nothing. Both Burke and Vreeland appeared nervous and distracted while the officers searched the area. During the search, Vreeland asked Byrnes what kind of sentence they faced for the robbery. Byrnes told him it was a mere one year in jail and a $250 fine. Hearing this, Vreeland and Burke refused to cooperate any further in the search. Whatever connection they might have had with the case, a mere year in jail and a small fine was nothing the two men couldn't handle.

At one point Vreeland told authorities of a specific spot along the Passaic River where they would find the body. Police laboriously dug where Vreeland had told them to and came up with a sack of bones, only to discover they were dog bones.

After returning from their sojourn to Chatham, where police turned up nothing, neither Burke nor Vreeland had anything more to say about the case. Although Byrnes had only circumstantial evidence linking Burke and Vreeland to the case, he appeared determined to pin the crime on them, if not solely for the fact that they had taken him on a wild goose chase to Chatham, only to clam up about the whereabouts of the body.

A reporter for the *New York Herald* managed to conduct a quick interview with Burke following the first hearing, and Burke told the reporter that only after being coerced by Byrnes did he admit that "we had buried a stiff." But, according to Burke, it had all been a lie. Neither he nor Vreeland had anything to do with the case, and they only led Byrnes to New Jersey to embarrass the illustrious detective. According to Burke, they had resolutely decided to give Byrnes "the kid to his heart's content."

According to Wayne Fanebust, in his book, *The Missing Corpse: Grave Robbing a Gilded Age Tycoon*, "Unquestionably the whole thing was rather smelly. The grisly crime, the vacant fascination of the public, the irresponsible reporting by the press, and the hapless antics of the police all combined to leave anything but a good impression. . . None of the pursuers were up to the challenge of finding the grave robbers."

The police, especially Byrnes, were in no mood for any pranks by Burke or Vreeland, and he pursued charges against them with a vengeance.

<hr />

At the hearing held on November 18, Judge Morgan asked Byrnes if Vreeland had confessed to the removal of the body from St. Mark's graveyard, and Byrnes testified, "No."

". . . He was one of the parties to the robbery after it left the cemetery?" Morgan asked.

"Yes," Byrnes told the court.

"Have Burke and Vreeland confessed that they had the body in their possession?" Morgan asked.

"Yes, in Burke's room in Twelfth Street. They told me they would show me where it was if I would give them the reward," Byrnes said.

Following lengthy testimony by Byrnes, Judge Morgan recessed the hearing and remanded Burke and Vreeland to be held until the hearing resumed the next day.

By the next day, November 19, Captain Byrnes had filed his formal complaint against the two men.

POLICE COURT—SECOND DISTRICT
STATE OF NEW YORK, CITY AND COUNTY
OF NEW YORK.

Thomas Byrnes, Captain of the Fifteenth Precinct Police, being duly sworn, says that on or about the 6th day of November, 1878, at the City of New York, in the County of New York, Henry Vreeland and William Burke (both now here) did, then and there acting in concert together, feloniously remove the dead body of a human being from the place of its interment, for the purpose of selling the same, and for the purpose of dissection, and with mere wantonness did remove the dead body of the late Alexander T. Stewart from the vault in the church-yard of St. Mark's Church, situated on the Second-avenue, between Ninth and Tenth streets, being a grave-yard in the said City, from the fact that the said Henry Vreeland and William Burke did acknowledge and confess to this deponent, in the presence of witnesses, that they had possession of the aforesaid dead body of the said Alexander T. Stewart, as more fully appears from the sworn statement of deponent hereto attached, and forming part of this complaint.

—THOMAS BYRNES

Sworn to before me this 19th day of

November 1878, B. T. Morgan, Police Justice

Counsel for the defense, Joseph H. Stiner, had an opportunity to cross-examine Byrnes during the second day of the probable-cause hearing before Judge Morgan. The testimony was recorded as follows:

Stiner: You said yesterday the prisoners admitted taking the body of A. T. Stewart from St. Mark's grave-yard?

Byrnes: Yes.

Stiner: When did they admit this?

Byrnes: On Thursday night, between 6 and 9 o'clock.

Stiner: A question was asked by the court yesterday, does the prisoner Vreeland confess that he was a party to the removal of the body from St. Mark's grave-yard, and you answered, no. How do you reconcile your statements?

Byrnes: Vreeland said to me that the stench was frightful. That the body had been placed in a rubber bag and other things which I detailed. It was about taking the body out of the church yard that the court asked me. That I did not know about.

———

Stiner went on to contend to the court that the two prisoners were entitled to know any and all information that led to their arrest and demanded that Byrnes reveal the name of the person who originally told him about Burke's involvement in the grave robbery. Byrnes again refused to reveal his source.

"I shouldn't like to tell you at the present stage of the proceedings. I do not think it prudent. It would interfere with the ends of justice," Byrnes said.

Judge Morgan agreed with Byrnes that the identity of his source did not have to be revealed.

"I now ask the court for the production of the witness who first gave the information," Stiner argued to the judge.

"The captain declines to produce him, and the court sustains the captain," Morgan ruled.

Stiner motioned for the court to release Vreeland for lack of any credible evidence.

"I now move that Henry Vreeland be discharged, first on the ground that Vreeland has not at any time confessed to the stealing of A. T. Stewart's body. Second, because the testimony of Captain Byrnes is entirely hearsay in relation to Vreeland, and third because there is nothing in the evidence whatever tending to show that Vreeland was one of the parties to the crime," Stiner said.

"Do you want a ruling?" Judge Morgan asked.

Stiner said he did.

"Denied," Morgan said.

Stiner next moved for the discharge of Burke on the grounds that if he had made a confession, it had been done under duress.

"Motion denied," Morgan said.

Stiner asked that bail for the two men be fixed at a reasonable amount, arguing that both men were poor and that the crime they were charged with would not require punishment of any consequence even if they were convicted.

Judge Morgan disagreed.

"The punishment is state prison for five years. There is not much question about that," Morgan said.

He set bail at $5,000 each.

Vreeland and Burke were led from the hearing room and jailed pending the decision of the grand jury.

———

VREELAND AND BURKE COMMITTED.

CAPT. Byrnes's FORMAL COMPLAINT AGAINST THEM—HE IS CROSS-EXAMINED BY PRISONER'S COUNSEL—BAIL FIXED AT $5,000.

. . . The prisoners were on hand under their usual strong escort of detectives. They looked haggard and nervous, particularly Burke, whose natural sneaking, cur-like expression of countenance would seem difficult to improve upon. He is one of the meanest looking of thieves. How any person could trust him with a secret seems as much a puzzle as to explain how the sharp, pretty woman who calls him husband can possibly live with such a wretch. Vreeland is a manly-looking fellow in comparison. He has a hard, villainous face, but there is a redeeming dash of pluck in it. . . .

—*New York Times*
November 20, 1878

With Burke and Vreeland charged in the crime and being held, the question remained: Where was A. T. Stewart's body? No one knew.

Reporters asked Judge Hilton on several occasions if he knew where the body might be, and his response each time was a curt, "No."

Again and again Hilton told reporters that he would not pay a red cent for the return of the body. He claimed he would, however, pay any amount for the capture and conviction of those who had stolen it. Hilton subsequently increased the reward for the capture of those responsible from $25,000 to $50,000.

Once again, with the arrest of Burke and Vreeland, it appeared that the illustrious Captain Byrnes had gotten his men. He had solved another one of the city's high-profile cases and in an incredibly short time. It was, however, for Byrnes, a short-lived success.

The evidence in the case against Burke and Vreeland was turned over to the district attorney's office. The extent of the evidence consisted of only the complaint filed by Captain Byrnes and Byrnes's testimony before Judge Morgan. Apparently, the district attorney's office was not as impressed by Byrnes's testimony as Judge Morgan had been. There was not enough evidence to charge the two men with the crime of stealing Stewart's body, but since the district attorney's office neither wanted to appear soft on crime nor publicly embarrass Captain Byrnes and the New York City Police Department, it decided to try to charge the two men with unrelated crimes.

Byrnes might not have arrested the right criminals, but he had nonetheless arrested some criminals, and that seemed good enough for the public at large, especially Judge Hilton and those directly connected with the case.

The grand jury indicted William Burke on charges of forgery stemming from an October 1878 incident in which he was involved in forging a $400 check drawn on the West Side Bank. There was little or nothing to charge Vreeland with, and he was held until December 3, 1878, when he was finally released from jail.

———

HENRY VREELAND DISCHARGED

Two weeks ago Capt. Byrnes, of the Fifteenth Precinct, had Henry Vreeland, of Brooklyn, and William Burke, of No. 402 East Twelfth-street, the two men who pretended to know the whereabouts of Mr. Stewart's remains in New Jersey, committed to await the action of the Grand Jury, on suspicion of their implication in the stealing of the body. No evidence connecting them with the offense was produced, however, and the Grand Jury did not inquire into the case. Burke, however, was identified as a man who had uttered a forged check on the West Side Bank, and an indictment for forgery was found against him. Yesterday, Vreeland was taken before Judge Gildersleeve, in the General Sessions, and discharged, Assistant District Attorney Horace Russell stating in his endorsement of the papers that there was no evidence to connect him with the offense charged. Burke still remains in the Tombs, awaiting trial on forgery charges.

—*New York Times*
December 4, 1878

———

Reports in the *New York Times* following the release of Vreeland claimed that Captain Byrnes's actions were "fully approved by his superiors, one of whom said yesterday that he would have deserved dismissal from the force if he had neglected to follow up the information given by Burke, which, however, proved utterly valueless."

Even Judge Hilton praised the efforts of Byrnes, telling reporters that he had offered Byrnes $1,000 to cover the costs of his personal expenses in the investigation but that Byrnes had refused the money. Hilton told reporters that, regardless of the outcome surrounding Burke and Vreeland, the work done by Byrnes and the New York City Police Department had not cost him or the Stewart family any money, and that he (Hilton) ". . . would be grateful to them as long as he lived."

In March 1881, nearly three years after the body of her husband was stolen from its crypt, Cornelia Stewart regained possession of what was claimed to be her husband's remains. Judge Hilton struck a deal with the unidentified grave robbers, agreeing to pay them a $20,000 ransom for the return of Stewart's body. The exchange was carried out on a deserted country road in Westchester County, New York. For $20,000 Hilton was given a burlap bag of bones, reportedly the last earthly remains of Alexander Turney Stewart. The remains were buried in a new family vault in the Episcopal Cathedral of the Incarnation in Garden City, Long Island. Mrs. Stewart built the cathedral as a lasting memorial to her husband. It took nine years and cost approximately $1.5 million.

GARDEN CITY'S CATHEDRAL
A GREAT CROWD AT THE OPENING SERVICES
BISHOP LITTLEJOHN PAYS A WARM TRIBUTE
TO MRS. STEWART'S GENEROSITY AND
MR. HILTON'S JUDGMENT

The Cathedral of the Incarnation, in Garden City, Mrs. A. T. Stewart's costly memorial to her millionaire husband, was opened for public worship yesterday. . . .

— *New York Times*
April 10, 1885

The story of A. T. Stewart's fortune took an unpredictable turn when Judge Henry Hilton was named the executor of Stewart's will. Based on Stewart's last wishes, formally articulated in his will, Hilton became the overseer of the vast fortune he had left behind. An otherwise obscure lawyer and an elected judge of no real prominence, Hilton became one of New York's richest citizens at the expense of Stewart's millions. He became the owner and proprietor of any number of magnificent estates, hotels, and businesses, and also acted as a conduit for a multitude of substantial gifts to museums, churches, and a host of other charitable organizations.

I especially appoint Henry Hilton of the City of New York to act for me and in behalf of my estate in managing, closing, and winding up my partnership business and affairs, and I empower him in respect thereto as fully as I may or can, or am authorized to in and by the articles of copartnership of the firm of Alexander T. Stewart & Co. I further authorize and direct the said Hilton, while so acting in behalf of my estate and in my place and stead, to exercise a sound discretion in bringing my said partnership affairs to a termination and discharging all obligations connected therewith, trusting to his judgment that he will so act in respect thereto as to avoid so far as can be avoided any unnecessary loss to those connected with me in business. For which service, and as a mark of my regard, I give to aid Hilton $1,000,000.

—FROM THE LAST WILL AND TESTAMENT OF
ALEXANDER TURNEY STEWART

Although the fortune itself did not go directly to Hilton, the will gave Hilton access and oversight over the fortune, as well as the many businesses that Stewart had created during his lifetime. Hilton became indispensable to Cornelia Stewart during the decade that she survived her husband. His handling of her affairs and the Stewart fortune ultimately ended in disaster. The company he formed, Hilton, Hughes and Company, failed, and nearly all of Stewart's massive fortune was spent on a series of financial disasters. The more Hilton tried to duplicate the success of his benefactor, Alexander Stewart, by establishing business corporations to further the retail trade, the more significant his failures became. This, however, did not curtail Hilton from buying splendid hotels and lavish homes and showering himself and his own family with other luxuries—all at the expense of Stewart's fortune. Priceless extravagant works of art that had once hung in places of honor in the Stewarts' marble mansion on Fifth Avenue were sold or given away as charitable deductions. The downward financial spiral was unstoppable.

By 1898, just a year before Henry Hilton passed away, the $40 million Stewart fortune was gone.

The bones buried in the Stewart family vault have never been positively identified as belonging to Alexander Stewart, and the identity of the grave robbers has never been uncovered.

AMERICAN ALMANAC, 1880–86

The six-year period from 1880 to 1886 was a momentous one for Thomas Byrnes. Rising through the ranks of the New York City Police Department, Byrnes was promoted to detective in 1880, and a mere two years later, he was put in charge of the entire Detective Bureau.

These significant changes in Byrnes's life paralleled those of the changing face of New York City, as well as the rest of the country.

The 1880 Census showed that the country had a population of 50,155,783. In that year, New York State became the first state with a population of more than 5 million. And New York City had a population of 1.9 million.

James A. Garfield was elected president of the United States in 1880. A Republican congressman from Ohio, he barely beat his Democratic challenger, General Winfield Scott Hancock, by 10,000 votes. Garfield received 4,449,053 votes, and Hancock received 4,442,035. Garfield's vice president was Chester A. Arthur, who was part of the New York City political machine under the leadership of U.S. senator Roscoe Conkling. Arthur had served as collector of the Port of New York City, doling out patronage according to Conkling's orders. On July 2, 1881, Garfield was shot in a Washington, D.C., train station by a disgruntled office seeker, Charles Guiteau. Garfield lingered for eighty days after being shot. He died on September 19, 1881. Vice President Arthur served out the balance of Garfield's term. Arthur did not run for president in 1884.

> *. . . O Garfield! brave and patient soul!*
> *Long as the tireless tides shall roll*
> *About the Long Branch beaches, where*
> *Thy life went out upon the air,*
> *So long thy land, from sea to sea,*
> *Will hold thy manhood's legacy . . .*
> —POEM BY MINOT J. SAVAGE

William Kissam Vanderbilt built his $3 million mansion at 660 Fifth Avenue on the corner of Fifty-second Street in 1881. He was a member of the prominent Vanderbilt family, the second son of William H. Vanderbilt, the owner of the Grand Central Railroad. He inherited $55 million from his father. The mansion was built in the elite, royal chateau style with classical detailing. Ornate and luxurious, Vanderbilt's mansion was considered one of the most stately homes in New York City. It was torn down in 1926 to make room for a new office building.

The Brooklyn Bridge was officially opened in May 1883. It was designed by John A. Roebling, a pioneer in building suspension bridges. He began work on it in 1869 but died of tetanus in July of that year after his foot was crushed while working on the bridge. His son, Washington A. Roebling, took over the construction of the bridge. The bridge has a span of 1,595 feet and its towers are 272 feet high. It spans the East River, connecting Manhattan and Brooklyn.

Grover Cleveland was elected president in 1884. Cleveland, a Democrat, beat his Republican opponent, James Blaine, with a popular vote of 4,911,017 to 4,848,334. He had served as mayor of Buffalo and was later elected governor of New York. Cleveland was defeated in his reelection bid in 1888, but ran again in 1892 and won the presidency. He is the only president in American history to serve two nonconsecutive terms.

The Haymarket Riot occurred on May 4, 1886, in Chicago's Haymarket Square. During a labor rally held there, a bomb exploded, killing seven police officers and wounding more than fifty others. Anarchists were blamed, and the police arrested eight suspected anarchist leaders. Although no evidence was brought against the eight men linking them to the bomb, they were all convicted, with seven sentenced to death and one to life in prison. In November 1885, four of the men were hanged. One committed suicide in prison. The remaining two had their sentences reduced from death to life in prison. In 1893, Governor John Peter Altgeld of Illinois pardoned them all.

The Statue Of Liberty was dedicated by President Grover Cleveland in a ceremony in October 1886 that was held in the New York City harbor on Bedloe's Island (now called Liberty Island). The copper statue weighed 225 tons and was 152 feet tall. The French presented it as a gift to commemorate one hundred years of American independence.

QUIPS AND QUOTES

The chief duty of government is to keep the peace and stand out of the sunshine of the people.
—JAMES A. GARFIELD

I must go to dinner, but I wish it was to eat a pickled herring, a Swiss cheese, and a chop at Louis' instead of the French stuff I shall find.
—GROVER CLEVELAND

Don't go around saying the world owes you a living. The world owes you nothing. It was here first.
—MARK TWAIN

No man has the right to allow his ambition to stand in the way of the performance of a simple act of justice.
—GOVERNOR JOHN PETER ALTGELD OF ILLINOIS

Give me your tired, your poor,
Your huddled masses yearning to breathe free,
The wretched refuse of your teeming shore,
Send these, the homeless, tempest-tost to me,
I lift my lamp beside the golden door.
—EMMA LAZARUS, FROM THE POEM "THE NEW COLOSSUS"

8
CHIEF OF DETECTIVES

In which Thomas Byrnes is appointed chief of detectives and initiates some far-reaching changes within the Detective Bureau.

Thomas Byrnes was made an inspector in the New York City Detective Bureau in 1880. In 1882, the New York State Legislature passed an act to establish the Central Office of Detectives. The new bureau consolidated all the detectives from the various wards and precincts into one department that was stationed at police headquarters at 300 Mulberry Street. Detectives had been previously treated like any other police officer and had no special authority, as they were under the direction of the precinct captains. Now, all city detectives were under one roof and answerable only to the chief inspector, Thomas Byrnes, who was considered the second-ranking police officer in the department after the superintendent.

Under Byrnes's leadership, and because of his ability to garner political support and the backing of wealthy and influential New Yorkers, the Detective Bureau became an independent authority, free from any control by either the police superintendent or the police commissioners.

Byrnes made sweeping changes within the Detective Bureau. At the outset, he discovered that he was in charge of a fairly motley crew of approximately thirty detectives, many of whom he determined were not fit for service. Some were old. Many had no concept of what detective work entailed or what was expected from them. Many had not been held accountable for either their time or their actions or behavior. All that came to a screeching halt under Byrnes's command.

. . . the Police Commissioners propose to make the Detective Bureau one of the most efficient branches of the service. They

don't propose to hamper me in any way as long as I enjoy their confidence. In a few days, after I have had an opportunity to test the capabilities of such men as are in the office now, I will be prepared to recommend some changes, and I will endeavor to bring into this office the best men in the department.

—THOMAS BYRNES

NEW YORK TIMES

MARCH 14, 1880

———

Detectives were still assigned to various precincts when Byrnes became its chief inspector. It wasn't until 1882 that all city detectives were organized under one separate department under the leadership of Byrnes. Still, despite the lack of a centralized bureau, Byrnes was able to wield considerable power over the city's detectives.

In one of his first orders of business, Byrnes reassigned some of the men who had been designated as detectives within their various precincts to other posts, weeding out the loafers and those not equipped for the rigors of detective work, and filled their positions with younger men in whom he could ingrain investigative knowledge. It was Byrnes's intention to mold the Detective Bureau into an essential and productive part of the city's overall police force. and to make it one of the best in the world, bar none, not even Scotland Yard.

In addition to handpicking his own men, Byrnes instituted a formal process of intelligence gathering, a process he had personally been doing for years. He ordered his men to keep meticulous records of all their investigations, a procedure that had never been in force. Byrnes also maintained a statistical analysis of his bureau's effectiveness, including the number of arrests made, the number of convictions, and the number of total years of incarceration of criminals apprehended by the bureau. He used these statistics as a tool in proving the effectiveness of the bureau.

Under Byrnes's watch, all criminals were photographed as a matter of standard police protocol. The photographs, along with a history of the criminal's record, the types of crime they engaged in, previous crimes they had committed, time served, and identifying characteristics were kept and stored at the Mulberry Street detective headquarters. It was the beginning of what would ultimately become standard police procedure; however, at the time that Byrnes instituted the new practice, it was a groundbreaking initiative. Mug shots and rap sheets would become commonplace in police work in later years, but Byrnes was the one who pioneered their use. Few, if any, criminal records had been kept prior to Byrnes's ascension to the lofty position of chief of detectives.

In 1886, Byrnes instituted the revolutionary "Mulberry Street Morning Parade." Criminal suspects were paraded before his detectives in an effort to identify the culprits in connection to ongoing investigations. Once again Byrnes was a pioneer in criminal identification. Although police lineups would become a standard practice in later years throughout the country, it was Byrnes who initiated and perfected this procedure. Byrnes kept a "Rogues' Gallery," a vast collection of mug shots of known criminals. To add to his stature in 1886, Byrnes published his best-selling book, *Professional Criminals of America.*

ALL MEN DETECTIVES
Inspector Byrnes Writes a Book
About Great Criminals

This book is called "Professional Criminals of America." It contains copies of the original photographs of a large number of celebrated criminals now engaged in making their presence felt in various parts of the United States. There are over 200 pictures and pedigrees and a large number of additional records of other criminals, all of which have been collected and verified by the Inspector. The book also contains the dates of several of the principal bank robberies committed throughout the country during the past 20 years; also a list of several murders and executions, together with the prison commutation laws and other valuable information relating to criminals and their treatment.

There will be nothing but facts found in the book, and Inspector Byrnes believes that his work will be of great value to Chiefs of Police, detectives, Sheriffs, Marshals, constables, Judges, District Attorneys . . . in short to all persons liable to contact with criminals.

. . . The book is printed on heavy paper and substantially bound. The pictures are careful reproductions of those in the Rogues' Gallery in this city.

—*New York Times*
October 1, 1886

Byrnes's book was a huge success, reportedly selling twenty thousand copies. It was reprinted in 1970, and although it is now merely a nostalgic album of times gone by, in 1886, *Professional Criminals of America* was a well-regarded handbook intended to be used by law enforcement and judicial authorities to impede criminals by making their identities known.

Byrnes classified those who graced the pages of his book by criminal categories, ranging from sneak thieves and pickpockets to bank robbers, and everything in between. In some instances, Byrnes offered grudging admiration of several notorious bank robbers, even referring to one as "one of the smartest bank sneaks in America . . . very gentlemanly and intelligent man. . . ."

Byrnes's begrudging praise was not just limited to bank robbers. Writing about a well-known pickpocket, Byrnes said, "[He] . . . is without doubt the smartest pickpocket in America."

Of a well-known female swindler, Byrnes wrote, "Little Annie Reilly is considered the cleverest woman in her line in America. . . . She seldom remains in one place more than one or two days before she robs it."

Byrnes held that mug shots exposed a criminal's inner self. Along with photographs of the criminals, he provided a brief description of them and their arrest and conviction records.

Of what good can these twisted and unnatural faces be? Were their owners met in the streets their countenances would be composed. They would be altogether free of these distortions, by which they have tried to cheat the purpose of the police in photographing them. No one would know them then. Well, that is all wrong. The very cleverest hands at preparing a false physiognomy for the camera have made their grimaces in vain. The sun has been too quick for them, and has imprisoned the lines of the profile and the features and caught the expression before it could be disguised. There is not a portrait here but has some marked characteristic by which you can identify the man who sat for it. That is what has to be studied in the Rogues' Gallery—detail.

—CHIEF INSPECTOR THOMAS BYRNES

PROFESSIONAL CRIMINALS OF AMERICA, 1886

Byrnes explained that when he arrested criminals and they were made aware of the evidence against them, they knew that their photograph would be added to the Rogues' Gallery. Even if the criminals tried to disguise their appearance in some way, by grimacing or frowning or by any other means, the camera didn't lie. Their faces and inner criminal natures were captured forever in those photographs.

Byrnes hailed photography as a new and beneficial aid in law enforcement.

According to Byrnes, ". . . there are scores of men and women whose appearance in the streets gives no hint to their character. Deception is their business, and they have to study its arts carefully."

Still, Byrnes was adamant that photographing of criminals would help law enforcement authorities all over the country. He was right. Other states and federal authorities soon began the uniform practice of taking and recording mug shots.

"Remember that nearly all the great criminals of the country are men who lead double lives. Strange as it may appear, it is the fact that some of the most unscrupulous rascals who ever cracked a safe or turned out a counterfeit were at home model husbands and fathers. In a great many cases wives have aided their guilty partners in their villainy, and the children, too, have taken a hand in it," Byrnes said.

"I have seen victims of thieves when called upon in court to identify a prisoner seated among a number of on-lookers pick out his captors, or a court clerk, or a reporter as the offender," he said.

Byrnes said that one known criminal who had a scar on his face and one eye dressed so properly that few people noticed his unusual facial appearance.

". . . River thieves and low burglars are as hard-looking brutes as can be found. So are a good many of the more desperate fellows. . . . Nugent, the Manhattan Bank burglar, carried a good deal of his old business of a butcher about with him in his appearance, but there was something about him that suggested the criminal," Byrnes said.

"In fact, it is a bad thing to judge by appearances, and it is not always safe to judge against them. Experience of men is always needed to place them right," he said.

Publication of *Professional Criminals of America* added another dimension to Byrnes's growing reputation as the most famous and successful detective in America, a label he readily and frequently cultivated and relished.

Robbery is now classed as a profession, and in the place of the awkward and hang-dog-looking thief we have today the intelligent and thoughtful rogue.
—CHIEF INSPECTOR THOMAS BYRNES, 1886

During his tenure, Byrnes's detectives were given the nickname "the immortals" by the New York City press. Byrnes was reciprocal in his support of his men for their new and systematic work. He saw to it that every detective was given a pay raise and elevated to the rank equal to a sergeant in the regular police department. According to

New York City journalist Jacob A. Riis, author of the famous exposé on poverty and slum life in New York City, *How the Other Half Lives*, Chief Inspector Byrnes "made the detective service great."

Byrnes also enforced a code of absolute secrecy within the Detective Bureau. No one was to speak to the press or anyone else, politicians included, about ongoing investigations. This code of secrecy was a public relations sleight of hand for Byrnes, since only he or those he designated could speak to newspaper reporters. He put himself in a very advantageous light in terms of public scrutiny. If Byrnes and his detectives were working in secrecy from the press and the public with other police bureaus and the case was solved or the criminal apprehended, then Byrnes and his bureau could claim credit for it. And in those instances when a case could not be solved, then all the facts could simply be swept under the rug and his bureau's reputation would go unblemished. Through the loyalty of his men and his cloak of secrecy, Byrnes was able to control events and further keep his failures out of public view. If there were two things Chief Inspector Thomas Byrnes could not tolerate, it was failure and damage to his reputation as the country's premier police detective.

Along with modernizing the Detective Bureau, Byrnes became well known for perfecting the use of the third degree, a term given to many of the harsher interrogation methods used by the police to coerce a confession out of a prisoner. By today's standards the practice would be considered outright torture. Although Byrnes has been credited with introducing and even coining the phrase, the third degree had been used by police long before Byrnes. Byrnes simply perfected it. Some of these techniques included simply beating a confession out of a prisoner. Other methods included the use of various paraphernalia such as the thumbscrew, an instrument of torture used for compressing the thumb by a screw; a sweat box, where prisoners were forced to endure excruciating temperatures in a small cramped box; and solitary confinement, isolating a prisoner for days in a small, dark cell. All of these crude methods of torture were intended to and often did force a suspect to confess to his crime, or in other cases, inform on his associates.

Riis, who was both an admirer and detractor of Byrnes, wrote that Byrnes would "beat a thief into telling him what he wanted to know."

"Thieves," according to Byrnes, "have no rights a policeman thinks himself bound to respect."

Byrnes's perfection of the third degree included psychological as well as physical abuse. It didn't matter to Byrnes which technique he chose as long as it worked. There was little doubt that his often brutal interrogation methods greatly enhanced his reputation as a successful investigator.

In his article "The New York Affair, Part II," which appeared in *Casebook: Jack the Ripper*, Wolf Vanderlinden wrote that a Thomas Byrnes interrogation would begin simply enough, with a suspect being brought into his private office. The office was luxuriously decorated. Oxblood wingback chairs and green, billiard-cloth-covered tables adorned the room. Three of the four walls were lined from floor to ceiling with glass cases filled with an assortment of paraphernalia, including crowbars; hooks; clusters of villainous weapons of every type, including brass knuckles; knives of every size and sort; a collection of derringers, pistols, and rifles; stacks of playing cards; and a series of black hoods, each with a label designating which criminal was hanged in it and the date of execution. It was a complete crime museum collected over the years by the renowned Byrnes.

The floor was thickly carpeted so that any shoe would fall onto it without making a bit of noise. A thick, huge oak door opened into the room, which had no windows. On the wall behind the neat and substantial desk where Byrnes would sit in a cushioned chair were portraits of dozens of criminals, men and women staring out across the silent room in sullen, haggard, and cruel but defeated glares. All the rogues hung on the wall were identified with the dates of their capture, their crimes committed against society, the dates of their incarceration, and, in many cases, the dates of their deaths. It was a somber homage to wickedness and the countenance of sin and retribution.

Behind the desk Byrnes would sit, always well dressed in a suit, vest, and tie, all in subdued coloring. He was powerfully built and had a bushy handlebar mustache. The only thing on the desk in front of him was a marble ashtray that held a smoking cigar. Byrnes's face would give no clue as to his disposition. He would wear a pleasant expression but one that was impenetrable. His movements—from picking up his lit cigar to motioning for the suspect to be led into the room—were easygoing and almost affable.

The thick carpet would muffle the manacled suspect's steps as he was led into the room. Although a chair was positioned in front of the desk opposite Byrnes, the suspect would not be asked to sit down and was instead made to stand before Byrnes with a detective standing on either side. Byrnes would start asking questions in a clear and frank way. His voice was loud, his words direct. If the suspect hesitated or stumbled over his words, Byrnes would rise slowly, walk from behind the desk, and stand in front of the handcuffed man. He would ask the same questions once more.

Aside from the height of the burly Byrnes, who stood over six feet tall, and his big broad shoulders, the most striking thing the suspect would notice about the chief inspector was that he was wearing black leather gloves, the kind that someone might wear when riding or participating in some other genteel sport. Byrnes would have his cigar clenched between his teeth, and the cigar smoke would blow against the suspect's face. If the suspect again didn't answer Byrnes's questions, or if the answers weren't what Byrnes wanted, he would clout the suspect across the face, which usually sent the suspect tumbling backward to the floor. The two detectives would lift the suspect back to his feet where Byrnes would be waiting, this time standing so close that the glowing ember of his cigar was a mere inch or so from the suspect's face. Byrnes would ask his questions again. If the suspect still faltered, Byrnes would again hit him, but this time the two detectives would hold the suspect up. Eventually, some information would be beaten out of the man, or, if he was obstinate, other techniques would have to be used, such as tossing the suspect into solitary confinement in a dirty, dark, small cell, or using thumbscrews on him.

Other times, if the suspect was quick to answer Byrnes's questions or appeared to know more than he let on, Byrnes would allow the prisoner to sit in the comfortable chair opposite his desk. He would dismiss the two detectives. He would reach inside his desk and offer the suspect a drink and then a cigarette. Byrnes would engage the suspect in casual banter about the weather or some other innocuous subject, talking to him like a friendly uncle. He would cajole the suspect and observe him closely. When he had garnered the information he wanted, Byrnes would ask the suspect to leave, and if he had gotten more than he had expected, Byrnes would even walk the suspect to the door, where the two detectives would be waiting to take him back to his cell.

One way or the other, Byrnes would get what he wanted from a suspect.

THIRD DEGREE IN POLICE PARLANCE
What It Means, How It Is Operated and Some Famous Cases Of Its Application

Potential and mystical is the term "third degree," as used in police parlance. To the average mind the term is familiar only as applied to degree in secret societies, particularly in Masonry, where, when it has been taken by a member of the Masonic fraternity, it means that he has gone about as high in Masonry as he can go. . . . But when it is used in connection with the arrest of a criminal, it means the limit of police examination of an individual. . . . It really is a third degree in the examination of a criminal. The "first degree" is given when he is examined by the officers in a precinct station house. The "second degree" generally means his examination by a detective from headquarters, at the police court. The "third degree" means the big examination given to him at Headquarters by the Chief of the Detective Bureau and whatever subordinates he may employ in the operation when the case warrants it. . . .

—*New York Times*
October 6, 1901

————

Jacob Riis and Lincoln Steffens were the premier New York City newspaper reporters and social reformers of Byrnes's time. Riis and Steffens became associated with the famous "muckrakers" school of crusading journalism. With the advent of inexpensive newspapers and magazines during the late nineteenth century, a flood of reporters and writers steadily began to expose and criticize political corruption, social injustice, and corporate greed, propelled by public outcry. These authors focused their attention on widespread malicious and moral exploitation and abuse of trusts, politicians, slums, poverty, food processing, and a host of other visible social ills. Although considered one of the era's most passionate reformers, Theodore Roosevelt was credited with coining the term *muckrakers* as a bitter indictment of the excesses of this form of investigative reporting. While intended as a derogatory phrase, the term quickly developed an affirmative connotation among the public, who viewed these writers as their slingshots in the David and Goliath battle between themselves and the greedy businessmen and corrupt politicians. Both Riis, an immigrant from Denmark, and Steffens, who was born in San Francisco, were among New York City's predominant muckrakers.

Riis became a police reporter for the *New York Tribune* in 1877. Having grown up in poverty, Riis dedicated himself to exposing the plight of the poor and their squalid living conditions in New York City slums. In 1888 he became a photojournalist for the *New York Evening Sun*. Riis was one of the first photographers to use flash powder to take pictures, which allowed him to photograph interiors and exteriors of the city's slums at night.

In 1890 Riis published the book, *How the Other Half Lives*. Illustrated with photographs, it depicted the unspeakable living conditions of the poor in New York's tenements. The book had a remarkable impact on how the poor lived. Because of it, the city adopted new housing and sanitation regulations to benefit the poor. As a crusading journalist, Riis wrote more than a dozen books, among them *Children of the Poor* (1892), *Out of Mulberry Street* (1898), and *Children of the Tenement* (1903).

As a newspaper reporter for the *New York Evening Post*, Steffens uncovered and reported on corruption at all levels of state and municipal government. In 1904 he published *Shame of the Cities,* a collection of articles exposing government corruption in New York and other cities across the country. This book was followed by an exposé of state politicians called *The Struggle for Self-Government*, published in 1906.

Riis had covered the police department for seventeen years and became Steffens's tutor when it came to reporting the ins and outs of the department. Over the years, Riis had uncovered the contamination of the city's drinking water supply, and his stories forced the city to fix the entire water supply system. Riis had fought for stricter building codes for schools and clinics, and for the creation of more city parks. He taught Steffens that as a newspaper reporter, he had a social obligation to make good things happen and to correct wrongs that no other person could.

Steffens took this philosophy to heart and put it into action, most notably during his coverage in 1894 of the Lexow Committee, which was established to investigate widespread corruption within New York City government. Very soon he found himself caught up in a war of words, as accusations and counteraccusations flew between the crusading Presbyterian minister, the Reverend Dr. Charles Parkhurst, and the police department, among the most vocal spokesmen being then-superintendent of police Thomas Byrnes. Although Parkhurst was merely an observer during the Lexow hearings, he became the public's most important source of information regarding police corruption. Steffens often met privately with Parkhurst in an effort to understand the underbelly of police corruption and its vast extent. Between his tutoring by Riis and the information he received from

Parkhurst, Steffens concluded that Parkhurst and other reformers were right about what was happening within the police department, which made him an immediate foe of Byrnes.

"Now I can go into a strange city and with my knowledge of New York methods understand their particular methods of corruption," Steffens said.

Byrnes established a detective substation in the heart of the city's financial district—Wall Street. In this way, Byrnes could assure the business community that his men would be on constant vigil to protect them and their assets. Byrnes personally promised bankers, financiers, and businessmen that they could rely on the city's police force to protect them. Because the Detective Bureau and police department had been in disarray and reportedly riddled with corruption, the Wall Street community had lost confidence over the years in the abilities of the city's law enforcement community. Many times, Wall Street businessmen were forced to hire private detectives, like the Pinkerton Detective Agency out of Chicago, to protect them and their wealth. Byrnes guaranteed the Wall Street community that under his leadership a new era of integrity and ability would pervade the Detective Bureau, and that his department could provide them with as good if not better protection as the private detective agencies, and at no cost.

Byrnes opened a small office on the second floor of 17 Wall Street, in a building on the west corner of Wall and Broad Streets, close to the Stock Exchange. He assigned six to eight of his top detectives to the office during Wall Street's regular business hours. Two or three detectives from his bureau would always be on call at the substation, while a contingent of his men would always be on undercover patrol within the Wall Street vicinity. Byrnes established a telephone line from all the banks and investment houses directly to the substation, in case his men needed to be reached in a hurry.

The immense amount of money, both cash and securities, concentrated around Wall Street made it a prime target for criminals. Byrnes had a simple plan to protect the area. He decided that instead of waiting for a crime to happen, he would aggressively pursue a preemptive strike against the criminal element who tried to frequent the area, plotting their nefarious deeds. Byrnes gave orders to drive every known criminal out of the Wall Street district, whether they were a criminal mastermind or merely a petty thief. It didn't matter to Byrnes. Wall Street was off-limits to every criminal in the city. The new boundary was called a "dead line." Any criminal found crossing the dead line was picked up by Byrnes's detectives.

Through a series of well-calculated raids on hangouts, as well as random roundups of any criminals found in the area, Byrnes was able to get his message out to the criminal underworld: If you were found in the district for whatever reason, you would be arrested on the spot. Because Byrnes and his detectives kept scrupulous records on all known criminals, their whereabouts, and their proclivity for certain crimes, keeping them under surveillance was not a problem.

If a known criminal was discovered beyond the designated "dead line," he would first be taken to the detective substation for questioning. If the criminal wasn't able to come up with a satisfactory reason for being in the area, and often he could not, he was immediately taken to police headquarters on Mulberry Street. There, the criminal was given a second chance to explain himself, this time directly to Byrnes. If Byrnes wasn't satisfied with the explanation, he would automatically hold the criminal overnight in jail, releasing him with a stern warning and a promise that he would spend a lot more than one night behind bars if he was ever seen again around Wall Street. The same ultimatum was given to those who were able to satisfy Byrnes. In either case the message came through loud and clear: Stay away from Wall Street. Most, if not all, of those rounded up, were never again seen frequenting Wall Street. According to a *New York Times* article, for criminals given this prescription by Byrnes, ". . . a night in the station house was their reward. This was a dose which seldom, if ever, repeated with the same man, and he never again visited the Wall Street district."

The "dead line," as Byrnes defined it, extended from John Street to the Produce Exchange and from Broadway to Pearl Street. Within that area Byrnes's undercover detectives were on patrol, riding the trolley cars, casually strolling in the vicinity of Liberty Street where the safety-deposit company was located, hanging out by the Stock Exchange and the Treasury, and infiltrating the unknowing business community. They were everywhere, watching everything.

Byrnes visited the Wall Street district almost daily, making his larger-than-life presence known there. He would often tour the district alone and on foot, smoking his ever-present cigar, not only to let criminals know he was watching for them, but also to assure the financial community that he saw the protection of Wall Street as his top priority as chief of detectives. His presence also served as a warning to his own men. Byrnes never left anything to chance. Even his detectives never knew when he might show up to check on them, and it kept them on their toes.

According to the *New York Times*, in a very short period of time, Chief of Detectives Thomas Byrnes made the Wall Street district "the most dreaded place in America for thieves."

———

Inspector Byrnes's heroic measures at the outset, as already indicated, early had the effect of making the Wall Street bureau a bureau of prevention. Thieves of every kind were so thoroughly frightened that they never ventured into the forbidden district and hence they never got or took a chance to rob a bank or financial institution.

"'In fifteen years not even so much as a ten-cent piece,'" as one high police official yesterday put it, "'was lost in Wall Street through thievery by outsiders. Whatever stealing has been done has been accomplished by the employees of financial institutions. . . .'"

—*New York Times*
May 31, 1895

———

INSPECTOR BYRNES TO BE HONORED

Inspector Byrnes is to be given a dinner at Delmonico's next Monday night by a special committee of the New York Stock Exchange. Superintendent Murray, the Police Commissioners, and Inspector Byrnes's brother Inspector will be with him the guests of the evening. The Stock Exchange will be represented by President J. Edward Simmons, ex-president Donald Mackay, Vice-President James D. Smith, H. S. Wilson, E. A. Drake, G. L. Haight, and Brayton Ives. President Simmons will present Inspector Byrnes with the gold watch and chain and seal recently voted to him by the Governors of the Stock Exchange as a token of their appreciation for the thorough way in which he has protected Wall-street since, six years ago, he took charge of the Wall-street detective bureau. Resolutions of the Exchange in Inspector Byrnes's honor have been engrossed in an album. Upon the case of the watch is some handsome engraving, the front bearing the Inspector's monogram, and the back the monogram of the Stock Exchange. Upon the inside of the case is the inscription, PRESENTED TO INSPECTOR BYRNES BY THE NEW-YORK STOCK EXCHANGE FOR MERITORIOUS SERVICE.

—*New York Times*
February 3, 1886

During his tenure as chief of detectives, Byrnes distinguished himself in all areas of crime fighting. In May 1885, he was able to track down and capture one of the city's most notorious and cleverest safecrackers, Gustave Kindt. Kindt, though, was no match for the unrelenting Byrnes.

Kindt had led a charmed life until he ran into Byrnes's Detective Bureau. He had escaped twice from Sing Sing prison and boasted that he could open any safe ever made. Kindt credited himself with being the first professional criminal to use a "pump-blower," a tool used by burglars to force gunpowder into the locks and seams of a safe door in order to blow the door off its hinges. Kindt had a large collection of wax impressions of various keys used to unlock any number of bank doors and vaults. He also invented a circular safety lock and key that he claimed was impregnable, since it could not be picked and wax impressions could not be made of a key to unlock it. Kindt said that he intended to market and sell the impenetrable lock and key to banks and other financial institutions when he went "straight." Who better than a thief to know how to make a safe indecipherable?

The forty-seven-year-old Belgian native was by trade a watch-maker. He left the legitimate life for a life of crime early. Going by any number of assumed names, including Isadore Marchal and Frank Levoy, Kindt was first arrested in 1869 for breaking into the Wheeler & Parsons watch-case factory in Brooklyn. Kindt was working at the factory at the time. He stole hundreds of watch cases but was caught and sentenced to Sing Sing for ten years. He escaped from prison by cutting through the bars on his cell window with a miniature saw that had been smuggled in to him. In 1872 he was arrested for robbing the Marion Watch Works in New Jersey where he had also been employed. The robbery bankrupted the small company. He was ultimately arrested in Hackensack, New Jersey, for the break-in. The authorities in New Jersey agreed to send him back to New York to serve out his unexpired term in Sing Sing; once he was discharged, he was to be sent immediately back to New Jersey to stand trial for the Marion Watch Works robbery.

Back in Sing Sing, Kindt struck a deal with authorities. He promised to invent a lever lock for prison cells that could be used to lock and unlock cells simultaneously, so prison guards would not have to unlock row upon row of cells individually. In exchange, Kindt wanted a pardon. Sing Sing officials agreed with the deal as long as he could perfect such a lock and it would become the exclusive property of the prison. Kindt set to work and finally perfected a mechanism that allowed prison authorities to lock or unlock all the cells at once. He was later able to redesign his mechanism so that any given number of cells on the same corridor could be simultaneously locked or unlocked. In 1874 he brought the invention to prison officials, who were in awe of his mechanical genius. They approached governor Samuel Tilden, explaining the invention and requesting a pardon. Tilden could easily see the value in such a locking mechanism but refused to grant Kindt a pardon. Kindt, in turn, refused the prison request to use the locking mechanism he had invented. It did no good. He had made the locking mechanism while in prison, using prison tools and materials, and so prison officials argued that it belonged to the prison. Kindt refused to give prison officials the secret to the lock, so they could not use the mechanism.

After being refused the pardon, Kindt managed to bribe one of the guards, escape again from Sing Sing, and make his way to Canada. While in Montreal he broke into a pawnshop and stole a large quantity of jewelry and precious stones. He was arrested and sentenced to three years in a Canadian prison. Kindt gave prison officials there the secret to his lever-locking mechanism, which was later adopted for use in practically every prison in Canada and the United States, including Sing Sing.

Kindt was released from the Canadian prison in 1879 and returned to the United States, where he was arrested in Vermont and charged as an escaped convict. While riding the train from St. Albans, Vermont, to Sing Sing, Kindt attempted another escape, this time by jumping off the moving train. The New York City police detective who had him in custody jumped from the train as well and chased after the handcuffed Kindt. Unable to catch the speedy Kindt, the detective drew his revolver and fired two shots. One bullet hit Kindt in the left cheek, the other in the back of the head. Badly wounded, he was taken to the hospital at Sing Sing, where he recovered and served out the remainder of his sentence. Released in February 1884, he was taken by authorities back to New Jersey to stand trial for the Marion Watch Works burglary. Several witnesses in the case had subsequently died, and others could not be found. Unable to prosecute Kindt, the district attorney was forced to set him free.

Kindt made a beeline to New York City, loaded down with the most sophisticated burglary tools and a head full of insidious plans. As soon as he hit the city, Byrnes's detectives had him under surveillance. Byrnes had a thick file on Kindt and knew he would try his hand at some sort of robbery fairly soon. He told his men to keep him under surveillance and to notify him if Kindt made contact with any other known burglars in the city. Sure enough, just as Byrnes predicted, undercover detectives witnessed Kindt in the company of "Big" Frank McCoy, a known felon and burglar.

Not long after the meeting between McCoy and Kindt, the Smith & Vanderbeek wholesale grocers' shop was broken into. The safe was blown open. A $5,000 bond, a silver watch, and $60 in cash were taken. Although he had no concrete evidence to implicate Kindt in the robbery, Byrnes was sure that he was the mastermind. Detectives continued to keep Kindt under surveillance on Byrnes's orders. Not long after the grocers' robbery, burglars broke into G. B. Horton & Co. leather dealers. The safe's combination was cracked, and $234 in cash, a quantity of postage stamps, a steel tape measure, and a box of train tickets were stolen.

Byrnes examined the safes in both burglaries and concluded that they had been opened in a workmanlike way by the same group of men. Byrnes was positive that Kindt was the ringleader of whatever gang had robbed both places. Byrnes decided that with or without evidence, he would go with his hunch, so he had Kindt arrested. His hunch paid off.

Following Kindt's arrest, Byrnes's detectives uncovered the most complete set of safecracking tools that had ever been confiscated by city police. They were found in a tenement apartment house that Kindt was reported to have frequently visited. There was every tool and apparatus conceivable, including drills, fuses, gunpowder, saws, wrenches, hammers, claws, crowbars, wax used for taking impressions of keys, and close to one hundred skeleton keys of every shape and size. Kindt had stashed a veritable gold mine of burglary implements. He had kept all the tools in the tenement apartment of his daughter, Rose Kent, at 413 East Twelfth Street She lived there with her two-year-old child. Her husband had abandoned her, and Kindt was generously supporting her and his grandson with the loot he had stolen in several of his break-ins.

Besides the vast quantity of tools, detectives also found a box filled with train tickets, a steel tape measure, a stack of postage stamps, and the $5,000 security bond that had been stolen from G. B. Horton & Co. and the grocers' shop. When asked by detectives where the tools and the other incriminating evidence had come from, Kent said her father had brought it all to the apartment. She was arrested and taken to police headquarters, where Inspector Byrnes brought her and her child before her father. Seeing his daughter in handcuffs with the threat of prison time hanging over her head, which was what Byrnes threatened if Kindt didn't cooperate, Kindt broke down and confessed to both burglaries. Byrnes had once again gotten his man.

ARREST OF THE CLEVEREST CRACKSMAN IN THE COUNTRY.
A CRIMINAL WITH INVENTIVE GENIUS—BURGLAR'S TOOLS OF EVERY KIND

An important capture was made Saturday by officers of Inspector Byrnes's corps, the prisoner being the notorious Gustave Kindt, perhaps the cleverest and most successful burglar in the country. There is evidence to connect him with two safe burglaries in this city, which have occurred recently in this city. . . . Kindt is subject to two indictments for burglary, and on conviction, as this would be a conviction for a second offense, he can, under Penal Code, be sentenced to imprisonment for life. . . .

— *New York Times*
May 25, 1885

William Losey of Brooklyn, a fifty-year-old, well-respected bookkeeper, managed to rob his employers of $31,000 over a brief two-year period ending in 1892, losing most of his ill-gotten gains playing the numbers game. Molleson Brothers, a paper company on Beekman Street in the city, had employed Losey. He was regarded as one of the company's most trusted employees and worked as a confidential book-keeper for the business. The company began to notice a shortfall in its cash accounts, and, upon questioning Losey, he ascribed the shortfall to poor debt collections. This explanation seemed to satisfy the company since it was coming from a trusted employee. As the shortfall in cash continued, company officials became suspicious, despite what Losey had told them, and secretly called on the outside accounting services of their legal counsel, Chauncey Truax.

Truax's examination of the company books revealed that Losey was $8,000 short in his cash account. The matter was turned over to Inspector Byrnes, who confronted Losey. Losey, who had no previous run-ins with the law, had read the many newspaper accounts of Byrnes's exploits. He was well aware of Byrnes's reputation as a relentless investigator who always got his man. When confronted by Byrnes, Losey immediately blurted out his confession. Losey confessed not only to stealing the $8,000 that was missing in his cash account, but also to systematically stealing more than $31,000 total from the company. Despite engaging in this nefarious operation, Losey could not escape his training and further confessed to Byrnes that he had kept an exact accounting of what he had stolen from the company, $31,702.37, as well as the total amount he had lost at gambling, $32,303.95. Between what he had stolen and what he had won and then lost at gambling, Losey had lost a grand total of $64,006.32. He turned these accounts over to Byrnes, who later told newspaper reporters that Losey was the most systematic thief he had ever met.

Losey's accounts listed the addresses of various illegal gambling operations, including those on Park Row, William Street, Ann Street, and Pearl Street in New York City, as well as on Myrtle Avenue in Brooklyn. With Losey in custody, Byrnes next set the stage to raid all the gambling parlors the bookkeeper had listed. At nine o'clock in the morning, Byrnes authorized a series of simultaneous raids on the addresses Losey had provided, and the police rounded up more than a dozen people, along with the gambling paraphernalia found at their homes. The suspects were brought to police headquarters, where Losey identified them as the men in charge of the gambling operations he had frequented. All of the men were charged with operating illegal gambling houses, and their money was confiscated. Losey was charged with fraud, larceny, and forgery.

OVER THIRTY THOUSAND DOLLARS OF STOLEN MONEY GONE
ARREST OF MOLLESON BROTHERS' CONFIDENTIAL BOOKKEEPER—THE POLICY MEN WHO GOT THE MONEY LIKEWISE UNDER LOCK AND KEY

Chief Inspector Byrnes made public last night the details of the most remarkable case which occupied his attention for several days. It is the story of a confidential bookkeeper who robbed his employers in less than two years of over $31,000 which he played away in "policy" at shops in this city and Brooklyn. The dishonest bookkeeper is under arrest, as are also the keepers of the New-York policy shops.

—*New York Times*

March 9, 1892

(Note: Policy shops were illegal gambling institutions where customers bet on a variety of numbers, winning if their numbers were drawn and losing if they weren't. In later years this type of gambling went under the name of the "numbers racket.")

GEN. SHALER ARRESTED
TAKEN INTO CUSTODY ON A COMPLAINT OF BRIBERY.
A BENCH WARRANT ISSUED BY THE RECORDER— BROKER WILSON'S ADMISSIONS AND MAYOR GRACE'S CHARGES

—*New York Times*

December 1, 1885

Inspector Byrnes had no fear of politicians or those well-connected to the Tammany Hall crowd. Even with Boss Tweed dead and gone (Tweed died in prison in 1878), the political machinery of Tammany Hall remained in place, doling out patronage and keeping the wheels of its whole operation greased with kickbacks and bribes. None of this deterred Byrnes when it came to doing his job as chief inspector of the Detective Bureau. Besides, Byrnes had cultivated his own cadre of wealthy and influential friends like Jay Gould and many of Wall Street's high-rolling financiers.

And so it was with little trepidation that in December 1885 he arrested Major-General Alexander Shaler at his home on West Forty-eighth Street on bribery charges. Shaler, a hero at the Battle of Gettysburg, was the commander of the First Division of the city's National Guard and president of the Board of Health.

Byrnes remained deferential but determined when he informed Shaler that he had a warrant for his arrest and that the general had to accompany him to police headquarters. A startled Shaler read the particulars of the warrant that Byrnes had handed him.

Shaler asked that he be able to inform his family and bid them good-bye, a request that Byrnes readily allowed. Shaler was taken to Inspector Byrnes's office and questioned by Byrnes, as was the usual custom. Byrnes made no exceptions.

The criminal complaint against Shaler was based on evidence given to authorities by Monmouth Wilson, superintendent of the Fire Insurance Patrol. According to Wilson, Shaler had taken bribes in connection with the purchase of sites throughout the city for armories. The evidence was presented before New York City mayor William Grace, who had the charges filed with the district attorney.

Word of Shaler's arrest spread quickly among his many influential friends. He was held overnight in jail, and no bail was set for him. Franklin Edson Jr., the son of ex-mayor Franklin Edson and a close friend of Shaler's, went to police headquarters on Mulberry Street and asked to see the prisoner. Byrnes refused his request. Edson contacted his father and asked him to use his influence to have a magistrate set bail for Shaler so it could be paid and Shaler could be released until his arraignment the next day. Not even the former mayor could get anyone to set bail for Shaler. Mayor Grace remained steadfast that no one be allowed to set bail for the general. Byrnes upheld Grace's wishes.

Judge Gildersleeve, General Shaler's chief of staff, showed up at police headquarters with the intent of posting bail for Shaler, but since no bail had been set, Gildersleeve's trip was futile.

The gist of the bribery case against Shaler involved a real estate transaction to acquire a site for the Eighth Regiment Armory. According to testimony from Monmouth Wilson, the owner of the property agreed to sell it to the city for $350,000. The real estate agent representing the property was to receive a commission of $32,000 for negotiating the sale. Half of this amount was reportedly paid to Wilson for his efforts to secure the acceptance of the site by Shaler. Shortly after the transaction, Wilson testified, he paid off Shaler's mortgage of $9,000 in exchange for Shaler's approval in acquiring the property for the Eighth Regiment Armory. Subsequently, Wilson was involved in selling to the city, with Shaler's approval, three other sites designated for armory locations for the National Guard. For this, Wilson reportedly paid for several pieces of property in Shaler's name.

General Shaler had two trials, resulting in neither a conviction nor an acquittal. In both trials, the jury was deadlocked. Finally, the district attorney dropped criminal charges against Shaler because of a lack of evidence, and the indictment against him was dismissed. No one except Wilson ever saw Shaler take a bribe, and the $9,000 Wilson spent to pay off Shaler's mortgage and the other properties he purchased for Shaler were viewed as gifts. Besides, Wilson was not a reliable witness. It was brought out during testimony at both trials that he had lied to a Senate investigating committee as well as the district attorney.

Although Shaler was never convicted of taking a bribe, his political career was over. In May 1886 Governor David Hill asked for and received his resignation as commander of the National Guard, and in early 1887 he was removed as president of the New York City Board of Health.

THE MAN WHO SHOT DRAKE
A WEAK-MINDED MEMBER OF A
WEALTHY FAMILY
WILLIAM C. RHINELANDER'S ATTACK ON HIS
FATHER'S LAWYER—DRAKE SERIOUSLY
INJURED AND HIS ASSAILANT ARRESTED.

The man who shot Lawyer John Drake, in his office at No. 79 Cedar-street, Thursday afternoon, was William C. Rhinelander, a grandson of the late millionaire of the same name, and a beneficiary of his large estates. Mr. Drake is under treatment at the Roosevelt Hospital. His wound, to say the least, is a very serious one.

—*New York Times*

June 21, 1884

If the politically well connected, like General Shaler, were not immune to Byrnes's long arm of the law, neither were some of New York City's wealthiest citizens.

Even after William Rhinelander had shot him, John Drake refused to press charges. He wanted to keep the whole incident out of the press, and for good reason. Rhinelander believed that Drake was having an affair with his wife.

Rhinelander disappeared after the shooting but was tracked down by Byrnes at his home later the same day. When he was arrested, he freely admitted shooting Drake and said that Drake had turned his wife against him. He showed no remorse nor was he in any way rattled by being arrested. He went along quietly to police headquarters. Rhinelander was the black sheep of the family, and he was constantly engaged in outlandish and questionable behavior. He had ended up marrying one of his servants, which was the last straw as far as his family was concerned. Although his wealthy father continued to generously support him, he had nothing to do with his son socially. Rhinelander's living expenses, estimated at approximately $100 a week, were drawn on an account managed by Drake, who was an old friend of the Rhinelander family and served as its legal advisor.

Members of Rhinelander's family and friends frequently viewed him as a lunatic. Some even said he should have been institutionalized. He had often made threats to shoot Drake, his own father, his brother, and his wife, charging them all with trying to interfere with his business, whatever that was. (Rhinelander did not work.) Still, Rhinelander complained that he didn't like the way his share of the family fortune was being doled out to him. No one paid any attention to his threats, since Rhinelander was not known to carry a gun and he'd been making such outlandish threats for years. Drake knew that Rhinelander had been having troubles with his wife and had tried to mediate their differences, perhaps more than he should have. Rhinelander's young, uneducated wife told her husband she had fallen in love with someone else, and then she left him. Rhinelander blamed Drake.

On the day of the shooting, Rhinelander had gone to Drake's office and found Drake busy at his desk. Rhinelander sat in a chair opposite Drake, and they cordially engaged in polite conversation. Drake knew immediately that something was wrong. Most times, Rhinelander exhibited eccentric behavior when he visited Drake, talking loudly and boisterously. Suddenly, without warning, Rhinelander jumped up from his chair, swearing and accusing Drake of cuckolding him. He drew a revolver from the pocket of his coat, and Drake tried to wrestle it from him. The gun went off. Despite being wounded in the shoulder, Drake managed to race around his desk, grab Rhinelander, and pin him against the wall. Rhinelander, who was still holding the gun, tried to fire again but the muscular Drake twisted the weapon from his hand and it fell to the floor.

Two employees at Drake's law office rushed into the room when they heard the shot and helped subdue Rhinelander. Rhinelander was shouting incoherently, accusing Drake of carrying on an affair with his wife and stealing his money. Drake picked up the small Remington revolver that Rhinelander had used to shoot him and put it on his desk. He had his two employees take Rhinelander into an adjacent office and hold him there.

"That fellow shot me," Drake told them.

"Send for a policeman," one of his employees said.

"No. No," Drake protested. "I don't want that. Send for a doctor."

Rhinelander was subsequently freed at Drake's request and left the law offices. By then he had calmed down and acted as if nothing had happened. One of the employees heard him whistling as he left the building.

Drake was taken to the hospital later that afternoon where he underwent surgery. Rhinelander was arrested.

A report by the New York Commissioners in Lunacy found William Rhinelander insane and ordered him committed to an asylum. The courts disagreed with the commissioners' decision, finding Rhinelander sane and ordering him to stand trial for the shooting of Drake. He was released from custody on $10,000 bail. In May 1885, before Rhinelander was brought to trial, Drake died suddenly of pneumonia, and the indictment against Rhinelander was dropped. In a twist, Rhinelander's estranged wife, Margarita, agreed to testify on his behalf, claiming that she never had an affair with Drake and that Drake had routinely tried to drive a wedge between her and her husband. She said that Drake had caused her and her husband great harm in the past and that her husband had withstood any number of insults from Drake. She and Rhinelander reunited after Drake's death.

HE WANTED TO KILL GOULD
A DANGEROUS CRANK FROM THE WEST CAPTURED.
CHARLES J. DICKSON'S WILD STORY OF A MYSTERIOUS AND HOMICIDAL ORDER—AN INITIATION ON THE CANADIAN BORDER

At the instance of Jay Gould's physician, Dr. Joseph P. Munn of 18 West Fifty-eighth Street, Inspector Byrnes and Detectives Frink and McClusky stationed themselves near Dr. Munn's house on Tuesday night and, when a signal was given, entered and arrested Charles J. Dickson of Pueblo, Col., a crank who

had come to kill Mr. Gould if he did not comply with the terms
of a mythical organization, Christ's Followers.

—*New York Times*

May 7, 1891

———•••———

The capture of forty-year-old Charles Dickson was another veritable
feather in Byrnes's already plumage-filled cap. Jay Gould, one of New
York City's wealthiest financiers, had become an intimate of Byrnes
following the murder of James Fisk Jr. The capture of the man intent
on killing Gould only further cemented their relationship. Byrnes had
gone out of his way as chief of detectives to curry favor with the city's
wealthiest and most influential inhabitants, and his endeavors to
ingratiate himself with the rich and the powerful, including establishing the Wall Street detective substation, paid off in spades. By 1891,
when he captured Gould's thwarted assassin, Byrnes was the most
powerful law enforcement officer in the city, and he had his sights
set on even more power—superintendent of the New York City Police
Department—a position he eventually attained in 1892, with the full
support of the city's financial community.

After the arrest of Dickson, Byrnes took the suspect to police headquarters for questioning. In his usual fashion—part coercion, part
cajoling, all psychological—Byrnes was able to get a complete confession out of Dickson. Dickson told Byrnes that he was a native of
Hartford, Connecticut, and that he had moved to Colorado to work as
a land agent and as the proprietor of the Jacksonian, a hotel in Pueblo.
According to Dickson's confession, in 1888, he had began an association with a religious group called Christ's Followers. Dickson said the
group hired him as a messenger for $25 a month. Later his salary was
increased to $100. Dickson said the group began to depend on him
in ways other than merely being a messenger. He told Byrnes that he
found favor in the eyes of the religious group because of his brav-
ery. According to Dickson, ten masked men had ridden into Pueblo
to steal county records several years before, and he had stopped them
by blocking their path. In a gunfight, Dickson claimed to have killed

four of them. His heroism led to his being initiated as a full member of the organization. According to Dickson, he was initiated into the secret Christ's Followers during a ceremony at Owl's Head Lake, along the Canadian border. Dickson went to the lake after dark and was met by forty or fifty masked men. He was ordered to kneel in the center of the ring while the men made him swear his allegiance to the group. He was given the title of Vice President No. 71 and took his orders directly from the leader, who was named Adonia.

Finally, several weeks before arriving in New York City, Dickson said he had received word from the group that it had tried Jay Gould in absentia and found him guilty of reneging on the financial demands the group had placed upon him. Gould was sentenced to die unless he immediately gave the organization $5 million and pledged to give $15 million more within the next ten years. Christ's Followers also demanded that Gould will his entire fortune to them after he died. The group told Dickson to go to New York and carry out its orders. When he arrived in the city, Dickson had $350 in cash, a blackjack, and a revolver. He also had a letter of introduction to Dr. Munn. He revealed to Dr. Munn the intent of his visit and assured Munn that the matter could be amicably resolved with Munn's help. He told Munn that, instead of carrying out the orders of Christ's Followers, he would be willing to forego all the demands and was prepared to guarantee Gould's protection if Gould would pay him $60,000 in cash. Munn went directly to Byrnes and informed him of Dickson's outlandish story and demands. Byrnes advised Munn to invite Dickson back to his offices, where Byrnes would set a trap for him.

Dickson said he had an elaborate plan to escape from the hold that Christ's Followers had on him. He would be condemned to death if he didn't carry out their orders. Dickson told Byrnes that he intended to go back to Hartford once Gould had paid him the $60,000, and there he would find a deserted spot, break his watch and chain so that authorities could find it, and scatter some of his personal papers around. He intended to buy another pistol, fire off several rounds, and leave the gun behind for authorities to find. Both the police and members of Christ's Followers would think he had been murdered and his body dumped elsewhere. With the money from Gould, Dickson said he would assume a new identity and serve as a vigilant bodyguard for Gould if Christ's Followers decided to come after Gould again.

Dickson was taken to the Jefferson Market Police Court where a hearing was held to determine Dickson's sanity. Armed with the bizarre confession, Byrnes testified that Dickson was a dangerous crank. He testified further that he was unable to corroborate anything Dickson had told him about his identity, his business, or the existence of any secret organization called Christ's Followers. Dickson was found to be insane and taken to the city's mental institution at Bellevue Hospital.

Byrnes used his methodical investigative abilities not only to capture criminals but also to free innocent men. One such case involved a burglar known as Red Jack. Byrnes had a file on Jack, as well as several mug shots from previous arrests, at police headquarters.

A burglary was reported in Tarrytown, New York, and there was an eyewitness to the crime. Someone had broken into a woman's home and had stolen jewelry and a small amount of cash. The victim was next door when the break-in happened and watched as the burglar slipped out the back door of her house. Although she was unable to stop him, she could identify him. She informed police of the burglary and gave them a description of the criminal. The police arrested a Tarrytown storekeeper who had no criminal record and steadfastly professed his innocence. Still, the woman identified him in a police lineup as the man who had broken into her home.

At the same time the break-in occurred in Tarrytown, Inspector Byrnes, as was his wont, had Red Jack under surveillance. Jack was a slippery character, and Byrnes was sure he was planning a burglary. The undercover detectives that Byrnes had assigned to trail Red Jack reported that Jack had been seen boarding a train and heading to Tarrytown. Although Tarrytown was out of his district, Byrnes contacted the police there to alert them that a known burglar was headed their way and to be on the lookout for him. When the Tarrytown police told Byrnes that they had arrested a local shopkeeper and charged him with the burglary, Byrnes had grave misgivings. Red Jack, he felt, was too slick to be caught on his first try at a burglary in Tarrytown. Besides, Byrnes thought, the Tarrytown police were not sharp enough to catch someone as clever as Red Jack.

Byrnes needed to prove that Red Jack, not the lowly Tarrytown shopkeeper, was the real culprit. Byrnes told his detectives to be on the lookout for Red Jack and posted several men at the train station to await the train coming back from Tarrytown. Sure enough, like clockwork, Red Jack arrived at the train station looking fit and pleased with himself. Byrnes had Red Jack picked up for questioning and, using one of his many methods of persuasion, was able to get a full confession out of him.

With Red Jack in custody, Byrnes took the train to Tarrytown, where he presented Red Jack before the police. He showed them the confession and asked that the man they had in custody be brought out of his cell. As it turned out, the innocent storekeeper and the notorious Red Jack looked practically identical, right down to the shock of wavy red hair. The much-relieved storekeeper was freed, and Red Jack was placed behind bars in Tarrytown.

During his twelve-year tenure as head of the New York City Detective Bureau, from 1880 until 1892, the criminals Byrnes and his men apprehended and prosecuted received prison sentences totaling ten thousand years.

Byrnes earned an international reputation as one of the world's greatest detectives. He became the subject of numerous books by author Julian Hawthorne and the central crime-fighting character in a number of dime-store books. A day didn't go by that Byrnes's name didn't appear in most of the major New York City newspapers. He seemed to be everywhere all the time, a cigar-chomping, derby-wearing, well-dressed, larger-than-life nemesis to criminals throughout the city and beyond.

His exploits earned him the attention of law enforcement professionals throughout the country who often modeled their own police departments and procedures after what Byrnes had done with the Detective Bureau.

His fame extended well beyond America. In 1891, King Humbert of Italy, learning of Byrnes's reputation as a crime fighter, conferred on him the Order of the Italian Crown in recognition of the services that Byrnes had rendered to the Italian authorities and the Italian Consulate in New York City in the arrest and extradition of Italian criminals. Despite it being offered, Byrnes turned down the honor on the grounds that it wasn't right for an American citizen who was just doing his job to accept such recognition from a foreign country.

INSPECTOR BYRNES DECORATED
HONORED BY KING HUMBERT AND MINISTER CRISPI

. . .Byrnes will now have a handsome decoration that he can disport on his left breast on parade or other special occasions, or even every day if he so chooses. It is the Order of the Italian Crown, which has been conferred on Mr. Byrnes by King Humbert of Italy in recognition of services . . .

—*New York Times*
February 26, 1891

Regardless of the national and international fame and honors bestowed on him, or the number of times he was used as a central character in a detective novel or magazine, Byrnes maintained a workmanlike perspective on the job of being a detective.

In one extensive interview with the *New York Times*, Byrnes offered advice to would-be detectives: "My advice to boys who want to become young sleuths is to stick to school till they graduate and then learn trades. The detective of fact owes nothing to the detective of fiction. . . . There is nothing like that in real detective work.

"One thing wrong about the detective of fiction is that it is all the same. Read one detective story and you have read them all. In real life the cases that come at you are all different. The detective of fiction tells the criminal all he knows. It would be hard to conceive a more senseless proceeding. The French detectives of fiction proceed to confound the criminals by laying before them proofs of their crimes. All the criminal has to do is to deny. Then if the proof fails, he is free," Byrnes said.

"When I arrested a man charged with a serious crime, I never told him why he was arrested. I might talk with him about his mother, his home, his employer, but not a word about his crime. I knew that he was not listening to me. The thought of his crime was whirling about in his head and he knew that I knew what he was thinking about. It worried him that I should not talk about the crime. He strained himself trying to think how much I knew. If he saw any accomplices march past the window or any of the clothing of the victim or the weapon of the crime, he was more uneasy. After a time he felt that he would be easier if he told all than constantly straining and worrying. So he confessed and slept easily after it. That was exactly the way we got them."

According to Byrnes, "It is not remorse that makes the hardened criminal confess; it is anxiety, mental strain.

"Neither West Point or the law schools give men training for the Police Department," Byrnes said. "And police inefficiency is due chiefly to the incompetent head and incompetent deputies who know practically nothing of the work they are called upon to supervise. The force is all right at the bottom and its head officers should be men who have risen through its ranks and not through the ranks of military men upon the battlefields, no matter how valorous their deeds."

THE CASE OF THE MURDERED WINE MERCHANT

In which Inspector Byrnes solves the case of murdered wine merchant Louis Hanier using a pioneering form of forensic science and establishes himself as the preeminent American detective.

Although there remains little doubt that New York City Chief Inspector Thomas Byrnes was the great American detective and the father of modern crime-scene investigation, he owed a great deal of his fame and many of his investigative techniques to French detective Eugène François Vidocq. It was Vidocq who, in the 1820s, first saw the potential for the use of fingerprints as an investigative and crime-fighting tool. It was not until nearly one hundred years after Vidocq's first attempt to incorporate fingerprinting into the arsenal of available investigative tools that the practice could be used by law enforcement agencies throughout the world. In 1901, Edward Henry, an Englishman, discovered a method of categorizing fingerprint patterns so they could be used to identify criminals. Still, it was Vidocq who was the first to apply these fundamental forensics to detective work.

Vidocq attempted to record fingerprint impressions by having the criminals dip their fingers into ink and press them onto a piece of paper, leaving behind an inky impression. The ink, though, dried too quickly on the criminal's fingertips before Vidocq could record the impressions. Although unsuccessful, he innately knew the potential value that fingerprints would have in scientifically identifying criminal suspects, and he continued throughout his life to experiment with the idea, including trying to preserve fingerprints in clay molds. When he died in 1857, no one had yet perfected the fingerprinting process, and few if any foresaw the immense value fingerprinting would have within the realm of forensic science.

The first detective department in America wasn't established until 1857 in New York City, and its fundamental investigative techniques were not modernized until Thomas Byrnes assumed control of the department. The first modern police department in England, Scotland Yard, was created in 1829. In France, the first detective bureau, the Sûreté, was formed in 1811, as part of the Paris Police Department. Vidocq was put in charge of it.

Byrnes pioneered the psychological and scientific approach to criminal detection in the United States. Although he did not delve into the use of fingerprinting as Vidocq had, Byrnes put into practice many of Vidocq's other means of criminal detection, from collecting criminal rap sheets into a central data bank to his use of criminal informants. Byrnes's scrupulous recordkeeping included making notes of the criminals' distinguishing physical characteristics, from height, weight, and hair color to tattoos, scars, and any other memorable features.

It was not until the 1900s that the use of blood as an identifying factor became a part of criminal investigations, since the ability to properly categorize human blood into blood groups was not discovered until then. And the use of DNA testing did not come about until the 1980s. Men like Vidocq in France and Byrnes in America were the forerunners of the modern detective and pioneers in the use of forensic science.

———

By the time Byrnes assumed the role of chief of detectives for the New York City Police Department in 1880, Eugène François Vidocq had been dead for more than twenty years. He died in 1857 at the age of eighty-two.

Vidocq's career was remarkable. An ex-convict, he had shot and killed a man in a duel. The man was reportedly having an affair with Vidocq's wife. Placed in some of France's most secure prisons, Vidocq was able to break out time and again. His adventures as a jailbreaker became fabled throughout Paris, and he acquired an envious respect from law enforcement authorities. Since Vidocq was not guilty of any crime other than defending his honor in a duel, and since his lengthy prison sentences were mostly due to his escapes, the chief of the Paris

Police Department saw in him the perfect match for the city's detective bureau, the Sûreté. The thirty-four-year-old Vidocq was hired as an undercover detective and soon after, as head of the Sûreté.

Vidocq began his investigative career with a simple principle: It takes a thief to catch a thief. His own experience as a prison convict made him familiar with the workings of the criminal underworld, and he quickly put his knowledge of criminal tendencies to work, solving—rather than committing—crimes. One of his first orders was to have his men placed in jail on fabricated charges, so they could keep the incarcerated criminals under surveillance and gather information about their plans once they were released, or identify their criminal cohorts on the outside. Using disguises Vidocq would frequently visit the hangouts of known criminals, easily mingling with many of Paris's most notorious and dangerous criminals. If his undercover work or investigation led to an arrest, Vidocq would give the culprit two options: go to prison, or work as a snitch for him. Many of those apprehended chose the latter, and Vidocq was able to create a small army of criminal informants.

Besides using informants on such a large scale, another of his innovations was to collect and record vital information on professional criminals, keeping track of everything from their physical descriptions and identifying characteristics to their methods of operations. Both the use of informants and criminal histories were innovations that Byrnes adopted.

With no real forensic science to draw on, Vidocq had to rely on his own rudimentary ideas, including handwriting analysis. In one famous case a professional criminal had swindled a widow out of her savings using a forged letter. When the man went on trial, his attorney attempted to prove that it was a case of mistaken identity and that the suspect was an upstanding citizen with no criminal record. This was quickly disproved when Vidocq took the stand and produced a lengthy criminal record on the man, including past cases of forgery and his physical description. Next Vidocq testified that he had taken the letter used by the suspect to swindle the widow to several University of Paris professors, who agreed that a person's handwriting was in fact unique. He presented the judge with a copy of the forged letter and samples of the prisoner's handwriting, which he assured the court were a perfect match. Faced with this unique evidence, the swindler immediately changed his plea to guilty and begged the court for mercy. The case demonstrated the first time forensic science had been used to examine a document.

Vidocq was also the first to use forensic firearms identification. When the wife of a wealthy Paris businessman was shot in the head and killed, the police immediately suspected her husband. His wife was much younger and had been known to have been carrying on an affair. The police suspected that the husband had shot her with one of his dueling pistols, but Vidocq, who was knowledgeable about dueling pistols, checked the barrels of the pistols and discovered no powder residue in either one. Vidocq concluded that neither of the pistols was the murder weapon. And after taking an inventory of the woman's possessions, it was discovered that some of her most expensive jewelry was missing. Vidocq concluded that robbery, not jealousy, was the motive for the murder, and that the husband had not used his dueling pistols to shoot his wife. He was no longer considered the prime suspect.

But Vidocq's investigation did not end there. Although he had proved the husband wasn't the killer, he still needed to prove who was. This would take some dark skullduggery. Although autopsies were used in America and England in murder cases, they were not legal in France. Vidocq had to persuade the undertaker to secretly remove the bullet that was lodged in the dead woman's forehead. After discovering who the murdered woman's secret lover was, he went to the man's apartment and searched it. There he discovered a small pistol. Using the fatal bullet that the undertaker had given him, Vidocq fit the bullet perfectly into the man's gun. A further search of the apartment turned up the stolen jewelry. The man confessed to the crime on the spot, telling Vidocq that the woman intended to break off their affair, and that he needed money. He then killed her and stole her jewelry.

Chief Inspector Byrnes used this same rudimentary forensic firearms identification procedure in 1882 when trying to uncover the killer of a wealthy New York City wine merchant, Louis Hanier.

Vidocq was also the first to attempt to use forensic science to identify blood found at the crime scene. In 1825, when Vidocq attempted to use blood identification to solve a case, there was no scientific way to identify blood. That would not happen until 1900. Still, Vidocq once again used an instinctive and rudimentary technique that turned out to be more ploy than science, but still managed to solve the case.

A wealthy Parisian citizen was found beaten to death in his mansion. Examining the crime scene, Vidocq found traces of blood throughout the house and on the latch to the door where he surmised the killer escaped. The blood on the door latch had to belong to the killer and not the murdered man. The killer had somehow been scratched or cut during his struggle with the victim. In disguise, Vidocq went to a seedy waterfront tavern, where many of the city's worst criminals were known to frequent. There he just happened upon a known burglar who looked as if he had recently been in a fight. Vidocq decided that, in order to get a blood sample from the man, he would have to pick a fight with him, which he did. Vidocq bloodied the man's nose and then offered the man his handkerchief. He took back his handkerchief with the man's blood sample smeared all over it. Back at police headquarters, he soaked the handkerchief in a chemical agent that turned the bloodstains a bright red color. He next applied the same chemical agent to the blood left behind by the killer on the door latch. It turned the same bright color. Vidocq concluded that the two blood samples matched and that he had his killer. He had the burglar arrested and brought to police headquarters where Vidocq showed him the results of his blood tests, telling the man that the tests conclusively proved he was the murderer. The man blurted out his confession when confronted with such "scientific" evidence. There was no way of proving the man's blood and the blood on the door latch were the same. There was no scientific proof, merely Vidocq's innate suspicion that blood types could be identified and used to apprehend criminals. This experiment used by Vidocq wasn't it, but it was, however, the beginning of the scientific methods that would later be commonplace in forensic crime-scene investigations.

In 1882, Byrnes tackled one of his most difficult cases, one that brought to the forefront his keenly perceptive investigative abilities as well as his use of several innovative tactics that would become the foundation for today's forensic-science field. Louis Hanier was a well-known and highly regarded wine merchant who was shot and killed by an unknown assailant during a midnight robbery of his liquor store. There were no eyewitnesses to the crime, although Hanier's wife and son were home in an upstairs apartment at the time. Furthermore, the killer left behind no clues—at least none that were perceptible to the naked eye. The case remained a mystery for weeks.

After undertaking an extensive study of the murder scene, sifting through the most minute details and using his acute powers of inductive reasoning, Byrnes made a startling revelation.

"It was Hanier's rum that killed him," Byrnes proclaimed.

To most of his detectives, this bewildering revelation made little sense, but to Byrnes, it was a key element in the investigation. One of the only clues that had been found at the murder scene was four half-filled glasses of brandy on the counter. No money had been stolen from the till, and no other objects of any worth had been taken.

From this, Byrnes concluded that four people had broken into Hanier's wine tavern that night—hence, the four glasses of unfinished brandy—and that they broke in to steal liquor, not to rob the place of money. Based on his conclusion, Byrnes surmised that the break-in and subsequent murder were not the work of professional burglars, since most of them were only interested in money and valuables. Their modus operandi was to get in and out as quickly as they could, most of the time without ever harming anyone, never mind murdering a defenseless wine merchant. Byrnes theorized that whoever broke in to the wine shop and killed Hanier had probably been one of the many shiftless young men who hung around the neighborhood. All Byrnes had to do was find him and prove it. No small matter.

MURDERED BY BURGLARS
A FRENCH SALOON-KEEPER SHOT
IN HIS OWN HOUSE
MOVEMENTS OF THREE SUSPICIOUS MEN
PREVIOUS TO THE MURDER—THIEVES ENTER
THE HOUSE AND KILL THE PROPRIETOR
—A MAN ARRESTED ON SUSPICION

Louis Hanier, a respectable Frenchman, the proprietor of a
beer saloon at No. 144 West Twenty-sixth street, was murdered by thieves, who at an early hour yesterday morning
entered his saloon for the purpose of robbery. . . . The house,
though situated in a very bad neighborhood, bore an excellent
reputation. The Police never had any trouble there. The second
floor of the building over the saloon was used as sitting rooms
and bed-rooms. His wife Aurelie, is a native of St. Quentin. . . .
They had been married 18 years, and had five sons and two
daughters. . . . Hanier closed the saloon at midnight, and at
12:30 he retired to bed in a room immediately over the saloon.
At 2 o'clock he was aroused by a noise in the rear of the
saloon, and he got up, slipped on his trousers, and started to
go down a steep staircase which leads to the front entrance
of the saloon, and at the foot of which is a door leading out of
the bar-room. Hanier, who was unarmed, had gone down but
three steps when the thieves, who had evidently taken possession of the saloon, heard him moving about. As he reached the
third or fourth step of the staircase a person appeared at the
door of the bar-room at the foot of the stairs and thrust out
a hand which held a large pistol and fired. The shot was evidently fired at random in the dark. The bullet however struck
Hanier in the left side. . . . Mrs. Hanier, alarmed by the shot
and the shrieks of her husband, threw open the window and
shouted for help. She then went to the assistance of her husband, helped him into the room and laid him down on the bed.
A policeman was promptly on hand but before he arrived the
thieves, alarmed at the result of the shot, had fled. A physician
was summoned. When he arrived Hanier was still breathing

but beyond human aid. He expired from internal hemorrhage in less than 15 minutes after receiving the wound. . . .

—*New York Times*

December 31, 1881

———⚬⚬⚬———

Hanier's saloon and wine shop was in an old house on West Twenty-sixth Street. The neighborhood was primarily made up of French immigrants, and many were regular customers of Hanier's. Afternoons and evenings men gathered at Hanier's small saloon where they sat playing cards, drinking wine or brandy, and talking about the news of the day. The old wooden house where the saloon was located was only two stories tall. On one side of the house was a brick wall, the remains of an old building, and on the other was an abandoned lumberyard where mounds of trash and rubbish collected.

The small single-room saloon was decorated with garlands, a few ornaments, and a small spindly Christmas tree in celebration of the recent holiday. Half the front door was made of glass, and it was locked nightly by the most simple lock and bolt. The back door to the saloon was old and wooden, latched on the inside. The men who broke in and fatally shot Hanier had come in the back door, nearly knocking it off its rusted hinges.

A wooden counter ran along one whole wall of the saloon, and behind the counter were shelves with bottles of wine and brandy on display. Clean glasses were strategically stacked along the counter, and a cask of beer with a spigot sticking out of it rested in the middle of the long counter. Several stools of different sizes and types sat in front of the counter, facing the shelves of wine and brandy, and several tables and chairs were scattered randomly throughout the room. The tables and the counter were lit by kerosene lamps and candles, but mostly the saloon was dark. As dim as it was, the atmosphere was always friendly. Most customers knew each other, and they all knew Louis Hanier. Occasionally, some rough trade from the neighborhood might wander in, but they were usually met with stony silence and seldom stayed long. Hanier discouraged the rough crowd from coming in and would often double the price for a glass of brandy or wine when a stranger or some of the neighborhood thugs happened to drop in.

Hanier was a soft-spoken man and a good husband, father, and provider. He was tall, with narrow features, and was thin and bony. His eyes were dark blue, and his hair, the little he had left, was blond and wispy. He had a prominent proboscis and protruding ears. He was seldom seen without a smile on his face, which wrinkled his brow and forced furrows along his mouth and cheeks. Hanier was a fastidious man who was almost always wearing a white apron wrapped around his waist with a rag in his hand to wipe off the counter and tabletops. No sooner was an empty glass put down than Hanier was there to take it away and wipe the table clean. Behind the wooden bar, all his wines and brandies were arranged by date, with the newest wines and brandies on the lower shelves and the older, more expensive ones on the top shelf. When he was not tending bar at his saloon, which he did six days a week, taking only Sundays off in keeping with his religious beliefs, he could be seen strolling through the neighborhood, usually wearing a black beret over his bald head and a dark frock coat. He carried a silver-topped cane that he used to poke at this and that along the sidewalk, gutter, or on the stoops. He did not need it for walking.

About one o'clock in the morning on December 30, Aurelie Hanier, who was a light sleeper, awoke with a start a feeling that something was wrong. At first, however, she did not arouse her husband, who lay asleep in bed beside her.

It was a windy and rainy night so it could have been the weather that had awakened her. Or it could have been the mice or rats scrambling down the stairs in the saloon below, looking for some discarded bit of food. If they were looking for crumbs, they were looking in the wrong place. Louis Hanier meticulously cleaned up his saloon every night, sweeping the floors, wiping down the counter and tables, and washing and putting away all the glasses. Still she listened. Now she heard the noise clearly coming from the saloon in the floor below the bed. It was not a sound she was unfamiliar with. She was used to hearing the clinking of glasses and the low drunken mumble of men, but not at one o'clock in the morning after the saloon had been closed for more than an hour. People were in the saloon below and they were drinking. She heard muffled laughter. Aurelie Hanier was overcome with a sickening feeling of dread. Her heart beat faster. Her intuition told her something was terribly wrong. She awoke her husband.

Louis Hanier had just fallen asleep. He was groggy and disoriented. His wife whispered and pointed below to the floor, and Hanier was obliged to listen. He could hear the clinking of glasses, the muffled voices, and the shuffling of footsteps. Some people had broken in.

Hanier had locked the front door that night as he always did, and neither his wife nor he had heard what would have been a loud and clear sound of breaking glass. There was nothing of any worth downstairs in the saloon. Hanier always cleaned out the till, putting the money in a small safe upstairs in the bedroom. There were no other valuables, no silver or gold or even expensive paintings. He wondered why anyone would break into his saloon. It didn't matter. Some people surely had, and they were downstairs doing God-knows-what, perhaps ransacking the place looking for money or valuables. Like the mice and rats looking for some morsel of food in Hanier's saloon, the robbers too would be frustrated.

Hanier slipped quietly out of bed, walking across the bedroom rug as if walking on eggshells, and put on a pair of pants over his nightshirt. With very few words he told his wife to slip out of bed as he had done, go down the hall, and check on the children. She did as she was told. She awoke her eldest son, a boy of ten years old, thinking that he might be of some assistance to his father. Louis Hanier walked slowly in the darkness through the hallway to the top of the stairs. He waved Aurelie and his son away. His wife held out his silver-topped cane, thinking he might need it for defense, but he brushed it aside as well.

It was still raining, and the raindrops pelted the flat cedar shingles on the roof. The wind howled and shook the old house. Suddenly there was a loud banging noise downstairs, followed by a noisy scuffle. Hanier heard the old wooden back door squeal on its rusted hinges. Whoever was downstairs, they were making their getaway. Hanier was at the top of the narrow and steep staircase. He could easily have let them go now that they had done their damage, whatever it might have been, but he was overcome with a sense of injustice and this impulse carried him down the stairs.

Aurelie waited anxiously in the hallway upstairs with her small son by the hand, waiting for some word from her husband. She expected at any moment for him to call out that it was all clear. But she didn't hear a word from him. Instead there was a golden flash in the staircase followed by a loud, short explosion. She heard pounding footsteps. Somebody raced up the stairs from below and bolted past her, nearly knocking her over. The shadowy figure ran into one of the children's rooms and climbed out onto the old balcony. From there he jumped off the porch into one of the many piles of rubbish and old wood stacked in the abandoned lumberyard. She spun around and saw her husband staggering backward up the stairs into the hallway. He cried out to her. It was a bone-chilling cry that sent shivers up Aurelie's spine. Hanier stumbled down the hall and into their bedroom, collapsing onto the bed. Aurelie rushed to him, reaching out in the darkness to grab him. Hanier rolled off the bed and onto the floor where he died of a single gunshot wound. Aurelie screamed to the heavens and fell beside him, clasping his hand, lifting him by the shoulders into her bosom, rocking back and forth, and weeping uncontrollably.

The Haniers' son had been standing by the bedroom door when the man ran by him in the darkness. He watched as the man climbed out onto the rickety balcony and jumped from there to the lumberyard. The boy ran to the balcony and looked down just in time to see a dark figure running away. He was not able to see who it was, but the man, running wildly through the yard, looked back over his shoulder just long enough to catch a glimpse of the boy. He saw the boy even if the boy didn't see him. But the killer didn't know the boy couldn't identify him and wouldn't know it right up until the moment that Inspector Byrnes coaxed a full confession out of him.

———

It would ultimately take every trick in Byrnes's arsenal of investigative ploys—strategies, deceptions, even rudimentary forensic firearm identification—to capture Hanier's killer. When the police arrived at the scene, Aurelie Hanier was on the floor, sitting in a pool of her husband's blood, still clutching him to her. Neighbors had been awakened and found their way to Hanier's second-floor apartment. All of the couple's children, except for the ten-year-old boy who had witnessed most of the events, were being taken care of by a woman friend of the Haniers, who lived just down the street. It was still raining when the police arrived, wearing their long waterproof cloaks and boots.

Candles and lamps now lit the upstairs rooms, and several officers surveyed the crime scene, while others went downstairs to the saloon to look around. Police attempted to question the inconsolable Mrs. Hanier. The story she told to police was, as expected from a woman who had just lost her husband so violently, confused and disjointed. Her ten-year-old's recollection of the events that had transpired was more cohesive. He told police that he saw a man rush by him in the darkness and jump off the balcony into the lumberyard below, but that he did not see the man's face and could barely describe his physical characteristics, aside from the fact that he appeared from a distance to be small and dark.

Downstairs, police found the saloon ransacked from end to end, tables turned over, wine bottles smashed, chairs tipped over, drawers and cabinets opened and rifled through, and the small cash register behind the counter ripped apart. The whole place had been wrecked. The only thing untouched was the front door, which remained locked. Police went to the back door and found it nearly torn from its hinges. This was not the work of any professional burglar. Every sign indicated that whoever had broken into Hanier's saloon had used brute force rather than finesse.

Word of the brutal murder spread quickly through the neighborhood and to the newspapers. A crowd of curious people gathered in front of the Haniers' house. Friends and relatives were allowed inside to try to comfort Aurelie Hanier and her children.

Police questioned everyone in the immediate neighborhood who had known Hanier, trying to determine if they knew of anyone who might hold a grudge against the wine merchant, but no one could think of anyone who might have had it in for him. Hanier had no enemies. Everything about him was aboveboard.

It was mid-morning before Inspector Byrnes arrived on the scene. After paying his condolences to Mrs. Hanier, he went downstairs to the saloon to investigate. The place was in a shambles. He stepped carefully over the broken glass and around the upturned tables and chairs. Byrnes inspected the back door that was barely hanging by its hinges. He had already heard from the coroner, who reported that Hanier had been killed by a single shot to the heart. The bullet remained inside Hanier's body. Byrnes's first directive was to have the coroner retrieve the bullet from the body and bring it to him.

Byrnes slowly began to piece together what he imagined had happened. The burglars were not professional thieves. The way they had broken in and the damage they had done demonstrated that, and no tools of any sort were left behind in their rush to get out. Nothing was stolen, not that Hanier had left anything of value downstairs in the saloon. Most of the expensive brandy and wine bottles had been either smashed or were still sitting along the top shelf behind the bar. Byrnes's conclusion was that whoever had broken into the saloon and killed Hanier were strangers to the French wine merchant. Since they weren't professional criminals, they had to be street thugs, and the neighborhood was filled with gangs of young, unemployed petty thieves and hoodlums to choose from. But the motive for the break-in and murder eluded Byrnes, until he went to the end of the bar along the wall where he found four glasses, each half filled with brandy— expensive brandy. The bottle was nearby. Now, he thought, he had his motive.

"It was Hanier's rum that killed him," he later told his men.

The gang of three men who had broken in had done so on a lark, after nothing more than some of Hanier's expensive liquor. After drinking their fill, they must have begun to drunkenly wreck the place. Hanier heard them downstairs and surprised them. One of the drunken three shot into the dark staircase where Hanier was and killed him. He then ran upstairs through the house and jumped off the balcony. Byrnes knew he had his work cut out for him, but at least he knew what type of criminal he was looking for—young street thugs—and why they had broken in—for the liquor. To find out who the killers were, he would have to begin with the murder weapon. Since he didn't have a murder weapon, he had to begin with the bullet that killed Hanier.

The bullet extracted from Hanier's body was determined to fit a .32 caliber revolver. Under normal circumstances, any other police detective might have given up on the idea that he could match the lone bullet with the gun, since whoever killed Hanier would likely have disposed of the weapon, probably tossing it into the river. But Byrnes had a different idea. If it was a group of three youthful street thugs who had broken in and killed Hanier, Byrnes wasn't about to assume they were smart enough to know to dispose of the gun. And guns don't come cheap to such lowly and impoverished youths. Rather than simply toss the gun away, Byrnes thought it more likely that they would pawn it for the money. But there were hundreds of pawnshops in the immediate vicinity of Hanier's saloon, and thousands of them throughout the city.

Searching all of them would be impossible. He would narrow his search based on the timeline. If the revolver used had been pawned, it would probably have been done within a day or two of the crime. If it was done within that time period, it was more than likely pawned at a neighborhood shop. Traveling across the city to some distant shop might arouse suspicion in the shop owner, especially if someone he didn't know came in, wanting to pawn a weapon. It was more than likely the killer would pawn the gun locally to someone who knew him or at least wouldn't be surprised that he had a gun to begin with. This allowed Byrnes to narrow his possibilities within a two-mile radius of the murder site.

Byrnes ordered his detectives to fan out and check the local pawn-shops. He told his men not to divulge why they were looking for the gun, since the pawnbrokers might deny having the gun for fear they might be implicated. Worse, they might warn the person who had pawned it that the police were looking for him.

Within twenty-four hours his detectives came back with reports of two .32 caliber revolvers recently pawned at shops within the neighborhood. The bullet from Hanier's body could easily have fit into either one of them. At the time of the investigation, 1882, there was no scientific way of identifying what gun a bullet had come from, so Byrnes had to work with his instincts, but his instincts were good—he knew a bullet came from one of the guns, even if he couldn't scientifically prove it. The pawnshop owner would have kept a receipt on the weapon identifying who had pawned it, but the likelihood that whoever pawned it would use his own name was slim to none. Still, Byrnes had little else to go on.

He personally went to the two pawnshops where the guns were reported to have been. At the first shop the owner easily identified the man who had pawned it as a carriage driver. He knew the man and knew exactly where Byrnes could find him. The carriage driver, an elderly man with no criminal record, admitted to Byrnes he had pawned the revolver and asked if he was in some sort of trouble because he had. Byrnes assured him he wasn't. The driver told Byrnes he had found the gun stuck between the seats of his carriage, and since he didn't know who had left it, he had kept it a few days and then pawned it. It seemed plausible to Byrnes, so he moved quickly to the next pawnshop. There, his luck turned better.

The pawnbroker told Byrnes that the revolver was pawned by a barkeeper, Charles Gooley, who owned a well-known, disreputable bar in the neighborhood. Gooley, who was an African American, had been a professional boxer. His face and his demeanor showed it. His ears were cauliflower, his nose smashed, and his chin a river of scars. He walked with a limp, and was hard of hearing and forgetful, often repeating himself or asking the same question over and over again despite being given the answer.

Gooley had no extensive criminal record, but his small, dingy bar had been the site of any number of altercations requiring police assistance. Upon questioning by Inspector Byrnes, Gooley freely admitted pawning the gun. He couldn't remember where he had pawned it, only that he did pawn it. He told Byrnes that it wasn't his gun in the first place but had belonged to one of his customers. When Byrnes pressed him on who the customer was, Gooley couldn't recall. Gooley explained that the man had given him the revolver to pay off his bar debt. He complained that the .32 caliber pistol hadn't fetched nearly as much as the man's debt, but that he was thankful, since the man who owed him, a young street thug, had always been trouble and seldom paid his bill. Byrnes tried a different approach with the forgetful former fighter and inquired how much the man owed him after the gun was pawned. Gooley told him that "Mike" owed him a lot. When he asked what Mike's last name was, Gooley responded, "Mike who?"

It wasn't much, but it was a lot more than he had had to go on before. Byrnes took a chance that the young thug, Mike, who had given the revolver to Gooley in exchange for his bar tab, might return to Gooley's bar, so he stationed an undercover detective there. The detective wasn't at Gooley's long when he came back and reported to Byrnes that a young thug named Mike had been in the seedy bar acting boisterously and claiming he was destined to make a reputation for himself. Further investigation by Byrnes led to the identity of the young man. His name was Mike McGloin.

HANIER'S MURDERER FOUND
THE ASSASSIN AND HIS ACCOMPLICES RUN DOWN AND ARRESTED

Inspector Byrnes and Central Office Detectives Rogers and Lanthier have arrested Michael McGloin, who on the morning of the 30th of December shot and killed Louis Hanier, a saloon-keeper at No. 144 West Twenty-sixth-street. McGloin's accomplices, Thomas Moran and Robert Morrissey, are also in custody, with two persons who were indirectly connected with the crime. When Hanier was killed Inspector Byrnes placed the murderer among four men who had failed in a scheme to rob Hanier's. . . .

—*New York Times*
February 2, 1882

Finding Mike McGloin was easy enough, but proving he had killed Louis Hanier would require all of Inspector Byrnes's best investigative abilities. McGloin and two of his partners in crime hung out at Gooley's bar, and with one of Byrnes's undercover detectives stationed at Gooley's around the clock, McGloin and his gang of fellow street ruffians met there soon enough. The nineteen-year-old McGloin appeared to be the leader of the ragtag gang of street punks that included Robert Morrissey, Thomas Moran, Frederick Banfield, and Oscar Healey. McGloin was the loudest and the most boastful. His speech was peppered with the most sordid profanities. All and all he was a hectoring bully to his friends and strangers alike. Byrnes had seen McGloin's type before in his years in law enforcement—the loudmouth, contemptible bully who roamed the city streets looking for trouble, and, if unable to find any, making it up on his own. He knew the type inside and out. He also knew that most of these coarse street types, filled with swagger and bravado, seething with lowlife vanity, liked nothing more than to boast of their deeds and bask in their friends' admiration. Byrnes knew that McGloin, like every other petty criminal, craved notoriety, and Byrnes was determined to prey on that flaw in the hopes McGloin might incriminate himself. Byrnes was already working on a way to make that happen.

Byrnes was also depending on another one of his theories: There was no honor among thieves, and for the right price, whether for money or immunity from prosecution, any criminal would be willing to squeal on another. Byrnes was banking on it. He was not sure which of McGloin's friends—Morrissey, Moran, Banfield, or Healey—might crack under interrogation, but he was certain one of them would, given the right inducement. Byrnes decided to begin with the most reliable inducement of all—money.

It was all adding up as far as Byrnes was concerned. McGloin already had a series of arrests for petty crimes. He lived in the neighborhood not very far from Hanier's saloon. He was known as a bully on the streets and was known to prowl the neighborhood, looking for trouble. The bullet taken from Hanier's body fit the revolver that had belonged to him. And according to Charles Gooley, the barkeeper who had actually pawned it, McGloin was in a big hurry to get rid of the weapon not long after the murder. Things were stacking up against McGloin quickly. All of these pieces might merely have been coincidences, but in Byrnes's mind, it was not a matter of determining McGloin's guilt, but rather determining his innocence. If he wasn't guilty, then Byrnes would give him ample opportunity to prove it, beginning with a reward.

Byrnes waited for an opportune time, and it arrived soon enough. He had stationed one of his undercover detectives at Gooley's bar with a poster tucked in his pocket. His orders were to hang up the reward poster in Gooley's, but not just anywhere. He was ordered to wait until McGloin and his friends came in for drinks and then to post the reward on the wall nearest them. McGloin, Banfield, and Morrissey came in early one evening and took a table in the farthest corner of the bar. Smoking cigarettes and cigars, the three young hoodlums ordered a round of brandy. As they sat drinking, the detective made his move. He excused himself, asking politely if Banfield would move his chair so that he could put something up on the wall. At first Banfield grumbled until the detective let his topcoat open enough for the three men to see his badge. Seeing the badge, Banfield moved quickly out of the way. Without saying a word, the detective, using the butt end of the small revolver he wore in his belt, nailed the reward poster onto the wall so that it hung within perfect view of the three men. The detective excused himself again and left. At first, McGloin, Banfield, and Morrissey pretended not to notice the poster. They waited until the detective had left Gooley's. On the way out the door, the detective nodded politely as he passed another man who was entering the small bar. He was a detective as well, assigned to keep an eye on McGloin and his friends after the first detective had left. He found a seat at the bar, ordered a drink, lit a cigar, and snapped open a newspaper. From his perch, Byrnes's detective was able to watch their every move.

Thinking that no detectives were in the bar, Banfield was the first to point out the reward poster. He seemed agitated and animated, pointing at the poster and then waving his hands at McGloin.

The poster read: FIVE HUNDRED DOLLARS REWARD WILL BE PAID FOR INFOR-
MATION LEADING TO THE ARREST OF THE PERSON OR PERSONS WHO SHOT THE WINE
MERCHANT LOUIS HANIER.

Anyone with information was asked to contact Inspector Thomas
Byrnes at police headquarters, in private. Anonymity was guaranteed.

McGloin ordered another round of drinks. He appeared unfazed
by the reward poster. The detective overheard McGloin boast that,
whenever the police resorted to issuing a reward, they were stumped
and couldn't catch the criminal. He laughed out loud. Banfield and
Morrissey were less than amused. The detective reported what he saw
back to Byrnes. The seed had been planted. Now Byrnes intended to
use another ploy. He would play on McGloin's vanity.

In his arsenal of tricks, Byrnes maintained any number of undercover snitches, each with their own special quality. One of them was
a young, attractive waif, known on the streets as Pretty Charlotte. She
was best at seduction, and she was just what Byrnes needed. Just seventeen, she had been a prostitute for the past five years. She had managed
to stay out of trouble and out of jail at the behest of Byrnes, who had
found many ways to use the young girl in his investigations. This time
he wanted her to seduce McGloin in the hopes that he might incriminate himself in an effort to impress her. Byrnes set up a small apartment
where Pretty Charlotte could take McGloin. He had several detectives
hide in the apartment next door, where they could listen in on whatever
conversation transpired between Pretty Charlotte and McGloin. It was
easy enough for the young girl to seduce McGloin and take him to the
apartment. There, she plied him with champagne and brandy. Byrnes
had supplied the liquor as well. Pretty Charlotte was all too adept at
playing on a man's vanity, and soon enough she had McGloin boasting
of his many exploits, but he didn't say a word about the Hanier murder.
What he did tell the young girl was that he and three of his friends,
Banfield, Healey, and Morrissey, had stolen a keg of beer from in front
of a local saloon in broad daylight. He told the girl that when the police
tried to catch them, he gave the officer a crack across the head that sent
him flying. McGloin laughed loudly after he told the story. Pretty Charlotte wasn't able to get McGloin to incriminate himself in the Hanier

murder, but she had done her job as far as Byrnes was concerned. He had more than enough reason to bring McGloin and his friends in for questioning—not on the Hanier murder, but for stealing the beer keg and assaulting a police officer. Everything McGloin had told Pretty Charlotte was true: Someone had reported a keg of beer stolen by a gang of street thugs, and the police officer dispatched to stop them had been beaten. By the end of the evening, McGloin had drunk himself into a stupor, helped along by some knockout drops with which Pretty Charlotte had laced one of his drinks.

When McGloin woke up the next morning, Charlotte was gone and his head was pounding. By the time he dressed and hit the streets, his friends, Morrissey, Moran, Banfield, Healey, and Charles Gooley had been arrested and taken to police headquarters. They were placed in separate cells far enough apart from one another so that they could not communicate. None of them had been told what they were charged with. Gooley, who was not implicated in the crime, had been arrested as a material witness. He was the one whom McGloin had given the revolver to and he was the one who had pawned it. They all demanded to know the charges against them, and regardless of what the charge might be, they all maintained their innocence.

McGloin was the last of the suspects brought to police headquarters. Byrnes arrested him himself. He was locked in a cell alone and left there overnight, not knowing the charges against him. He didn't know that the others were being held as well. Byrnes decided to let him stew in his own juices through the night.

The next morning Byrnes had McGloin escorted to his office, where he strategically placed him in a chair facing the door. He left the door open so that McGloin could see people passing in the hallway outside Byrnes's office. It was for good reason.

Byrnes began his questioning, asking McGloin his name, address, and age. McGloin protested, wanting to know the charges against him. Byrnes continued to ask his innocuous questions: name, address, age.

Byrnes stopped when one of his detectives came to the doorway and beckoned him. Byrnes went to the doorway, where the detective handed him something wrapped in a handkerchief. Byrnes took it, and as he crossed the room in front of McGloin, he let the handkerchief slip away revealing the .32 caliber revolver that McGloin had given to Gooley. Byrnes made sure that McGloin had a good look at the weapon. He placed the revolver on his desk without saying a word and went back to questioning McGloin. McGloin didn't say anything about the gun and kept asking Byrnes what he was being charged with. Still, Byrnes didn't answer him.

Another detective showed up at the door. This time he had Frederick Banfield with him. Banfield was in handcuffs. Again Byrnes went to the door. The detective whispered something to Byrnes. Byrnes nodded. He looked at Banfield, put his hand on Banfield's shoulder, and nodded approvingly at him. The detective led Banfield away without saying another word. Byrnes went back to where McGloin was and resumed his questioning, never once mentioning the Hanier murder, the gun, or Banfield.

McGloin wanted to know what Banfield was doing there. The thoughts must have begun churning in his head. First the gun. Now Banfield. Had Banfield betrayed him for the money? Had any of his friends sold him out? Had they all? Were any of them faithful friends? Or would they have easily betrayed him for the $500 reward? Had Byrnes traced the revolver back to him? His head must have begun to spin. Byrnes wasn't giving him anything to go on. He kept asking the same stupid questions: name, address, age. Byrnes could see McGloin growing restless, like a caged animal.

Suddenly, without warning, McGloin sprang from his chair and tried to shake off the demon thoughts racing through his head. Byrnes ordered him to sit back down. McGloin did as he was told. He glanced cautiously around Byrnes's office, with its shelves filled with photographs of criminals and an array of weapons—guns, knives, chains—and burglary tools—drills, crowbars, hammers. His eyes fixated on the series of photographs of the various gallows. Beneath the photographs were the names and dates of the criminals who had met their deaths at the end of a rope. It must have sent shivers through him.

Another detective arrived at the door, this time with Gooley in custody. Byrnes went to the door and whispered something to the detective. He next did what he had done to Banfield. He put his hand on Gooley's shoulder and nodded at him approvingly. The detective took Gooley away.

Byrnes went back, but before he could return to questioning McGloin, another detective appeared at the door. This time the detective had a small boy with him. He was holding the boy by the hand. It was Louis Hanier's ten-year-old son. Byrnes went to the door. He asked the boy to step through the threshold. The boy did as he was told. McGloin recognized the little boy immediately. He stared at him with shocked dismay. He tried to look away, but he couldn't. The little boy stared at McGloin with a cold, penetrating gaze. Byrnes knelt down beside the boy, and the boy whispered something into his ear. The boy said what he had said all along about the man who had bolted past him that night—he didn't see who he was. McGloin had no way of knowing that. He had seen the boy, but he didn't know that the boy hadn't seen him well enough to recognize him.

Byrnes patted the boy on the head and had the detective lead him away. This time Byrnes made a slow and calculated march back to the chair opposite McGloin. The series of detectives at the doorway had been a deliberate trap. Now Byrnes sprung the trap. He asked McGloin a new question, one that made him bite his lip, the color draining from his face.

"Can you verify your whereabouts on the night of Louis Hanier's murder?" he asked in a solemn monotone.

McGloin became dumbstruck. He tried to speak, but no words would come out.

He shifted uneasily in his chair.

"I already know the answer," Byrnes said, his voice unwavering. "And I have eyewitnesses who will back my claim up, including one of your own gang. I've even got the murder weapon, and the bullet we dug out of Hanier's body matches the gun you gave to Charles Gooley."

Not a word of what Byrnes told McGloin was true. Banfield hadn't betrayed him. The boy couldn't identify him, and there was no way of scientifically proving the bullet came from McGloin's gun. It didn't matter. McGloin's worst fears had been realized. He'd been betrayed by one of his own friends for the reward, he thought. Byrnes had found the gun he had used to shoot Hanier and the bullet was a perfect match. And the little boy had identified him.

McGloin's face twitched uncontrollably. His lips trembled. He clenched his teeth to stop them from chattering.

"The charge against you is murder," Byrnes said, looking straight into McGloin's wide eyes. He revealed to McGloin that every one of his accomplices, Moran, Morrissey, Healey, and Banfield, had been arrested and charged. Byrnes confided to McGloin in a low whisper that, if there was any mercy to be handed out in the case, it would rest on his full confession, here and now.

McGloin slipped from the chair onto his knees and burst into tears.

"I did it. I swear it was an accident. Can you save me from hanging?" McGloin cried, begging for his life at the feet of Inspector Byrnes. Byrnes grew silent. He had won. Once again, his mastery of detective work had solved an almost unsolvable case.

McGLOIN CONVICTED
THE JURY QUICKLY FIND HIM GUILTY OF
MURDER IN THE FIRST DEGREE

The trial of Michael E. McGloin, aged 19 years, for the murder of Louis Hanier, a French saloon-keeper, residing at No. 144 West Twenty-sixth-street, on the morning of Dec. 30, was concluded in the General Sessions yesterday and resulted in the conviction of the accused man of murder in the first degree.

—*New York Times*
March 4, 1882

YOUNG McGLOIN'S SENTENCE
TO BE HANGED ON FRIDAY, THE 28TH DAY OF APRIL

—*New York Times*
March 7, 1882

—•••—

McGLOIN AND MAJONE SUFFER DEATH FOR THEIR CRIMES

TWO FELONS UNDER THE GALLOWS IN THE EARLY MORNING—A WAVE OF A HANDKERCHIEF AND THE LAW SATISFIED

In the prison yard of the Tombs yesterday morning at 8:12 o'clock, two convicted felons, Michael E. McGloin and Pasquale Majone, suffered death on the gallows.

The crime for which McGloin paid this penalty was the murder of Louis Hanier, a French wine dealer . . .

—*New York Times*

March 10, 1883

AMERICAN ALMANAC, 1892–95

After almost thirty years on the New York City police force, Thomas Byrnes was appointed superintendent of the police department in 1892. He had come a long way from growing up in the slums of Five Points. His life had changed exponentially, as had the world around him.

Democrat Grover Cleveland was elected president in 1892, beating the Republican incumbent, Benjamin Harrison. Cleveland, who had served as president from 1885 to 1889, was the only president to serve two nonconsecutive terms. Cleveland garnered 5,554,414 votes to Harrison's 5,190,802. It was Harrison who beat Cleveland in his 1888 re-election bid.

The World's Columbian Exposition in Chicago began in May 1893. The event marked the four-hundredth anniversary of Christopher Columbus's discovery of America. Popularly known as the Chicago World's Fair, the event encompassed more than six hundred acres along the shores of Lake Michigan. The fairgrounds included approximately 150 buildings designed by some of America's most noted architects. By the time it closed in October 1893, more than twenty-seven million people from around the world had reportedly visited the fair.

"After The Ball," written by American songwriter Charles K. Harris, became the first million-selling song hit. The song was made popular by John Philip Sousa, who played it at the 1893 World's Columbian Exposition. It eventually sold five million copies.

After the ball is over,
After the break of morn,
After the dancers' leaving;
After the stars are gone;
Many a heart is aching,

If you could read them all;
Many the hopes that have vanish'd
After the ball.
—Words and music by Charles K. Harris

Henry Ford built the first successful two-cylinder gasoline engine in 1893. Three years later he built his first car.

Eugene Debs led a successful workers' strike against the Great Northern Railroad in 1894. Debs was the leader of the American Railway Union (ARU). On May 18 of that same year, the violent Pullman Strike began at the Chicago railroad car plant. A court injunction brought under the Sherman Antitrust Act ended the strike and broke the back of Debs' union.

An unsolved murder in Fall River, Massachusetts, made headlines across the country. The high-profile Lizzie Borden murder case seemed like a natural for master crime solver Thomas Byrnes, but he was never consulted on the case.

Lizzie Borden was charged in the brutal hatchet murder of her father, Andrew Borden, a prominent Fall River, Massachusetts, businessman, and his second wife, Abby, who were found slain in their home in August 1892. Andrew's thirty-two-year-old unmarried daughter, Lizbeth Borden (Lizzie), was accused of the brutal murder. Lizzie Borden did not testify at her trial. Although she was acquitted, the case was never officially solved.

Lizzie Borden took an ax,
Gave her mother forty whacks,
When she saw what she had done,
She gave her father forty-one.

QUIPS AND QUOTES

Sensible and responsible women do not want to vote. The relative positions to be assumed by man and woman in the work-

ing out of our civilization were assigned long ago by a higher intelligence than ours.

—GROVER CLEVELAND

We Americans have no commission from God to police the world.

—BENJAMIN HARRISON

I knew there was an old axe down cellar; that is all I knew.

—LIZZIE BORDEN

A business that makes nothing but money is a poor business.

—HENRY FORD

When great changes occur in history, when great principles are involved, as a rule the majority are wrong.

—EUGENE DEBS

AN UNSPEAKABLE ROTTENNESS

In which Thomas Byrnes is named superintendent of police and faces charges of corruption in the police department from the Reverend Dr. Charles Parkhurst, a special legislative investigative committee, and police commissioner Theodore Roosevelt.

The murder of Carrie Brown in 1891 and the apprehension and conviction of Ameer Ben Ali as her killer was the last major case Byrnes worked on as the head of the New York City Detective Bureau. In 1892 the police commissioners appointed Byrnes superintendent of the police department when William Murray retired. Byrnes claimed the appointment was a surprise to him and told reporters when his appointment was made public that he had never actively campaigned for the position. Byrnes had to pass a civil-service exam before being officially appointed. He passed the exam and was certified eligible for the position of superintendent.

SUPT. MURRAY DROPS OUT
CHIEF INSPECTOR BYRNES WILL SUCCEED HIM
THE CHANGE AT POLICE HEADQUARTERS—
THE EX-SUPERINTENDENT'S CAREER IN AND OUT
OF THE FORCE—
PROBABLE CHANGES OF CAPTAINS.

. . . When the Police Commissioners were in session yesterday, Major Kipp, the chief clerk, read a letter from Mr. Murray, addressed to the board, in which he placed in the Commissioners' hands his application for retirement. In taking this step, he said, he had been influenced by the advice of his physician.

. . . Commissioner Martin then moved that Chief Inspector Byrnes be appointed Superintendent of Police, "subject to a civil service examination" and the motion received four affirmative votes. Mr. Byrnes, when congratulated, he said the action of the board was a surprise to him. . . .

—*New York Times*
April 13, 1892

I am not a member of any political organization, nor have I ever been such; consequently, in the performance of my duty I shall have but one supreme object, the protection of life and property, the prevention and suppression of crime, and, above all, the enforcement of the laws without fear or favor against whomever may be found violating them.

—Chief Inspector Thomas Byrnes

UPON BEING PROMOTED TO SUPERINTENDENT OF POLICE,

APRIL 1892

. . .To Capt. Byrnes was given the task of bringing order and decency out of inefficiency and corruption. How well he succeeded is fully proved by the record of the Detective Bureau from the time he became its head. His force of character soon made itself felt among the officers at that time connected with the bureau. They found they had a new sort of commandant to deal with, one who would enforce obedience and demand honest work and who could not be moved by politicians or political influence. . . . If there is one trait in the Superintendent's character more prominent than another, it is his wonderful tenacity and patience, and this is an element which has won success. . . .

—*New York Times*
April 14, 1892

Thomas Byrnes was appointed superintendent only a short time after the Reverend Dr. Charles H. Parkhurst of the Presbyterian Church in

Madison Square began his campaign against vice and police corruption. From his pulpit Parkhurst indicted New York City politicians and police alike for getting rich on the city's vast network of debauchery and vice—gambling, prostitution, and the illegal sale of alcohol to minors and on Sundays. Tammany Hall politicians, newspapers, and police department officials, including Byrnes, called Parkhurst a political opportunist, a crank who was only interested in making a name for himself, and a dupe for the Republican Party. According to Parkhurst, New York City was "rotten with a rottenness which is unspeakable. . . ."

———

The Reverend Dr. Charles H. Parkhurst was a fifty-year-old Presbyterian minister in 1892. He was a graduate of Amherst College in Massachusetts and had taught at Amherst High School. Parkhurst married one of his students at the high school. The scholarly Parkhurst was tall and lean and had a thin, ruddy face. His hair was long in the back, and he wore rimless glasses. By nature he was a stubborn and obstinate man. However, during the previous twelve years he had served as the minister at the Presbyterian church in New York City, he had not shown any inclination toward being a social reformer. Then, in 1891, after joining the Society for the Prevention of Crime, a private reform-minded organization made up of merchants, lawyers, and clergy, his attitude changed. When he was elected president of the group, he said he would accept the position only if the organization agreed to radical tactics in order to bring social change to the city. Little did anyone suspect the extent to which Parkhurst intended to take his radical tactics.

Parkhurst began his campaign against citywide vice and political corruption on February 14, 1892, in a sermon called "Ye Are the Salt of the Earth." In it, Parkhurst claimed that both politicians and police made enormous profits from blackmail and bribes from prostitutes, gambling parlors, opium dens, and saloon keepers. He denounced the Tammany Hall boss, Richard C. Croker, and his underlings. The 350-pound Boss Croker was not as brazen a leader of Tammany Hall as Boss Tweed had been, but he was crafty and equally corrupt. Parkhurst accused politicians and police of collusion with illegal gambling operations throughout the city, prostitution, and the illegal sale of liquor, and of protecting these various criminal operations through bribes.

The public outcry was resounding, especially from Tammany Hall, the district attorney, and several newspapers controlled by Boss Croker's crowd. The *Sun* called for Parkhurst's resignation. Mayor Hugh Grant demanded that Parkhurst prove his vicious allegations. And District Attorney De Lancey Nicoll ordered Parkhurst to appear before a grand jury to prove his claim.

When Parkhurst appeared before the grand jury, he reluctantly admitted that he had no legal evidence to support his allegations. He told the grand jury that he had based his claims on recent newspaper articles. The grand jury admonished him and called his charges of widespread political corruption groundless. An onslaught of vicious attacks on Parkhurst soon followed.

The best employment to which the Reverend Dr. Parkhurst can now devote himself is prolonged prayer and repentance to atone for the grievous sin of which he has been guilty. An appropriate place wherein to give him the opportunity to subject himself to such spiritual mortification would be a penitentiary cell.

—EDITORIAL APPEARING IN THE *SUN*, 1892

But Parkhurst was not to be deterred in his mission to expose the city's vast network of vice and corruption. He decided to conduct his own undercover investigation to gather the evidence he needed. He hired a private detective, Charles Gardner, who agreed to act as his guide through the seedy underbelly of the city. For a fee of $6 a night, plus expenses, Gardner took Parkhurst and John Langdon Erving, a close friend of Parkhurst's, on a guided tour of illegal drinking establishments and whorehouses throughout the city. On March 5, 1892,

Parkhurst, Gardner, and Erving began their odyssey. On the advice of Gardner and with his help, Parkhurst and Erving disguised themselves as country bumpkins. Parkhurst wore flashy black-and-white-checked trousers, a red tie, and a dandified derby. No one would ever recognize him as the scholarly, dour Presbyterian minister he truly was. Over the next several nights, Parkhurst, with Gardner and Erving as witnesses, conducted a personal tour of the city's brothels, flophouses, saloons, opium dens, and gambling parlors, all of them operating out in the open and sanctioned by the police department.

They stopped at a saloon on Cherry Street and observed the usual goings-on. Parkhurst was not against legitimate drinking establishments. What he was against was the illegal sale of alcohol to minors and the illegal sale of liquor on Sundays. At the Cherry Street saloon, Parkhurst watched as time and again young children came up to the bar in plain sight and were able to buy liquor. He watched as several times, little girls, no older than ten years old, purchased liquor, they said, for their fathers.

On one occasion Gardner took Parkhurst and Erving to a whorehouse on Water Street where two young girls, their faces painted and wearing nothing but see-through nightgowns, solicited Parkhurst and Erving, practically dragging them inside. Parkhurst and Erving managed to elude the two girls. At another brothel, Parkhurst was dragged inside and led to a chair, where a young girl tried to sit naked on his lap. When Parkhurst refused, Erving consented to dance with the girl, for the going rate, of course. In Washington Square, Parkhurst was shown dozens of whorehouses, all operating within clear view of patrolling police officers. One house of ill repute was directly across the street from the police precinct house.

At the Golden Rule Pleasure House, Parkhurst was taken into a series of rooms where young boys waited. Their faces were painted like women's. They spoke in falsetto voices and called each other by women's names. The sight of these young male prostitutes sickened Parkhurst, and he was forced to run from the building. At an upscale brothel located at 31–33 East Twenty-seventh Street, operated by Hattie Adams, the trio watched as five naked young girls performed a cancan and played a game of leapfrog. Parkhurst and Gardner watched as Erving consented to play the role of the frog in the debauched display.

Parkhurst recorded it all and collected sworn affidavits from Gardner, Erving, and four more of Gardner's detectives he hired to visit the various dens of inequity. Parkhurst, Erving, and the crew of detectives visited 284 saloons, gambling dens, and brothels and documented each and every visit. Among the stack of sworn affidavits was a list of thirty houses of prostitution within the Nineteenth Precinct, where his own church was located.

On March 13, 1892, a month after he had given his first sermon on vice and corruption from the pulpit of his church, Parkhurst delivered another biting sermon on rampant corruption in the city. This time, on the lectern, was the stack of sworn affidavits. Parkhurst called New York City "hell with the lid off." He called it a "Tammany-debauched town."

"Calling for particulars. I have given you particulars, 284 of them," Parkhurst railed. "Now what are you going to do with them?"

"Anyone who . . . with all the . . . ascertainable facts in view, denies that drunkenness, gambling, and licentiousness in this town are municipally protected, is either a knave or a fool," Parkhurst said.

This time the cry of "crank" and "publicity seeker" by Boss Croker, his Tammany Hall gang, and the newspapers was silenced by the public outcry calling for reform. People were shocked by the descriptions of the vice and crime that infested the streets of New York City.

There were still some who, despite being shown the extent of the vice and corruption in the city, tried to discredit Parkhurst, angry at the messenger instead of the message. Some people felt Parkhurst was guilty of impropriety for crawling through the raunchy depths of the city. But most people applauded his tenacity and courage.

Parkhurst and his citizens' organization, the Society for the Prevention of Crime, demanded that the district attorney and the courts close the places Parkhurst had visited, but no action was taken. Judges, most of whom were Tammany Hall appointees, refused to issue warrants, and even if they had, it was doubtful that the police department would have acted, since whorehouses, gambling dens, and liquor sales were all sources of illegal income for many officers. Members of the Society for the Prevention of Crime who testified at the Essex Market Court on neighborhood vice and corruption were attacked by an angry mob waiting for them outside the courthouse, and the police refused to protect them from the violence.

When the next grand jury convened, Parkhurst was invited to testify. The grand jury accepted his 284 affidavits and ultimately handed down indictments against two whorehouses, including the one operated by Hattie Adams, where the infamous naked game of leapfrog was reportedly played. Adams was found guilty of operating a brothel and sentenced to one year in jail.

The grand jury called and questioned the city's four police commissioners, who denied any police wrongdoing or knowledge of any bribes solicited by police from the various whorehouses, gambling dens, or saloons. Several police captains and inspectors were also called to testify, and they too denied any knowledge of corruption within the department.

The grand jury issued a statement at the close of the session: "[The police] are either incompetent to do what is frequently done by private individuals with imperfect facilities for such work, or else there exists reasons and motives for such inaction which are illegal and corrupt. The general efficiency of the Department is so great that it is our belief that the latter suggestion is the explanation of the peculiar inactivity."

Parkhurst continued to hammer away at vice and corruption in his sermons, week after week. Finally, because of the public outcry for reform and because the New York City Chamber of Commerce began to worry about the city's reputation, the chamber asked the state legislature in 1894 to investigate the city's police department.

To say that the police do not know what is going on and where it is going on, with all the brilliant symptoms of the character of the place distinctly in view, is rot.

—The Reverend Dr. Charles Parkhurst

April 1892

Dr. Parkhurst on the floor,
playing leapfrog with a whore.
Ta-ra-ra-boom-de-ay.
Ta-ra-ra-boom-de-ay.

—RIBALD SONG CIRCULATED AFTER PARKHURST DISCLOSED

HIS UNDERCOVER FINDINGS

The newly appointed superintendent of police, Thomas Byrnes, remained loyal to the men under his command and engaged in his usual self-promotion and the promotion of his department. In an April 1892 letter to the police commissioners, Byrnes wrote, "As the result of this system inaugurated by me, I am enabled to report that within less than two months in the First Inspection District, commanded by Inspector Williams, 6 reputed gambling houses and 93 policy shops were closed and vacated, and 104 disorderly houses were raided. In all the latter cases the proprietors have been held to bail, and the inmates have been fined or imprisoned."

According to Byrnes, forty-two houses of prostitution were raided and the proprietors arrested. Contrary to what Parkhurst had uncovered, Byrnes vowed that there wasn't a single house of prostitution in the city's Third Precinct. And, according to Byrnes, "From the reports made to me by the Inspectors of several districts, and the Captains of the various precincts, I am convinced that there is no public gambling in this city at the present time."

Byrnes also contended that, although the law called for the closing of certain saloons and brothels, it would be difficult if not impossible to do so.

"The problem involved in the suppression of houses of prostitution and assignation is difficult of solution. While it is an illegal traffic under the laws of the State, and the police are charged with the execution of all laws regardless of consequences, it is a grave question in my mind, and one which deserves the serious consideration of the general public and future legislators, whether good results are obtained by the closing of such houses and the scattering of the inmates," Byrnes wrote to the commissioners.

". . . This department has been sometimes criticized by both the public and press for what they assert is the non-enforcement of the law," he wrote. "The difficulty in the proper and uniform enforcement of the law lies not with the police, but with the courts that deal with offenders against this law . . ." Byrnes wrote.

But Byrnes's defense of the police department was not limited to letters to the police commissioners. Byrnes took an active (if not illegal) role in attempting to discredit Parkhurst's investigation and campaign by attacking Parkhurst and the private detectives he hired to help him in his exposé, and by limiting the authority of the public to request warrants for the arrest of known violators. According to Byrnes, he saw potential abuse in allowing what he called "irresponsible persons" receiving warrants and serving them when it best suited their cause. Byrnes asked for and received approval of his request to forbid judges from issuing warrants, except to "persons authorized by the law," meaning that Parkhurst and his Society for the Prevention of Crime had no authority to appear before justices asking for warrants to be issued.

"I have no hesitation in declaring that this rule was aimed to hurt me, to harass me, and prevent me and the Society for the Prevention of Crime from carrying on our work," Parkhurst told newspaper reporters.

"Superintendent Byrnes understands us, and we understand him. There is no common ground between us, and he antagonizes us, and we mean to keep our eyes on him," he said.

DR. PARKHURST AND THE POLICE
He Thinks Supt. Byrnes Is
Determined To Antagonize Him

Every obstacle put in our way by the Superintendent of Police is but an admission on his part of the antagonistic spirit he harbors and the means he will employ to thwart us if possible, and at least to hamper us in all that we may undertake.

—*New York Times*
December 2, 1892

———•••••———

Shortly after Parkhurst identified Byrnes as a hindrance to his concerted efforts to clean up the city, Byrnes came out swinging. On December 7, 1892, Byrnes publicly declared war on Parkhurst, claiming to newspaper reporters that all the trouble instigated by Parkhurst was the result of a difficult divorce suit. According to Byrnes, the plaintiff in the divorce case was the daughter of a well-known member of Parkhurst's congregation. Byrnes claimed that the woman married a prominent member of New York high society and that she won her divorce suit just prior to Parkhurst's crusade to rid the city of vice and corruption.

According to Byrnes, the husband was involved with another woman whom he kept in style at one of the more upscale houses of prostitution. When the wife found out, she filed for divorce. When she demanded that the police testify on behalf of her suit, claiming that they knew of the relationship between her husband and the woman, they refused. Their refusal was at the heart of Parkhurst's crusade, Byrnes claimed.

"I have correspondence in my possession and it shows that Dr. Parkhurst and certain members of his congregation have resorted to everything that was dishonorable to get evidence of any and every kind through which to compromise the Chief Magistrate of this city, the Judges of the higher courts, the magistrate, the District Attorney, myself, and high officials . . . ," Byrnes told reporters.

Parkhurst was quick to counter Byrnes's allegations.

"If Inspector Byrnes supposes that I have hung my crusade against his department on any such miserable hook as what he hints at, he entirely mistakes the man he has to deal with. I would like to have Superintendent Byrnes understand that as to the entire animus of the society he is barking up the wrong tree," Parkhurst responded to reporters.

Parkhurst produced a copy of the law, Section 282, that governed the duty of police officers to prevent the maintenance and operation of gambling houses, houses of ill repute, and disorderly places of other kinds.

"Now, these things Mr. Byrnes does not do," Parkhurst told reporters.

"We unofficered people can break up these disreputable places, and why does not Superintendent Byrnes? For Byrnes to make these statements that we have no ground for our action is impudence. It is damnable impudence," Parkhurst said.

Byrnes responded by having Parkhurst's lead private detective, Charles Gardner, arrested on a series of trumped-up charges and held on $7,500 bail. The charges were extorting money from several prostitutes whom he, Parkhurst, and Erving had exposed during their undercover operation. Gardner was ultimately released from jail and the charges were dropped.

The transparency of Byrnes's attacks on Parkhurst and the Society for the Prevention of Crime wore thin very quickly as others in the religious community began to attack prostitution and police corruption in the city. For the first time in his life, Byrnes was losing the public relations war and he didn't like it.

DR. PARKHURST HITS BACK
HIS PROMPT REJOINER TO THE
POLICE SUPERINTENDENT
MR. BYRNES MUST NOT TRY TO SHIFT
THE BURDEN OF THE SITUATION—
"COLOSSAL IMPUDENCE" OF HIS
ASSERTIONS—NEGLECT OF DUTY

He is trying to blacken me as a means of whitewashing himself and his department. . . . He thinks that by showing the community what I am doing he will make the community forget what he isn't doing. Mr. Byrnes is one of our municipal servants. I am helping to pay his salary. His opposition to having our public officials watched has a bad look. I have been shadowed off and on for the last nine months. I have never thought it necessary though to fly into print about it nor to call the reporters together and give out sensational material for the press. There is an element of childishness about such petulance that I regret that Mr. Byrnes found necessary to stoop to . . .

—*New York Times*
December 8, 1892

The tide was turning against Byrnes. The Reverend Dr. D. C. Potter of the Baptist Tabernacle in the city preached a sermon to his congregation entitled "Delivering the City from Crime."

"Wealth is just as lawless as poverty," Potter said. "It is more reprehensible in its wickedness because it has better intelligence and no need."

The Reverend B. F. De Costa at the Church of St. John the Evangelist told his congregation, "Superintendent Byrnes told us last week that he had proceeded against 400 houses, but not against a landlord. He has arrested 2,572 women, but does not tell us that he has arrested a single man. Until there is a common moral standard for men and women, no progress can be attained."

During the course of the Lexow hearings and his ongoing public relations battle with Parkhurst, Byrnes resorted to an old standby to help reinforce his illustrious position—a full-scale public relations campaign in the newspapers, beginning with an extended front-page feature story in the December 10, 1893, issue of the *New York Times*. Changes were made to reflect it as part of an ongoing battle. In it the reporter praised Byrnes's accomplishments throughout his nearly thirty-year career as a police officer, captain, detective, chief inspector, and superintendent.

The article ended with incredible over-the-top praise of Byrnes, gushing, "Police Superintendent Byrnes's record is an open book, which all can read. His methods are unique, according to the old fogies, but they are effective, and that is what people want. The end aimed at is attained. Therein lies the strength of the man. It is a strength that is potent. That it may long continue to exist is the earnest wish of every citizen of New York, who sleeps more peacefully because he knows that Thomas Byrnes is at the head of the Police Department."

The public relations ploy by Byrnes didn't satisfy the general public, which was clamoring for reform. Byrnes decided to resort to another one of his tried-and-true methods of recouping the public's adulation. He was losing the public relations battle with Parkhurst in the newspapers, but he could do one thing to reclaim his once-lofty position in public opinion—solve a high-profile case. And he already had a suspect in mind: the anarchist, Emma Goldman.

Following the Haymarket Riot in Chicago on May 4, 1886, the country had been gripped by fear of a workers' revolt. Workers throughout the country and mostly in the major cities like Chicago, New York, and Philadelphia began to unionize and strike against companies for fair wages and shorter workdays. The major capitalists, with the help of police and Pinkerton agents, cracked down on any efforts to unionize. The country's elite businessmen claimed that the workers' unionizing demands were spearheaded by socialists and anarchists who wanted to ruin the American way of life. At the height of America's Gilded Age, that way of life meant that 1 percent of the country controlled 90 percent of the wealth, and they were bound and determined to keep it that way, at any cost.

A nationwide strike calling for an eight-hour workday began on May 1, 1886. In Chicago, on May 4, a mass meeting of workers was held in the Haymarket district, where farmers traditionally sold their produce. Approximately two thousand workers and their families gathered there to protest an unprovoked police attack on union pickets at the McCormick Harvesting Machine Company.

When the Chicago police ordered the demonstrators to disperse, a bomb was thrown. The explosion killed seven police officers and injured sixty others. The police fired into the crowd, killing four workers. Police dispersed the crowd by using clubs, randomly striking men, women, and children. Hundreds of workers were arrested and beaten. Eight reported anarchist leaders were arrested and charged with inciting a riot and murder. Seven of the men were convicted of conspiracy to commit murder and were sentenced to death, and one was sentenced to life in prison. Four of the men were hanged in November 1887. One committed suicide while in jail. Governor John Peter Altgeld of Illinois subsequently pardoned the three remaining prisoners. Neither the Haymarket Riot nor subsequent riots and strikes were able to stop the unionization of American workers.

Socialism in the United States may be regarded as synonymous with Anarchy.

—AUTHOR AND CHICAGO POLICE

CAPTAIN MICHAEL J. SCHAACK

ANARCHY AND ANARCHISTS, 1889

Ever the opportunist, Superintendent Byrnes quickly decided that tackling the anarchist scare that gripped the business community in New York City could serve as a remedy for his recent public relations losses to Parkhurst. On August 21, 1893, several hundred unemployed workers gathered in a small East Side hall to listen to anarchist Emma Goldman deliver a zealous speech on workers' rights. Byrnes and his police detectives infiltrated the meeting. They reported to the anxious press that the meeting was an ardent call for a citywide strike and riot provoked by Goldman. Byrnes had his men round up union leaders, known socialists, and anarchists. Goldman had already fled to Philadelphia by the time Byrnes instigated his crackdown on anarchists and workers.

On August 31, 1893, Byrnes traveled to Philadelphia to arrest Goldman on charges of inciting a riot based on her speech to the unemployed workers. Goldman denied the charge, saying she was there to argue for public support for unemployed workers. It didn't matter. Byrnes had got his man—this time a woman—again. Byrnes made front-page headlines for his arrest of the notorious Goldman. The rich and well-to-do could sleep more easily knowing that Byrnes had once again made the city's streets safe, this time from anticapitalists like Goldman. Byrnes won acclaim as a fearless foe of anarchists everywhere.

———

. . . little bit of a girl, just 5 feet high, not showing her 120 pounds; with a saucy, turned-up nose and very expressive blue-gray eyes that gazed inquiringly at me through shell-rimmed glasses.

—Description of Emma Goldman written by

Nellie Bly, appearing in the *World*,

August 1893

———

. . . I don't believe that through murder we shall gain, but by war, labor against capital, masses against classes, which will not come in 20 or 25 years. But some day, I firmly believe we shall gain, and until then I am satisfied to agitate, to teach, and I only ask justice and freedom of speech.

—Emma Goldman

August 1893

———

Emma Goldman's trial in New York City lasted four days. In October 1893, she was found guilty of one charge of conspiracy to incite a riot. She was sentenced to one year in the city's women's prison on Blackwell's Island.

———

. . . the philosophy of a new social order based on liberty unrestricted by man-made law; the theory that all forms of govern-

*ment rest on violence, and are therefore wrong and harmful,
as well as unnecessary.*

—Emma Goldman's definition of anarchism

But even Byrnes's effort to whip up a frenzy about anarchists was futile. The public spotlight remained on Parkhurst's crusade to rid the city of vice and corruption, and the public outcry for reform was deafening. Parkhurst's undercover work and his weekly sermons decrying the vile state of affairs within the city and corruption in the police department led to the formation of a legislative investigative committee chaired by state senator Clarence Lexow. The Lexow Committee was charged with investigating police and municipal corruption.

In March 1894, the Lexow Committee, made up of five Republicans, including its chairman, state senator Clarence Lexow, one independent Democrat, and one Tammany Hall–controlled Democrat, began its hearings into crime and police corruption. The first person the committee interviewed was the Reverend Dr. Charles H. Parkhurst, considered the leader of the anti-vice forces in the city. At Parkhurst's suggestion, the committee named John W. Goff, an incorruptible and accomplished lawyer, as its counsel. At one point during the investigation, Goff was reportedly offered $300,000 to abandon the probe of police corruption, but Goff rebuffed the bribe and the Lexow Committee went on with its work.

During the investigation the committee took testimony from 678 witnesses over the course of seventy-four sessions that ended in late December 1894. More than ten thousand pages of transcripts covering the testimony were compiled. The findings of the committee were collected into six huge books comprising close to six thousand pages.

In January 1895, the committee issued a scathing report on New York City police corruption. The network of corruption, according to the committee, ran through the entire municipal government system with police officers, judges, politicians, and a host of criminals all interconnected in a web of deceit, bribery, and fraud. The release of the committee's findings was so damaging that the Tammany Hall leader, Boss Croker, resigned his position and fled to Europe.

According to the report, police corruption began at the bottom with police officers. Anyone wanting to be appointed to the police force, according to the committee's findings, had to pay a $300 bribe just to be hired. Under questioning by Goff, police commissioner James Martin testified that 85 percent of appointments to the police force were made based on recommendations by Tammany Hall politicians. Martin informed the committee that over a five-year period only two men had ever been promoted within the department based solely on merit. According to the committee's findings, a police officer had to pay $2,500 to be promoted to sergeant, while it cost upward of $10,000 in bribes for an officer to obtain a rank of captain. Being appointed an inspector cost close to $20,000 in bribes. The committee found that this pay-for-appointment-and-promotion scheme netted Tammany Hall politicians—as well as police department officials—close to $7 million a year in bribes. No proof was presented that Byrnes had ever paid for any of his promotions, nor did he ever admit to paying for any. Despite the stiff payoffs, police officers were all but guaranteed to make their money back tenfold through bribes they accepted on behalf of saloon keepers, gambling salons, and houses of prostitution. Some brothels paid upward of $50 a month for police protection.

One brothel madam testified before the committee that she had paid $150 per month in bribes to the police over the course of ten years. Not only did the police receive bribes from known criminals and the operators of criminal establishments, but they also received tribute from various peripheral sources, such as the sale of liquor, cigarettes, and food at the illegal establishments. Police commissioner John McClave resigned when it was uncovered that, after making a series of police appointments, he made huge deposits of money into his private bank account.

The committee interviewed Byrnes for four hours, and although he denied any wrongdoing, he was grilled on how he had come to amass somewhere between $300,000 to $350,000 in real estate and securities on his paltry salary of $5,000 a year. Byrnes claimed that he had made his small fortune legally and that many Wall Street investors—most notably, Jay Gould—had helped him make wise and financially successful investments over the years. No one on the committee and least of all Reverend Parkhurst, who sat through the entire series of hearings, believed Byrnes's story. The shadow of doubt cast over Byrnes's reputation spelled the end of his long career.

The Lexow Committee handed out approximately seventy indictments against various police officers, two former police commissioners, twenty police captains, and three police inspectors. Although many of these men were convicted, the verdicts against them were overturned in a higher court, which was overseen by handpicked Tammany Hall appointees. Many of those indicted were reinstated to the police force. Although the indictments didn't stick, the city's reform-minded citizenry forced out the Tammany Hall mayoral candidate in the 1894 election. William L. Strong, a reform-minded Republican, was elected mayor and came into office with the clear and abiding mandate to reform the city's police department. One of Strong's first acts was to get rid of all the Tammany Hall–appointed police commissioners and appoint his own men to the positions. Strong named thirty-six-year-old Theodore Roosevelt, a former member of the state legislature and a former New York City health commissioner, as president of the newly organized Board of Police Commissioners. One of Roosevelt's first orders of business was to get rid of the upper echelon of the police department, including Superintendent Thomas Byrnes. Byrnes clearly saw the handwriting on the wall and resigned before Roosevelt had the chance to tarnish his reputation by firing him.

CREEDEN'S CAPTAINCY COST HIM $15,000
CONFESSES TO THE LEXOW COMMITTEE THAT THE MONEY WAS FOR BRIBERY

HE SWEARS THAT HE PAID JOHN MARTIN $10,000
VOORHIS, THEN POLICE COMMISSIONER
POLICE BOARD SUSPENDS CREEDEN UPON BYRNES
SUGGESTION
SENATORS INDIGNANT, HAVING PROMISED THE
CAPTAIN PROTECTION—PRESIDENT MARTIN AND THE
SUPERINTENDENT SUMMONED BEFORE THEM—THE
OFFICIALS PROMISE TO TAKE STEPS TO REINSTATE
THE POLICEMAN—JUSTICE VOORHIS MAKES A
DENIAL OF THE CHARGES

Police Captain Timothy J. Creeden yesterday made a clean breast of the circumstance connected with his appointment to a Captaincy. He swore before the Lexow committee that he paid $15,000 for his appointment, and that he understood the money went to ex-Police Commissioner John R. Voorhis, now a Police Justice. . . . Upon receiving intelligence of Capt. Creeden's testimony Police Superintendent Byrnes reported the matter to the Police Commissioners who were in session, and the Commissioners ordered Capt. Creeden suspended. . . .

This action aroused the indignation of the members of the Senate Committee, who had commended Capt. Creeden and promised to protect him against such proceedings. . . .

—*New York Times*
December 15, 1894

Byrnes is considered by many influential men of all parties as a valuable aid to the committee. . . . For that reason he should not be required to give evidence to discredit the value of his testimony in the public estimation.

—SENATOR CLARENCE LEXOW
DECEMBER 25, 1894

BYRNES AND HIS MONEY
DEFIES ANY MAN TO PROVE HE TOOK A DISHONEST DOLLAR
STRONG HAS HIS RESIGNATION
INFLUENTIAL FRIENDS IN WALL STREET
TOLD THE SUPERINTENDENT HOW TO WIN ON STOCKS

The last session of the Lexow committee was brought to a dramatic close last evening by Superintendent Byrnes, who, just before stepping from the witness stand, handed to Mr. Goff a copy of a letter addressed to Mayor-elect Strong tendering his resignation from the office of Superintendent of Police. . . .

Superintendent Byrnes was the last witness, and in many respects the most interesting. His account of how he rose from ordinary circumstances to be a man of wealth, with nearly $300,000, was very interesting, but was given with apparent candor and without hesitancy. . . .

He said he knew the police department was honeycombed with corruption and declared that the fault was largely with the system. . . .

—*New York Times*
December 30, 1894

Goff: Can you say if blackmail ever found its way higher than inspectors?

Byrnes: I defy any man, either inside or outside of the police force, to point his finger at me and say he ever gave me one dollar dishonestly. I want to say to you now I would have retired from the department once or twice, but I thought I owed it to the people of New York to stay at the head of affairs.

Goff: And you have stayed until the Police Department has become rotten?

Byrnes: No, it is not rotten.

Goff: But you said here it was honeycombed with corruption?

Byrnes: I said honeycombed with abuses.

Goff: We have it now that as you stand today your property is worth $295,000?

Byrnes: Yes.

Goff: Have you been in any business outside of the Police Department?

Byrnes: No.

Goff: Then explain right here how you acquired so much property?

Byrnes: After I was assigned to the Detective Bureau and had reorganized the bureau I was brought into intimate contact with men connected with Wall Street. I had business with them, both public and private, and they helped and assisted me in speculations in which I made money.

Goff: How did you first acquire money to enable you to invest with Mr. Gould?

Byrnes: In 1879 a relative of mine, named Byrnes, died in Duchess County, leaving $4,200. I was made Captain in 1870 and had saved $5,000 or $7,000. In 1875 I had $8,000 or $9,000. Part of this was the proceeds of my relative's property, which was sold after his death. His wife received one third and I got the rest. In 1880 I had $15,000 or $20,000. It was with that much when I got acquainted with Gould.

Goff: Can you give a more definite statement about your money?

Byrnes: No.

Goff: Had you a bank account?

Byrnes: I have no recollection of one.

Goff: How did your capital of $12,000 or $15,000 develop into nearly $300,000.

Byrnes: Through speculation.

—Testimony from the Lexow Committee
hearing with Superintendent Thomas Byrnes
December 30, 1894

———•◦•◦•———

Dear Sir:

I appreciate as fully as any man can the tremendous responsibilities that will come upon you when you assume the duties of Mayor and undertake the reform of the various departments of the City Government.

On the contrary, I wish to aid you in any way I can. I assume you are now considering what action you are going to take and what legislation will be required to make such action practical.

I now place in your hands my request to be retired from the post of Superintendent, the request to be used by you or not at any time after the 1st of January as you see fit.

Let me further say that you may be entirely free to command my services, advice, and information at any time in regard to the affairs of the Police Department, with which I have been so long connected. Your obedient servant,

Thomas Byrnes

—Letter of resignation by Superintendent Byrnes sent to Mayor-elect
William Strong, December 30, 1894

———•◦•◦•———

I regard the tender as an evidence of good faith on the part of Mr. Byrnes. By this act he made it plain that he did not desire to embarrass the incoming administration in any plan that might be adopted for the reorganization of the police department.

I will not do anything with it at least until I have been installed as Mayor.

—Mayor-elect William Strong

December 31, 1894

———•‡•———

Byrnes hated us and kept tabs on us and tried to make us contemptible in public esteem by showing that our agent was levying blackmail, which, as shown by the Lexow committee, was precisely what his agents were doing and precisely what we were obliged to presume he knew his agents were doing. . . .

He lied all the same, and the object of the lie was to break the power that I was exercising against the viciousness of his department. He even perpetrated a vile sneaking insinuation against my church, by saying that he knew of a well-trodden path that conducted from my vestibule to a disreputable resort. . . .

If Mr. Byrnes, with characteristic disposition to get his own neck out of the yoke, says that he has been so handicapped as to be practically powerless, I want to say that all such excuse is evasive and cowardly. . . .

—The Reverend Dr. Charles Parkhurst's response to Superintendent

Byrnes's letter of resignation, December 31, 1894

———•‡•———

I have nothing at all to say at present. Dr. Parkhurst is a real nice man, that is my New Year's greeting to him.

—Superintendent Byrnes's response to Parkhurst's statement,

December 31, 1894

———•‡•———

Mayor Strong did not accept Byrnes's resignation and asked him to remain on as superintendent of the police. The Lexow Committee issued a statement praising and exonerating Byrnes.

"There was not a bit of evidence to show that Superintendent Byrnes was guilty of corruption," the committee chairman, state senator Clarence Lexow, wrote in his statement to newspapers.

Although Strong publicly made it a point of retaining Byrnes as superintendent, his career was over. Strong would not have to do the dirty work of firing Byrnes. He left that to his new president of police commissioners, Theodore Roosevelt.

In May 1895, Byrnes officially tendered his resignation to Roosevelt and the police commissioners. This time, his resignation was accepted.

According to Byrnes, he had decided to retire if it was the desire of the commissioners. Under Roosevelt's leadership, it was. Although rumors circulated that Byrnes was forced out of his position with the threat of corruption charges being filed against him, neither Mayor Strong nor the police commissioners verified this rumor.

Asked by reporters if he had any comment on his retirement, Byrnes said, "If any statement is to be made to the public, let the Commissioners make them."

Byrnes's many friends in the business community rushed to his defense.

"One of the main reasons why Byrnes has been forced into retirement is the fact that some newspapers and his personal enemies have continuously charged that he paid too much attention to the men in Wall Street, and profited by the friendship of men of wealth," one unnamed businessman was quoted as saying in the *New York Times*.

"It must be conceded that under his administration life and property were safer than ever before in this city," the unnamed source said.

And so ended the illustrious public police career of Thomas Byrnes. In the years following his retirement, he opened a private detective agency on Wall Street, catering to the needs of his many wealthy and prominent friends.

In early 1896, a minor flare-up regarding Byrnes's retirement and Police Commissioner Roosevelt made it into the papers. Byrnes made a comment to reporters that he ". . . may yet have something to say" about his departure from the New York City Police Department. The comments riled Roosevelt, who shot back in the newspapers, "If Mr. Byrnes deems it necessary to state at any time what, in his opinion, were the reasons that led to his retirement from Mulberry Street, I shall, in my turn, take the trouble to state what were the real reasons for his retirement from the force." Neither Byrnes nor Roosevelt pursued the matter publicly any further, and Byrnes settled into a comfortable retirement. Byrnes had been able to shield his wife, Ophelia, and their five daughters, Adelaide, Isabelle, Jessie, Amy, and May, from the public glare. He kept the sordid, dirty, often gruesome, and unsettling work of criminal investigations as far as he possibly could from his family. Despite his name appearing so frequently in newspaper headlines, associated with many of the city's most high-profile cases, Byrnes refused to discuss the particulars of any case with his family. Although they were proud of his many accomplishments, they seldom knew any of the details surrounding them. For most of their lives, Ophelia and the children lived at the family's comfortable home at 318 West Seventy-seventh Street, far from any taint of crime or corruption.

Following his retirement from the police department, Byrnes traveled with his family to Europe several times, maintained his membership in many clubs and civic organizations, and ran his successful Wall Street detective agency.

Whatever his flaws or human foibles, whether guilty of corruption or not, and whether his tactics were abusive or his behavior self-serving, one thing remains clear: Byrnes's legacy as the father of modern American detective work cannot be disputed. His use of mug shots, police lineups, early forensic methods, interrogation tactics, and crime-scene investigation techniques, including his manipulation of the press, remain as the foundation of law enforcement procedures all over the world.

Although many in New York City government undoubtedly wished that the Reverend Dr. Charles H. Parkhurst were dead and gone, Parkhurst managed to outlive almost all of his foes, including Thomas

Byrnes. Parkhurst retired in 1918. He remarried at the age of eighty-five in 1927, and died in 1933 at the age of ninety-one.

The citywide reform that was a result of Parkhurst's crusade on vice and corruption was short-lived. The Tammany Hall mayoral candidate won the 1897 city election.

Thomas Byrnes died of stomach cancer on May 7, 1910. He was sixty-eight years old. He left behind his wife, Ophelia, and five daughters. At the time of his death, three of his daughters, Adelaide, Isabelle, and May, were married to successful young men. Even at the end of his life, Byrnes sought to keep his family away from any unsettling news and did not divulge to any of them the seriousness of his illness. A *New York Times* article on his life and death called him ". . . the greatest policeman New York ever had." No one could ever dispute that claim.

EX-CHIEF BYRNES
DIES OF CANCER
Best Known of All the City's
Police Officials Had Been
Ill Since August.
WON FAME AS DETECTIVE
Made Fulton Street a "Dead Line" to
Crooks and Introduced His Own
Methods of Controlling Crime.

Thomas F. Byrnes, successively Inspector, Superintendent, and Chief of Police of this city and for many years before his retirement into private life the best-known and most picturesque figure in the department, died at 9 o'clock last night at his home, 318 West Seventy-seventh Street, of cancer of the stomach. . . . At his bedside when the end came were his wife and five children, three of whom are married; his physician, Dr. Casebeer, and Father Taylor of the Church of the Blessed Sacrament. . . . Many men on the force and off who served under Byrnes expressed sorrow last night on hearing of his death. Among them was ex-Chief Inspector Moses W. Cortright.

"Byrnes," said Cortright, "was a truly remarkable man . . ." For fifteen years or more the phrase "In Tom Byrnes's day" has been the standard way of introducing the best of the Police Department yarns. When Byrnes ruled the department with a mailed fist he made the detective Bureau famous. . . .

—*New York Times*
May 8, 1910

ACKNOWLEDGMENTS

I wrote much of this book on Block Island, a small island off the coast of Rhode Island. I have written most of my books on Block Island. It is a good place to write. It is quiet and peaceful, a dreamy sort of place. Writers need to dream.

Everyone on Block Island functions on *island time*, which means, as best as I can define it, that no one ever looks at a watch. Everyone eats, drinks, sleeps, hikes, walks, swims, and shops when the urge strikes, and everyone else is welcome to do the same, whenever the same urge comes upon him or her. Somehow, some way, everyone meets up with everyone else—island time.

———

I have been coming to Block Island since 1957 when my father first brought me. In 1982, I started bringing my boys, Nate and Andrew, to the island. And in 2000, they began bringing their children, my grandchildren.

Andrew's wife, Kelly, first came to Block Island during a near hurricane, bravely riding the small ferry over from Point Judith across Narragansett Bay in the high wind and waves. Good for her. Brave girl. True love, I say.

My son, Nate, proposed to his wife, Leah, on Block Island. More true love.

My brother-in-law, Bobby (he who must be referred to as Dr. Sullivan) and his wife, Lisa, had their honeymoon on Block Island.

Aside from riding the ferry in a hurricane, proposing, and honeymooning, there is not much to do on Block Island—bike riding, taking long walks, hiking nature trails, swimming at Scotch Beach, eating at Spring House and the Atlantic Inn, baking muffins, watching sailboats, and of course, for me, writing. Good for me. It gives me something to do with all the love, proposals, and hurricanes swirling all around me.

———

I would like to thank my agent, Tris Coburn, who has managed, some-how, to sell every book I've given him, and my editor, Keith Wallman, who has not only made *this* a better book, but has made me a bet-ter writer. (So much for not being able to show old dogs new tricks.) And Kristen Mellitt, who kindly helped correct the many errors of my ways.

———•••———

I have been a working writer most of my life. (Many people consider that an oxymoron.) Writing is a funny business. That is not to say that you have to be funny in order to be a writer, although it helps.

I have been a newspaper reporter, editor, business editor, a feature writer, a humor columnist, the editor of a computer magazine, and an executive editor for a major corporation. Good for me. How I ended up as a crime writer working on a trilogy about the Gilded Age I have no idea. Like I said, writing is a funny business.

This book, *The Big Policeman,* is the second book of a planned trilogy on New York City during the Gilded Age. The first book was *King of Heists.* I have told my editors that I would like to model my trilogy after J. R. R. Tolkien's trilogy, *Lord of the Rings.* Since my tril-ogy takes place during the extravagant, excessively greedy era of the Gilded Age, I have suggested to my publisher that we call my trilogy, *Lord of the Bling.*

I doubt they will. While writing is a funny business, publishing is deadly serious.

I would thank God, if I could, but I am a practicing "agnostic atheist"—I don't know which God not to believe in. So instead I would like to acknowledge the help, generosity, and forgiveness given to me by the people I've mentioned here.

———•••———

Lastly, I would like to thank my mother, Irma Conway, who passed away at ninety-one years old while I was writing this book. Even toward the end of her life she would ask me: "Jackie, are you a writer?" And I would say "Yes." And she would say, "What do you write?"

"Books," I'd say. "How many books have you written?" she'd ask. "About a dozen," I'd say. "A dozen books by my son the writer. Yes. Yes. Imagine that," she'd say. Then she'd start all over again: "Jackie, are you a writer?"

I became a writer because my mother and father always said yes to whatever it was I wanted to do. They let me think I could do anything, no matter how crazy it might seem. My father passed away when I was pretty young, but he always said yes, too. No matter what harebrained idea I had about what I wanted to be when I grew up, they always supported me, even when I wrapped myself from head to toe in aluminum foil and proclaimed to them that I wanted to be an astronaut.

I remember my father saying, "Yes, what an exciting career that's going to be, Jackie!" (Everyone in my family calls me "Jackie," even though I cringe when I hear it.) "Yes. Yes. Imagine that," my mother said. For Christmas they bought me a model rocket kit and a toy plastic space helmet. Being deathly afraid of heights helped end that career choice. But it didn't matter. They always said yes and always encouraged me to become whatever it was I wanted to, and so I became a writer.

I tell people I became a writer because the pen is mightier than the sword, and besides, you don't get stuck having to wear a scabbard. My mother was most proud of me for being a professor at a college and a university. "Are you a professor?" she would ask. "Yes," I'd say. "Yes. Yes. Imagine that. I never thought my son would become a professor," she would say proudly. She never graduated from high school. "It's better than being an astronaut," I would say. "And you don't have to wear aluminum foil, I bet," she would say, still, even at her age, able to remember my youngest occupational desire.

And so, I would like to thank my mother (and my father) for always saying yes. I try to say yes every chance I get. I am thankful that I have so many good friends and family who said yes when I told them I was writing this book. I am thankful my agent, Tris Coburn, said yes to representing it. I am thankful my publisher said yes to this book. And I am especially glad that you said yes when you bought this book Yes. Yes. Imagine that. Thank you.

BIBLIOGRAPHY

BOOKS

Ackerman, Kenneth D. *The Gold Ring: Wall Street's Swindle of the Century and Its Most Scandalous Crash—Black Friday, 1869*. New York: Carroll & Graf Publishers, 2005.

Adams, Charles F., Jr., and Henry Adams. *Chapters of Erie and Other Essays*. Boston: James R. Osgood & Company, 1871.

Albion, R. G. *The Rise of New York Port, 1815–1860*. New York: Charles Scribner's Sons, 1939.

Anbinder, Tyler. *Five Points: The 19th-Century Neighborhood that Invented Tap Dance, Stole Elections, and Became the World's Most Notorious Slum*. New York: The Free Press, 2002.

Anonymous. *James Fisk, Jr.: The Life of a Green Mountain Boy*. Philadelphia: W. Flint, 1872.

Asbury, Herbert. *The Gangs of New York*. New York: A. A. Knopf, 1928.

Atkins, Gordon. *Health, Housing, and Poverty in New York City, 1865–1898*. Ann Arbor: Edwards, 1947.

Bailey, William, ed. *The Encyclopedia of Police Science*. New York: Routledge, 1995.

Barnes, David. *The Draft Riots in New York*. New York: Baker & Godwin, 1863.

Bayor, Ronald and Timothy Meagher, eds. *The New York Irish*. Baltimore, MD: The Johns Hopkins University Press, 1997.

Beckert, Sven. *The Monied Metropolis: New York City and the Consolidation of the American Bourgeoisie, 1850–1896*. Cambridge, U.K.: Cambridge University Press, 2003.

Bernstein, Iver. *The New York City Draft Riots: Their Significance for American Society and Politics in the Age of the Civil War*. New York: Oxford University Press, 1991.

Blake, E. Vale. *History of the Tammany Society*. New York: Souvenir Publishing Company, 1901.

Brace, Charles Loring. *The Dangerous Classes of New York and Twenty Years' Work Among Them.* New York: Wynkoop & Hallenbeck, 1872.

Browne, Junius Henri. *The Great Metropolis: A Mirror of New York. A Complete History of Metropolitan Life and Society, with Sketches of Prominent Places, Persons and Things in the City as they Actually Exist.* Hartford: American Publishing Company, 1869.

Burrows, G. Edwin, and Mike Wallace. *Gotham: A History of New York City to 1898.* New York: Oxford University Press, 2000.

Byrnes, Thomas. *Professional Criminals of America.* New York: Cassell & Company, 1886.

Campbell, Helen. *Darkness and Daylight: Lights and Shadows of New York Life.* Hartford: The Hartford Publishing Company, 1891.

Clinton, H. L. *Celebrated Trials.* New York: Harper & Brothers Publishers, 1897.

Costello, Augustine E. *Our Police Protectors: History of the New York Police from the Earliest Period to the Present Time.* New York: C. F. Roper & Company, 1885.

Crapsey, Edward. *The Nether Side of New York or the Vice, Crime, and Poverty of the Great Metropolis.* New York: Sheldon & Company, 1872.

Dash, Mike. *Satan's Circus: Murder, Vice, Police Corruption, and New York's Trial of the Century.* New York: Three Rivers Press, 2007.

Diner, Hasia. *Erin's Daughters in America: Irish Immigrant Women in the Nineteenth Century.* Baltimore, MD: The Johns Hopkins University Press, 1983.

Dunlop, M. H. *Gilded City: Scandal and Sensation in Turn-of-the-Century New York.* New York: William Morrow, 2001.

Elias, Stephen N. *Alexander T. Stewart: The Forgotten Merchant Prince.* Westport, CT: Praeger Publishers, 1992.

Ernst, Robert. *Immigrant Life in New York City.* New York: King's Crown Press, 1949.

Evans, Stewart, and Paul Gainey. *Jack the Ripper: First American Serial Killer.* New York: Kodansha America, 1998.

Fanebust, Wayne. *The Missing Corpse: Grave Robbing a Gilded Age Tycoon.* Westport, CT: Praeger Publishers, 2005.

Fiske, Stephen. *Off-hand Portraits of Prominent New Yorkers.* New York: G. R. Lockwood & Son, 1884.

Franklin, Allan, and Thomas Nast (illustrator). *The Trail of the Tiger, Being an Account of Tammany from 1789; The Organization and Sway of the Bosses.* New York: Allan Franklin, 1928.

Fuller, Robert H. *Jubilee Jim: From Circus Traveler to Wall Street Rogue: The Remarkable Life of Colonel James Fisk, Jr.* New York: Texere, 2001.

Genung, Abram Polhemus. *The Frauds of the New York City Government Exposed. Sketches of the Members of the Ring and Their Confederates.* New York: Self-published, 1871.

Gilfoyle, Timothy J. *City of Eros: New York City, Prostitution, and the Commercialization of Sex, 1790–1920.* New York: W. W. Norton & Company, 1994.

Gold Panic Investigation—41st Congress, 2d Session, H. of R. Report No. 31. Washington, 1870.

Gordon, R. Michael. *The American Murders of Jack the Ripper.* Westport, CT: Praeger Publishers, 2003.

Green-Lewis, Jennifer. *Framing the Victorians: Photography and the Culture of Realism.* Ithaca, NY: Cornell University Press, 1996.

Grodinsky, Julius. *Jay Gould: His Business Career.* Philadelphia: University of Pennsylvania Press, 1957.

Harris, Leslie M. *In the Shadow of Slavery: African Americans in New York City, 1626–1863.* Chicago: The University of Chicago Press, 2003.

Hawthorne, Julian. *A Tragic Mystery: From the Diary of Inspector Byrnes.* New York: Cassell, 1887.

Howe, William F., and Abraham Hummel. *Danger: A True History of a Great City's Wiles and Temptations.* New York: Courier, 1886.

Hoyt, Edwin P. *The Goulds.* New York: Weybright & Talley, 1969.

Johnson, Marilynn S. *Street Justice: A History of Police Violence in New York City.* Boston: Beacon Press, 2004.

Jones, Willoughby. *The Life of James Fisk, Jr., Including the Great Frauds of the Tammany Ring.* Chicago: Union Publishing Company, 1872.

Josephson, Matthew. *The Robber Barons*. New York: Harcourt, 1934.

Kenny, Kevin. *The American Irish: A History*. New York: Longman, 2000.

Klein, Marcus. *Easterns, Westerns, and Private Eyes: American Matters, 1870–1900*. Madison: The University of Wisconsin Press, 1994.

Lardner, James, and Thomas Reppetto. *NYPD: A City and Its Police*. New York: Henry Holt & Company, 2001.

Lening, Gustav. *The Dark Side of New York, and Its Criminal Classes from Fifth Avenue down to the Five Points. A Complete Narrative of the Mysteries of New York*. New York: Frederick Gerhard, 1873.

Long, Kat. *The Forbidden Apple: A Century of Sex & Sin in New York City*. New York: Ig Publishing, 2009.

Lundberg, Ferdinand. *America's Sixty Families*. New York: Citadel Press, 1937.

Lynch, Denis Tilden. *Boss Tweed: The Story of a Grim Generation*. New York: Transaction Publishers, 2002.

Mandelbaum, Seymour. *Boss Tweed's New York*. New York: Wiley, 1965.

Maurice, Arthur B. *Fifth Avenue*. New York: Dodd, Mead & Company, 1918.

Mayer, Grace M. *Once Upon a City*. New York: Macmillan, 1958.

Mohl, Raymond A. *The Making of Urban America*. Lanham, MD: SR Books, 1997.

Morton, James. *Gangland: The Early Years*. New York: Time Warner Paperbacks, 2004.

Nevins, Allan, and Thomas Milton Halsey. *The Diary of George Templeton Strong*. (4 vols.). New York: Macmillan, 1952.

Newton, Michael. *The Encyclopedia of Robberies, Heists, and Capers*. New York: Facts on File, 2002.

O'Connor, Richard. *Hell's Kitchen*. New York: J. B. Lippincott Company, 1958.

Palmiotto, Michael. *Criminal Investigation*. Lanham, MD: University Press of America, 2004.

Panek, LeRoy. *The Origins of the American Detective Story.* Jefferson, NC: McFarland & Company, 2006.

Parkhurst, Charles. *My Forty Years in New York.* New York: Macmillan, 1923.

Parkhurst, Charles. *Our Fight with Tammany.* New York: Charles Scribner's Sons, 1895.

Patton, Clifford W. *The Battle for Municipal Reform: Mobilization and Attack, 1875–1900.* New York: American Council on Public Affairs, 1940.

Richmond, Rev. J. F. *New York and Its Institutions, 1609–1873.* New York: E. B. Treat, 1873.

Riis, Jacob. *The Making of an American.* New York: Macmillan, 1901.

Rovere, Richard. *Howe and Hummel.* New York: Michael Joseph, 1947.

Sante, Luc. *Low Life: Lures and Snares of Old New York.* New York: Farrar, Straus and Giroux, 2003.

Schecter, Barnet. *The Devil's Own Work: The Civil War Draft Riots and the Fight to Reconstruct America.* New York: Walker & Company, 2007.

Sloat, Warren. *Battle for the Soul of New York: Tammany Hall, Police Corruption, Vice, and Reverend Charles Parkhurst's Crusade against Them, 1892–1895.* New York: Cooper Square Press, 2002.

Smith, Matthew Hale. *Sunshine and Shadow in New York.* Hartford: J. B. Burr & Company, 1869.

Steffens, Lincoln. *Shame of the Cities.* New York: McClure, Phillips & Company, 1905.

Stone, William L. *History of New York City from the Discovery to the Present Day.* New York: Virtue & Yorston, 1872.

Swanberg, W. A. *Jim Fisk: The Career of an Improbable Rascal.* New York: Scribner's and Sons, 1959.

Swierczynski, Duane. *This Here's a Stick-Up: The Big Bad Book of American Bank Robbery.* Indianapolis, IN: Alpha Books, 2002.

Tagg, John. *The Disciplinary Frame: Photographic Truths and the Capture of Meaning.* Minneapolis: University of Minnesota Press, 2009.

Tomkins, Calvin. *Merchants and Masterpieces.* New York: Dutton, 1973.

Walling, George Washington. *Recollections of a New York Chief of Police.* New York: Caxton Book Concern, 1887.

Wood, Sharon. *The Freedom of the Streets: Work, Citizenship, and Sexuality in a Gilded Age City.* Chapel Hill: University of North Carolina Press, 2005.

NEWSPAPERS AND MAGAZINES

Brooklyn Daily Eagle

Harper's Weekly

McClure's

Nation

New York Times

SOURCES

CHAPTER 1: THE CASE OF JACK THE RIPPER

Notes on comments made by James Jennings, owner of the East River Hotel where Carrie Brown was found murdered, as well as comments from witnesses including Mary Miniter, the hotel housekeeper; Mamie Harrington's description of Carrie Brown, including her identity; Mary Healey; Dr. Bernard Shultz, the coroner; and Inspector Thomas Byrnes.

Newspapers:
"A Leap from the Bridge," *New York Times*, July 24, 1886.
"Choked, Then Mutilated," *New York Times*, April 25, 1891.
"Byrnes Says He Has a Clue," *New York Times*, April 26, 1891.
"Byrnes Names the Man," *Brooklyn Daily Eagle*, April 26, 1891.
"It Is Yet a Mystery," *New York Times,* April 27, 1891.
"Still Working in the Dark," *Brooklyn Daily Eagle*, April 27, 1891.
"The Murderer Still at Large," *New York Times*, April 28, 1891.
"Still Puzzled," *Brooklyn Daily Eagle*, April 28, 1891.
"He Has the Man," *Brooklyn Daily Eagle*, April 30, 1891.
"Is He the Guilty Man," *New York Times*, May 1, 1891.
"The East River Hotel Murder," *New York Times*, May 3, 1891.
"Jack the Ripper in Queens Jail," *Daily Star (Astoria)*, May 1891.
"Jury Ready for Frenchy No. 1," *New York Times*, June 27, 1891.
"Frenchy Trial Nearly Over," *New York Times*, July 3, 1891.
"Frenchy Found Guilty," *New York Times*, July 4, 1891.

Information regarding Byrnes's comments about Jack the Ripper:
"Under the headline: 'An American Detective's Opinion,' Byrnes was asked how . . ."
Vanderlinden, Wolf. "The New York Affair II." *Casebook: Jack the Ripper*. n.d.

". . . for Inspector Byrnes has said that it would be impossible for crimes such as 'Jack the Ripper' committed in London to occur in New York . . ."

"Choked, Then Mutilated," *New York Times*, April 25, 1891.

"An American Detective's Opinion . . . What's the good of talking? The murderer would have been caught long ago." Evans, Stewart and Paul Gainey. *Jack the Ripper: First American Serial Killer.* New York: Kodansha America, 1998.

General information regarding the Carric Brown murder case and investigation:

Barbee, Larry. "An Investigation into the Carrie Brown Murder." *Casebook: Jack the Ripper.* n.d.

Conlon, Michael. "A Tale of Two Frenchys." *Casebook: Jack the Ripper.* n.d.

Gordon, R. Michael. *The American Murders of Jack the Ripper.* Westport, CT: Praeger Publishers, 2003.

"Inspector Thomas F. Byrnes, Inventor of the Third Degree," *New York Press*, September 4, 2001.

CHAPTER 2: NO IRISH NEED APPLY

Notes on the plight of New York City's poor, its Irish population, treatment of the Irish in America, Five Points, and tenement housing.

Books:

Anbinder, Tyler. *Five Points: The 19th-Century Neighborhood that Invented Tap Dance, Stole Elections, and Became the World's Most Notorious Slum.* New York: The Free Press, 2002.

Asbury, Herbert. *The Gangs of New York.* New York: A. A. Knopf, 1928.

Bayor, Ronald, and Timothy Meagher. *The New York Irish.* Baltimore, MD: The Johns Hopkins University Press, 1997.

Brace, Charles Loring. *The Dangerous Classes of New York and Twenty Years' Work Among Them.* New York: Wynkoop & Hallenbeck, 1872.

Browne, Junius Henri. *The Great Metropolis: A Mirror of New York. A Complete History of Metropolitan Life and Society, with Sketches of Prominent Places, Persons and Things in the City as they Actually Exist.* Hartford: American Publishing Company, 1869.

Burrows, G. Edwin, and Mike Wallace. *Gotham: A History of New York City to 1898.* New York: Oxford University Press, 2000.

Crapsey, Edward. *The Nether Side of New York or the Vice, Crime, and Poverty of the Great Metropolis.* New York: Sheldon & Company, 1872.

Diner, Hasia. *Erin's Daughters in America: Irish Immigrant Women in the Nineteenth Century.* Baltimore, MD: The Johns Hopkins University Press, 1983.

Kenny, Kevin. *The American Irish: A History.* New York: Longman, 2000.

Lening, Gustav. *The Dark Side of New York, and Its Criminal Classes from Fifth Avenue down to the Five Points. A Complete Narrative of the Mysteries of New York.* New York: Frederick Gerhard, 1873.

Sante, Luc. *Low Life: Lures and Snares of Old New York.* New York: Farrar, Straus and Giroux, 2003.

Smith, Matthew Hale. *Sunshine and Shadow in New York.* Hartford: J. B. Burr & Company, 1869.

Articles:

Dolan, Jay P. "Immigrants in the City: New York's Irish and German Catholics." *Church History*, Vol. 41, No. 3 (1972).

Newspapers:

"Walks Among the New-York Poor," *New York Times*, February 11, 1853.

"A Scene in the Five Points," *New York Times*, April 30, 1853.

"Association for Improving the Condition of the Poor," *New York Times*, November 9, 1853.

"The Children of the Poor," *New York Times*, March 4, 1854 (Letter).

"New York City; City Mortality," *New York Times*, March 20, 1854.

"Walks Among the New-York Poor," *New York Times*, March 21, 1854.

"The Children of the City Poor," *New York Times*, May 16, 1854.

"Morals of Fashionable Society" ("People lately have been going down to the Five Points and expending their sympathy and labor on the children of depravity that swarm in those classic purlieus . . ."), *New York Times*, June 7, 1854.

"Walks Among the New York Poor," *New York Times*, June 16, 1854.

"Rents and Tenements in New-York," *New York Times*, September 15, 1854 (Letter).

"Relief for the Poor," *New York Times*, December 28, 1854 (Letter).

"Starvation at the Five Points," *New York Times*, January 4, 1855.

"The Hard Times; To the Public-Food for the Poor," *New York Times*, January 30, 1855.

"Relief for the Poor; The Policy of Soup-Houses," *New York Times*, February 6, 1855.

"Winter Among the Poor," *New York Times*, February 12, 1855.

"Condition of the Unemployed Poor," *New York Times*, March 1, 1855.

"Irish Emigration Society," *New York Times*, July 11, 1855.

"Tenement Houses . . . Human Beings Crowded Like Sheep into Pens," *New York Times*, March 14, 1856.

"Tenement Houses in New York; Examinations of the Legislative Committee," *New York Times*, March 28, 1856.

"Secrets of the Five Points," *New York Times*, June 11, 1856.

"Inspection of Tenement Houses," *New York Times*, June 20, 1856.

"The Sanitary Condition of the City," *New York Times*, August 22, 1856.

"New-York Association for Improving the Condition of the Poor," *New York Times*, December 9, 1856.

"The City Poor," *New York Times*, December 20, 1856.

CHAPTER 3: NEW YORK UNDER SIEGE

Sources for the New York City draft riots in 1863, the number of deaths and cost, Superintendent Kennedy, the role of the New York City Police Department during and after the riots, Byrnes's duties during the riots, and the burning of the Orphan Asylum for Colored Children.

Books:

Barnes, David. *The Draft Riots in New York*. New York: Baker & Godwin, 1863.

Bernstein, Iver. *The New York City Draft Riots: Their Significance for American Society and Politics in the Age of the Civil War*. New York: Oxford University Press, 1991.

Burrows, G. Edwin, and Mike Wallace. *Gotham: A History of New York City to 1898*. New York: Oxford University Press, 2000.

Harris, Leslie M. *In the Shadow of Slavery: African Americans in New York City, 1626–1863*. Chicago: The University of Chicago Press, 2003.

Schecter, Barnet. *The Devil's Own Work: The Civil War Draft Riots and the Fight to Reconstruct America*. New York: Walker & Company, 2007.

Walling, George Washington. *Recollections of a New York Chief of Police*. New York: Caxton Book Concern, 1887.

Articles:

Lut, Stephen. "Martha Derby Perry: Eyewitness to the 1863 New York City Draft Riots." *America's Civil War*, May 2000.

Man, Albon, Jr. "Labor Competition and the New York Draft Riots of 1863." *Journal of Negro History*, Vol. XXXVI, No. 4 (October 1951).

Newspapers:

"The Mob in New-York," *New York Times*, July 14, 1863.

"The Riots Yesterday," *New York Times*, July 14, 1863 (Editorial).

"The Murder of Colored People in Thompson and Sullivan Streets," *New York Times*, July 16, 1863.

"The Reign of Rabble . . . The Mob Increased in Numbers," *New York Times*, July 16, 1863.

"The Nationality of Rioters . . . An Appeal to the Irish Catholics," *New York Times*, July 16, 1863.

"A State of Insurrection . . . The Draft and Financial Confidence," *New York Times*, July 16, 1863 (Editorial).

"More Military Organizing . . . The Riots in New-York," *New York Times*, July 16, 1863.

"The Riot Subsiding . . . A Last Desperate Struggle," *New York Times*, July 17, 1863.

"A Colored Man Is Driven to Despair and Suicide . . . The Great Riots," *New York Times*, July 18, 1863.

"Quiet Restored . . . A Proclamation from the Mayor," *New York Times*, July 18, 1863.

"Another Victim of the Riots," *New York Times*, July 20, 1863.

"The Enforcement of the Draft," *New York Times*, July 20, 1863 (Editorial).

"Condition of the City . . . A Quiet Sunday," *New York Times*, July 20, 1863.

"Quiet Restored . . . A Proclamation from the Mayor," *New York Times*, July 20, 1863.

"A Victim of the New York Mob," *Albany Times*, July 21, 1863.

"How to Deal with Mobs," *New York Times*, July 21, 1863 (Editorial).

"Arrival of the Vermont Brigade," *New York Times*, July 21, 1863.

"The Riots in This City," *New York Times*, July 22, 1863.

"Arrests, Incidents . . . Important Arrest of a Ringleader," *New York Times*, July 22, 1863.

"Permanent Peace of the City," *New York Times*, July 22, 1863.

"Relief of Colored Sufferers," *New York Times*, July 22, 1863.

"Condition of the City; Quiet and Order Universal," *New York Times*, July 23, 1863 (Letter).

"The Recent Riots . . . Superintendent Kennedy . . ." *New York Times*, July 24, 1863.

"The Late Riots a Conspiracy," *New York Times*, July 24, 1863 (Editorial).

"The Mob on the Bench," *New York Times*, July 24, 1863 (Editorial).

"The Police and the Riots . . . An Address to the Police Force from the Board of Police Commissioners," *New York Times*, July 25, 1863.

"Losses by the Riots," *New York Times*, July 25, 1863.

"The Police and the Riots," *New York Times*, July 25, 1863.

"The Terrors of the Riot," *New York Times*, July 25, 1863 (Letter).

"How Rioters and Thieves Have Been Benefited," *New York Times*, July 26, 1863.

"A Large Number of Leaders Caught," *New York Times*, July 27, 1863.

"The Metropolitan Police . . . Their Services During the Riot Week," *New York Times*, July 28, 1863.

"The Colored Orphan Asylum," *New York Times*, July 29, 1863.

"The Military and the Late Riots," *New York Times*, July 30, 1863.

"A Victim of the New-York Riots," *New York Times*, July 30, 1863.

"Quiet and Order Universal," *New York Times*, July 31, 1863.

"The Riots," *New York Times*, August 1, 1863.

"Recorder Hoffman on the Riots, Charge to the Grand Jury," *New York Times*, August 5, 1863.

"Trial of the Rioters," *New York Times*, August 8, 1863.

"Gov. Seymour's Correspondence with the President," *New York Times*, August 11, 1863.

"The New York Riots," *New York Times*, August 12, 1863.

"The Metropolitan Police . . . Their Services During the Riot Week," *New York Times*, August 13, 1863.

"More Arrests of Ringleaders in the Riots," *New York Times*, August 14, 1863.

"The Doom of the Rioters," *New York Times*, August 14, 1863.

"The Draft and the Riots," *New York Times*, August 15, 1863.

"Awards to Policemen and Others," *New York Times*, August 15, 1863.

"Deaths from Riots," *New York Times*, August 18, 1863.

The Metropolitan Police . . . Their Services During the Riot Week," *New York Times*, August 20, 1863.

"The Cost of the Riot," *New York Times*, August 20, 1863.

"National Troops in New-York . . . Why Are They Here," *New York Times*, August 29, 1863 (Letter).

"Convict Three Men in Hawthorne Case," *New York Times*, March 15, 1913.

CHAPTER 4: THE MURDER OF JUBILEE JIM

Notes on the murder of Jim Fisk, the subsequent investigation and trials of Edward Stokes, the role of Josie Mansfield, and the partnership and friendship of Fisk with Jay Gould and Boss Tweed.

Books:

Ackerman, Kenneth D. *The Gold Ring: Wall Street's Swindle of the Century and Its Most Scandalous Crash—Black Friday, 1869.* New York: Carroll & Graf Publishers, 2005.

Anonymous. *James Fisk, Jr.: The Life of a Green Mountain Boy.* Philadelphia: W. Flint, 1872.

Asbury, Herbert. *The Gangs of New York.* New York: A. A. Knopf, 1928.

Browne, Junius Henri. *The Great Metropolis: A Mirror of New York. A Complete History of Metropolitan Life and Society, with Sketches of Prominent Places, Persons, and Things in the City as they Actually Exist.* Hartford: American Publishing Company, 1869.

Burrows, G. Edwin, and Mike Wallace. *Gotham: A History of New York City to 1898.* New York: Oxford University Press, 2000.

Franklin, Allan, and Thomas Nast (illustrator). *The Trail of the Tiger, Being an Account of Tammany from 1789; The Organization and Sway of the Bosses.* New York: Allan Franklin, 1928.

Fuller, Robert H. *Jubilee Jim: From Circus Traveler to Wall Street Rogue: The Remarkable Life of Colonel James Fisk, Jr.* New York: Texere, 2001.

Gold Panic Investigation—41st Congress, 2d Session, H. of R. Report No. 31. Washington, 1870.

Grodinsky, Julius. *Jay Gould: His Business Career.* Philadelphia: University of Pennsylvania Press, 1957.

Hoyt, Edwin P. *The Goulds.* New York: Weybright & Talley, 1969.

Jones, Willoughby. *The Life of James Fisk, Jr., Including the Great Frauds of the Tammany Ring.* Chicago: Union Publishing Company, 1872.

Josephson, Matthew. *The Robber Barons*. New York: Harcourt, 1934.

Lynch, Denis Tilden. *Boss Tweed: The Story of a Grim Generation*. New York: Transaction Publishers, 2002.

Mandelbaum, Seymour. *Boss Tweed's New York*. New York: Wiley, 1965.

Swanberg, W. A. *Jim Fisk: The Career of an Improbable Rascal*. New York: Scribner's and Sons, 1959.

Articles:

Kirkland, Edward C. "The Robber Barons Revisited." *The American Historical Review*, Vol. 66, No. 1 (October 1960), pp. 68–73.

Newspapers:

"The Gold Excitement," *New York Times*, September 25, 1869.

"The Gold Ring," *New York Times*, October 18, 1869.

"The President and the Gold Ring," *New York Times*, October 22, 1869.

"Jim Fisk vs. Brooklyn . . . He Seizes the Brooklyn Oil Refinery . . . E. S. Stokes, the Secretary, Arrested," *Brooklyn Daily Eagle*, January 9, 1871.

"Statement of Mr. Stokes Through His Counsel . . . A Little Scandal," *Brooklyn Daily Eagle*, January 13, 1871.

"The Fisk-Stokes Case," *New York Times*, October 22, 1871.

"Fisk and Mansfield," *New York Times*, November 19, 1871.

"Fisk and Stokes," *New York Times*, December 2, 1871.

"The Fisk Letters," *Brooklyn Daily Eagle*, January 6, 1872.

"The Fisk Mansfield Case," *New York Times*, January 6, 1872.

"The Fisk Mansfield Case . . . Judge Brady's Decision on the Publication of Fisk's Private Letters," *New York Times*, January 6, 1872.

"Sketch of James Fisk, Jr.," *New York Times*, January 7, 1872.

"The Origin of the Difficulty Between Fisk and Stokes," *New York Times*, January 7, 1872.

"Jim Fisk Murdered . . . He Is Deliberately Shot Down in the Grand Central Hotel," *New York Times*, January 7, 1872.

"Probable End of a Checkered Career," *New York Times*, January 7, 1872 (Editorial).

"Mrs. Mansfield Informed of the Shooting by a Reporter . . . She Discredits the Story," *New York Times*, January 7, 1872.

"The Mansfield Suit . . . Cross-Examination of Miss Mansfield . . . Spicy Developments," *New York Times*, January 7, 1872.

"His Antemortem Statement," *Brooklyn Daily Eagle*, January 8, 1872.

"Fisk After Death," *Brooklyn Daily Eagle*, January 8, 1872.

"The Murder of Fisk," *New York Times*, January 8, 1872 (Editorial).

"Obituary of James Fisk, Jr." *New York Times*, January 8, 1872.

"Fisk and the Police Force," *New York Times*, January 8, 1872.

"Was Stokes Watching for Fisk," *New York Times*, January 8, 1872.

"An Improbable Report—Rumored Threats of Lynching Stokes . . . Activity of the Police," *New York Times*, January 8, 1872.

"Death of James Fisk . . . Closing Scenes in the Life of the Great Speculator," *New York Times*, January 8, 1872.

"Fisk Funeral," *Brooklyn Daily Eagle*, January 9, 1872.

"Stokes on Trial . . . The Prisoner Testifies on His Own Behalf," *New York Times*, January 9, 1872.

"Imposing and Elaborate Funeral Services Yesterday," *New York Times*, January 9, 1872.

"Mrs. Mansfield Still at Home . . . A Reporter Interviews Her and Gets Arrested," *New York Times*, January 9, 1872.

"Funeral Ceremonies Yesterday at Brattleboro, Vermont," *New York Times*, January 10, 1872.

"The Servants at the Mansfield Mansion Under Arrest," *New York Times*, January 10, 1872.

"The Fisk Murder," *Brooklyn Daily Eagle Saturday*, January 13, 1872.

"Stokes Indicted . . . The Grand Jury Act," *New York Times*, January 16, 1872.

"The Murder of Jim Fisk," *New York Times*, January 24, 1872.

"What His Counsel Will Claim . . . A Singular Story About a Strange Bullet . . . Did Fisk Shoot Himself," *New York Times*, January 25, 1872.

"The Life and Times of Col. James Fisk, Jr., Being a Full and Impartial Account,"*New York Times*, May 11, 1872.

"The Stokes Case . . . The Prisoner's Last Plea Disallowed," *New York Times*, May 25, 1872.

"Fifth Day's Proceedings in the Fisk Murder Case," *New York Times*, June 25, 1872.

"A Jury Obtained Yesterday to Try Stokes," *New York Times*, June 27, 1872.

"The Fisk Murder," *New York Times*, June 28, 1872.

"The Evidence for the Prosecution Continued," *New York Times*, June 29, 1872.

"Testimony of the Physician Who Probed the Wound. . ." *New York Times*, July 2, 1872.

"The Evidence of the Physicians Continued," *New York Times*, July 3, 1872.

"Close of the Evidence for the Prosecution," *New York Times*, July 4, 1872.

"Stokes . . . More Medical Testimony," *Brooklyn Daily Eagle*, July 5, 1872.

"The Fisk Murder . . . The Theories of Self Defense and Insanity," *New York Times*, July 6, 1872.

"Further Evidence to Show," *New York Times*, July 7, 1872.

"Stokes and Mansfield . . . Both on the Stand Before Judge Ingraham," *New York Times*, July 9, 1872.

"Conclusion of the Prisoner's Testimony . . . Miss Mansfield's Story," *Brooklyn Daily Eagle*, July 10, 1872.

"Did Stokes Put the Pistol in the Sofa," *Brooklyn Daily Eagle*, July 13, 1872.

"The Jury Discharged . . . End of the First Trial of Stokes . . . Irreconcilable Differences among Jurors," *New York Times*, July 16, 1872.

"The Stokes Case . . . Newly Discovered Testimony," *New York Times*, October 16, 1872.

"The Tweed Trial . . . The Defendant Pleads Not Guilty," *New York Times*, December 17, 1872.

"Found Guilty, Close of the Second Act in the Fisk Tragedy," *New York Times*, January 5, 1873.

"The Death Sentence, Edward S. Stokes to be Hanged February 28," *New York Times*, January 7, 1873.

"Edward S. Stokes . . . Conduct of the Condemned Murderer in the Tombs," *New York Times*, January 8, 1873.

"The Third Trial of Stokes," *New York Times*, October 17, 1873.

"Stokes . . . New and Important Evidence in Favor of the Prisoner," *Brooklyn Daily Eagle*, October 21, 1873.

"Sketches of the Prisoner, the Witnesses, the Lawyers, the Spectators," *Brooklyn Daily Eagle*, October 23, 1873.

"The Verdict . . . Manslaughter in the Third Degree . . . Stokes Sentenced to Imprisonment for Four Years," *New York Times*, October 30, 1873.

"Stokes . . . Liberty Regained by the Slayer of Fisk," *Brooklyn Daily Eagle*, October 28, 1876.

"Edward S. Stokes Dead," *New York Times*, November 3, 1901.

"Fisk Murder Recalled by Death . . . Josie Mansfield," *New York Times*, October 29, 1931.

CHAPTER 5 : THE MURDER OF MAUDE MERRILL

Notes for the murder of Maude Merrill, her identity, her killer's identity, their backgrounds and relationship, the investigation of the case by Thomas Byrnes, the trial and outcome, and information regarding prostitution in New York City at the time.

Books:

Anbinder, Tyler. *Five Points: The 19th-Century New York City Neighborhood that Invented Tap Dance, Stole Elections, and Became the World's Most Notorious Slum*. New York: The Free Press, 2002.

Beckert, Sven. *The Monied Metropolis: New York City and the Consolidation of the American Bourgeoisie, 1850–1896*. Cambridge, U.K.: Cambridge University Press, 2003.

Dunlop, M. H. *Gilded City: Scandal and Sensation in Turn-of-the-Century New York*. New York: William Morrow, 2001.

Gilfoyle, Timothy J. *City of Eros: New York City, Prostitution, and the Commercialization of Sex, 1790–1920*. New York: W. W. Norton & Company, 1994.

Lening, Gustav. *The Dark Side of New York, and Its Criminal Classes from Fifth Avenue down to the Five Points. A Complete Narrative of the Mysteries of New York*. New York: Frederick Gerhard, 1873.

Long, Kat. *The Forbidden Apple: A Century of Sex & Sin in New York City*. New York: Ig Publishing, 2009.

Wood, Sharon. *The Freedom of the Streets: Work, Citizenship, and Sexuality in a Gilded Age City*. Chapel Hill: University of North Carolina Press, 2005.

Articles:

Robertson, Stephen. "Prostitutes, Runaway Wives, Working Women, Charity Girls, Courting Couples, Spitting Women, Boastful Husbands, Pimps, and Johns." *Journal of Women's History*, Vol. 20, No. 1, (Spring 2008), pp. 247–257.

Scobey, David. "Nymphs and Satyrs: Sex and the Bourgeois Public Sphere in Victorian New York." *Winterthur Portfolio*, Vol. 37, No. 1 (Spring 2002), pp. 43–66.

Wyman, Margaret. "The Rise of the Fallen Woman." *American Quarterly*, Vol. 3, No. 2 (Summer 1951), pp. 167–177.

Newspapers:

"Shocking Murder . . . A Fashionable Courtesan Killed by an Unknown Man," *New York Times*, December 11, 1872.

"No Clue to the Murderer," *New York Times*, December 11, 1872.

"The Latest Tragedy . . . Maude Merrill's Murderer in Custody of the Police," *New York Times*, December 12, 1872.

"A Sad Scene at Maude Merrill's Funeral," *New York Times*, December 13, 1872.

"The Record of Both Lives," *Brooklyn Daily Eagle*, December 13, 1872.

"Maude's Murder . . . Interesting and Important Developments Before the Coroner," *New York Times*, December 14, 1872.

"Maud Merrill . . . Conclusion of the Inquest," *Brooklyn Daily Eagle*, December 16, 1872.

"The Insanity Dodge . . . Bleakley, the Murderer, Makes a Sham Attempt at Suicide," *New York Times*, April 26, 1873.

"The Maud Merrill Murder," *Brooklyn Daily Eagle*, April 28, 1873.

"Maud Merrill's Murder," *Brooklyn Daily Eagle*, April 28, 1873.

"The Bleakley Murder Trial . . . Four Jurors Obtained Yesterday," *New York Times*, April 29, 1873.

"The Bleakley Trial," *Brooklyn Daily Eagle,* April 29, 1873.

"The Maude Merrill Murder . . . Trial of Bleakley for Shooting His Niece," *New York Times*, May 1, 1873.

"Murder of Maude Merrill . . . Alleged Blackmailing by Prisoner," *New York Times,* May 2, 1873.

"The Bleakley Trial . . . The Neilson-Place Murder Opening of the Case for the Defense," *New York Times*, May 3, 1873.

"Bleakley Feigns Suicide for the Second Time," *New York Times*, May 4, 1873.

"The Trial of Bleakley . . . Yesterday's Proceedings," *New York Times*, May 6, 1873.

"The Bleakley Trial . . . The Prisoner Testifies in His Own Defense," *New York Times*, May 8, 1873.

"Bleakley's Sentence," *Brooklyn Daily Eagle*, May 9, 1873.

"Sentenced for Life," *New York Times*, May 9, 1873.

CHAPTER 6: THE GREATEST BANK ROBBERY IN AMERICA

Notes for the Manhattan Savings Institution bank robbery, the investigation and capture of the thieves, the subsequent trials, and all other information related to the case.

Books:

Asbury, Herbert. *The Gangs of New York*. New York: A. A. Knopf, 1928.

Blake, E. Vale. *History of the Tammany Society*. New York: Souvenir Publishing Company, 1901.

Brace, Charles Loring. *The Dangerous Classes of New York and Twenty Years' Work Among Them*. New York: Wynkoop & Hallenbeck, 1872.

Burrows, G. Edwin, and Mike Wallace. *Gotham: A History of New York City to 1898*. New York: Oxford University Press, 2000.

Byrnes, Thomas. *Professional Criminals of America*. New York: Cassell & Company, 1886.

Clinton, H. L. *Celebrated Trials*. New York: Harper & Brothers Publishers, 1897.

Costello, Augustine E. *Our Police Protectors: History of the New York Police from the Earliest Period to the Present Time*. New York: C. F. Roper & Company, 1885.

Crapsey, Edward. *The Nether Side of New York or the Vice, Crime, and Poverty of the Great Metropolis*. New York: Sheldon & Company, 1872.

Howe, William F., and Abraham Hummel. *Danger: A True History of a Great City's Wiles and Temptations*. New York: Courier, 1886.

Klein, Marcus. *Easterns, Westerns, and Private Eyes: American Matters, 1870–1900*. Madison: The University of Wisconsin Press, 1994.

Newton, Michael. *The Encyclopedia of Robberies, Heists, and Capers*. New York: Facts on File, 2002.

O'Connor, Richard. *Hell's Kitchen*. New York: J. B. Lippincott Company, 1958.

Panek, LeRoy. *The Origins of the American Detective Story*. Jefferson, NC: McFarland & Company, 2006.

Sante, Luc. *Low Life: Lures and Snares of Old New York*. New York: Farrar, Straus and Giroux, 2003.

Swierczynski, Duane. *This Here's A Stick-Up: The Big Bad Book of American Bank Robbery*. Indianapolis, IN: Alpha Books, 2002.

Walling, George Washington. *Recollections of a New York Chief of Police*. New York: Caxton Book Concern, 1887.

Newspapers:
"The Great Bank Robbery . . . Manhattan Savings Institution Robbed," *New York Times*, October 28, 1878.

"The Responsibility for Yesterday's Bank Robbery," *Brooklyn Daily Eagle*, October 28, 1878.

"The Big Bank Burglary . . . Searching for a Clue to the Thieves," *New York Times,* October 29, 1878.

"The Vanished Millions of the Manhattan Savings Institution," *Brooklyn Daily Eagle,* October 29, 1878.

"No Trace Yet of Vanished Millions," *Brooklyn Daily Eagle,* October 30, 1878.

". . . The Police Say They Have a Clue," *New York Times,* October 30, 1878.

". . . The Police Entirely at Fault," *New York Times,* October 31, 1878.

"The Manhattan Securities . . . Rumored Negotiations for the Recovery of the Stolen Bonds," *New York Times,* November 10, 1878.

"Manhattan Bank Robbery," *Brooklyn Daily Eagle,* November 12, 1878.

". . . The Manhattan Bank Robbers . . . Attempted Negotiation," *New York Times,* November 14, 1878.

"Two Prisoners in Court . . . The Extraordinary Story Told by Capt. Byrnes," *New York Times,* November 19, 1878.

". . . The Manhattan Bank Burglars . . . The Prisoners Arrested on Friday," *New York Times,* December 15, 1878.

"Red Leary's Last Chance . . . An Attempted Rescue from the Officers," *New York Times,* December 17, 1878.

"Good News for Depositors . . . The Manhattan Savings Institution to Resume Payments," *New York Times,* December 17, 1878.

". . . Failure of the Negotiations with the Thieves," *New York Times,* December 27, 1878 (Special Dispatch to *New York Times*).

"The Manhattan Savings Bank . . . What a Trustee Says Regarding the Offers Made," *New York Times,* January 26, 1879.

". . . Police Captain Byrnes's Latest Prisoner," *New York Times,* February 10, 1879.

". . . Clearing Up the Manhattan Bank Mystery . . . One of the Burglars in Custody," *New York Times,* February 12, 1879.

"Geo L. Howard . . . How the Bank Burglar Is Said to Have Been Killed," *Brooklyn Daily Eagle,* March 10, 1879.

"A Bank Resumes Business," *New York Times,* March 12, 1879.

"Rushing for Their Money," *New York Times,* March 13, 1879.

"Tracing Some Stolen Bonds," *New York Times,* March 23, 1879.

"Johnny Dobbs in Custody . . . The Manhattan Burglary," *New York Times*, May 7, 1879.

"Johnny Dobbs in Custody," *New York Times*, May 7, 1879.

"A Night Watchman's Tale . . . How the Manhattan Bank Was Robbed," *New York Times*, June 2, 1879.

"The Manhattan Bank Burglars . . . Committed to the Tombs," *New York Times*, June 3, 1879.

"Shevlin and Kelley Examined and Committed to the Tombs," *New York Times*, June 6, 1879.

". . . Trial of John Hope for Robbery . . . How the Manhattan Savings Bank Was Robbed," *New York Times*, June 13, 1879.

". . . Patrolman John Nugent Arrested as One of Them . . . Implicated by Shevlin's Confession," *New York Times*, June 14, 1879.

". . . Patrolman John Nugent's Examination," *New York Times*, June 15, 1879.

". . . Watchman Shevlin Undergoes a Searching Cross-Examination," *New York Times*, June 18, 1879.

"John Hope's Trial . . . Witnesses Say He Was in Philadelphia When the Bank Was Robbed," *New York Times*, June 19, 1879.

". . . John Hope Sentenced to Twenty Years in State Prison," *New York Times*, July 19, 1879.

"Stolen Bonds Detected . . . Five of the Bonds Stolen from the Manhattan Bank Presented for Redemption," *New York Times*, July 31, 1879.

"The Manhattan's Stolen Bonds," *New York Times*, September 4, 1879.

"The Great Bank Robbery . . . Fortunes of the Men Who Took Part in the Crime," *New York Times*, October 6, 1879.

"Manhattan Bank Robbers . . . Patrolman John Nugent Arrested as One of Them," *New York Times*, October 6, 1879.

"The Manhattan Bank Burglary . . . Shevlin, the Watchman, Gives Account of the Conspiracy," *New York Times*, December 18, 1879.

"William Kelley's Trial," *New York Times*, December 19, 1879.

"The Manhattan Bank Burglars Two of the Three Still Remaining at Large Captured," *Brooklyn Daily Eagle*, April 30, 1880.

". . . Death of John D. Grady," *New York Times*, October 4, 1880.

"Old 'Mother' Mandelbaum Is Dead," *New York Times*, February 27, 1894.

"Jimmy Hope Dies," *New York Times*, June 3, 1905.

CHAPTER 7: BAG OF BONES

Notes on the theft of A. T. Stewart's body, the subsequent investigation by Thomas Byrnes, the apprehension of and hearings on Vreeland and Burke, and their involvement, and resolution of the case.

Books:

Asbury, Herbert. *The Gangs of New York*. New York: A. A. Knopf, 1928.

Browne, Junius Henri. *The Great Metropolis: A Mirror of New York. A Complete History of Metropolitan Life and Society, with Sketches of Prominent Places, Persons, and Things in the City as they Actually Exist*. Hartford: American Publishing Company, 1869.

Costello, Augustine E. *Our Police Protectors: History of the New York Police from the Earliest Period to the Present Time*. New York: C. F. Roper & Company, 1885.

Elias, Stephen N. *Alexander T. Stewart: The Forgotten Merchant Prince*. Westport, CT: Praeger Publishers, 1992.

Fanebust, Wayne. *The Missing Corpse: Grave Robbing a Gilded Age Tycoon*. Westport, CT: Praeger Publishers, 2005.

Lardner, James, and Thomas Reppetto. *NYPD: A City and Its Police*. New York: Henry Holt & Company, 2001.

Lening, Gustav. *The Dark Side of New York, and Its Criminal Classes from Fifth Avenue down to the Five Points. A Complete Narrative of the Mysteries of New York*. New York: Frederick Gerhard, 1873.

Riis, Jacob, *The Making of an American*. New York: Macmillan, 1901.

Tomkins, Calvin. *Merchants and Masterpieces*. New York: Dutton, 1973.

Walling, George Washington. *Recollections of a New York Chief of Police*. New York: Caxton Book Concern, 1887.

Articles:

Cantor, Jay E. "A Monument of Trade: A. T. Stewart and the Rise of the Millionaire's Mansion in New York." *Winterthur Portfolio*, Vol. 10, (1975), pp. 165–197.

Resseguie, Harry E. "Alexander Turney Stewart and the Development of the Department Store, 1823–1876." *The Business History Review*, Vol. 39, No. 3 (Autumn 1965), pp. 301–322.

Resseguie, Harry E. "The Decline and Fall of the Commercial Empire of A. T. Stewart." *The Business History Review*, Vol. 36, No. 3 (Autumn 1962), pp. 255–286.

Newspapers:

"Ghouls in New York City . . . A. T. Stewart's Body Stolen . . . Removed from the Family Vault," *New York Times*, November 8, 1878.

"Mr. Stewart's Body Not Found . . . Mrs. Stewart Offers a Reward of $25,000," *New York Times*, November 9, 1878.

"The Grave Desecrators . . . Tracing the Robbers of Mr. Stewart's Grave," *New York Times*, November 10, 1878.

"The Robbers of the Tomb . . . Judge Hilton Will Not Talk," *New York Times*, November 11, 1878.

"Seeking for the Ghouls . . . Mr. Stewart's Body," *New York Times*, November 12, 1878.

"Is Stewart's Body Found . . . Indications Pointing That Way," *New York Times*, November 13, 1878.

"Stewart's Stolen Body . . . The Prospect of Its Recovery," *New York Times*, November 14, 1878.

"A. T. Stewart's Body Found . . . The Guilty Persons All Known," *New York Times*, November 15, 1878.

"The Cemetery Robbery . . . Two of the Ghouls Arrested," *New York Times*, November 16, 1878.

"Closing on the Ghouls . . . Successful Efforts to Catch Them," *New York Times*, November 17, 1878.

"Light at Last . . . The Police Clearing Up the Stewart Mystery," *Brooklyn Daily Eagle*, November 18, 1878.

"The A. T. Stewart Outrage," *New York Times*, November 18, 1878.

"Working Up a Fine Clue . . . Reporters Following the Chief of Police in New Jersey," *New York Times*, November 18, 1878.

"Still in the Dark . . . A. T. Stewart's Body Not Found . . . Supposed Police Blundering in the Case," *Brooklyn Daily Eagle*, November 19, 1878.

"Stewart's Stolen Body . . . Capt. Byrnes Corroborates the *Times*'s Statement," *New York Times*, November 19, 1878.

"The Body of A. T. Stewart," *New York Times*, November 19, 1878.

"Stewart's Grave Robbers . . . Why Of Course We Have the Body," *New York Times*, November 20, 1878.

"Vreeland and Burke Committed . . . Captain Byrnes's Formal Complaint," *New York Times*, November 20, 1878.

"The Case of Vreeland and Burke," *New York Times,* November 21, 1878.

"Grave Robber Christian . . . He Turns Up in Stewart Case," *New York Times*, November 21, 1878.

"Search for the Robbers . . . Still No Arrests Made," *New York Times*, November 22, 1878.

"The Grave Robbers . . . Still Searching for the Thieves," *New York Times*, November 23, 1878.

"No Further Arrests Made," *New York Times*, November 24, 1878.

"The Stewart Mystery . . . Police Still Looking," *New York Times*, November 25, 1878.

". . . The Stewart Grave Robbery . . . A Number of Detectives Withdrawn From the Case," *New York Times*, November 26, 1878.

"Henry Vreeland Discharged," *New York Times*, December 4, 1878.

"Tracing a Dead Body . . . Is It a Relic of the Alexander Case," *New York Times*, December 13, 1878 (Special Dispatch to *New York Times*).

"Garden City's Cathedral," *New York Times*, April 10, 1885.

CHAPTER 8: CHIEF OF DETECTIVES

Notes on Thomas Byrnes's rise to the position of chief of detectives, his use of the third degree and its definition, his innovations to detective work including mug shots and criminal recordkeeping, and his earliest pioneering efforts in police forensics.

Books:

Asbury, Herbert. *The Gangs of New York.* New York: A. A. Knopf, 1928.

Bailey, William, ed. *The Encyclopedia of Police Science.* New York: Routledge, 1995.

Burrows, G. Edwin and Mike Wallace. *Gotham: A History of New York City to 1898.* New York: Oxford University Press, 2000.

Byrnes, Thomas. *Professional Criminals of America.* New York: Cassell & Company, 1886.

Campbell, Helen. *Darkness and Daylight: Lights and Shadows of New York Life.* Hartford: The Hartford Publishing Company, 1891.

Costello, Augustine E. *Our Police Protectors: History of the New York Police from the Earliest Period to the Present Time.* New York: C. F. Roper & Company, 1885.

Crapsey, Edward. *The Nether Side of New York or the Vice, Crime, and Poverty of the Great Metropolis.* New York: Sheldon & Company, 1872.

Green-Lewis, Jennifer. *Framing the Victorians: Photography and the Culture of Realism.* Ithaca, NY: Cornell University Press, 1996.

Howe, William F., and Abraham Hummel. *Danger: A True History of a Great City's Wiles and Temptations.* New York: Courier, 1886.

Johnson, Marilynn S. *Street Justice: A History of Police Violence in New York City.* Boston: Beacon Press, 2004.

Klein, Marcus. *Easterns, Westerns, and Private Eyes: American Matters, 1870–1900.* Madison: The University of Wisconsin Press, 1994.

Lening, Gustav. *The Dark Side of New York, and Its Criminal Classes from Fifth Avenue down to the Five Points. A Complete Narrative of the Mysteries of New York.* New York: Frederick Gerhard, 1873.

Morton, James. *Gangland: The Early Years.* New York: Time Warner Paperbacks, 2004.

Palmiotto, Michael. *Criminal Investigation.* Lanham, MD: University Press of America, 2004.

Panek, LeRoy. *The Origins of the American Detective Story.* Jefferson, NC: McFarland & Company, 2006.

Riis, Jacob. *The Making of an American.* New York: Macmillan, 1901.

Sante, Luc. *Low Life: Lures and Snares of Old New York.* New York: Farrar, Straus and Giroux, 2003.

Steffens, Lincoln. *Shame of the Cities.* New York: McClure, Phillips & Company, 1905.

Tagg, John. *The Disciplinary Frame: Photographic Truths and the Capture of Meaning.* Minneapolis: University of Minnesota Press, 2009.

Walling, George Washington. *Recollections of a New York Chief of Police.* New York: Caxton Book Concern, 1887.

Articles:

Bryk, William. "Thomas Byrnes, Inventor of the Third Degree." *City of Smoke: New York History, Commentary and Culture*, 2009.

Byrnes, Thomas. "How to Protect a City from Crime." *The North American Review*, Vol. 159, No. 452 (July 1894), pp. 100–107.

Fisher, Jim. "Eugène François Vidocq: The World's First Detective." *Forensic Science*, 2008.

Fox, Lorna Scott. "There Will Always Be Blood: True Crime Writing." *The Nation*, 2009.

Gunter, Whitney, and Christopher Hertig. "An Introduction to Theory, Practice, and Career Development for Public and Private Investigators." *International Foundation for Protection Officers*, 2005.

Newspapers:

"The Police View of Crime," *New York Times*, July 21, 1875.

"The Man Who Shot Drake," *New York Times*, June 21, 1884.

"Arrest of the Cleverest," *New York Times*, May 25, 1885.

"Gen. Shaler Arrested," *New York Times*, December 1, 1885.

"Inspector Byrnes to Be Honored," *New York Times*, February 3, 1886.

"All Men Detectives," *New York Times*, October 1, 1886.

"Inspector Byrnes Decorated," *New York Times*, February 26, 1891.

"He Wanted to Kill Gould," *New York Times*, May 7, 1891.

"Over Thirty Thousand Dollars of Stolen Money Gone," *New York Times*, March 9, 1892.

"He Rules Through Fear . . . The Life Work of Police Superintendent Byrnes," *New York Times*, December 10, 1893.

"The Third Degree—How It Was Worked on Suspects By Inspector Byrnes," *Lewiston Evening Journal*, January 1, 1894.

"Wall Street Guardians . . . The Most Dreaded District in America for Thieves," *New York Times*, May 31, 1895.

"A New Book About Criminals . . . Ex-Chief Byrnes Has Been at Work on One," *New York Times*, February 14, 1896.

"Third Degree in Police Parlance," *New York Times*, October 6, 1901.

"Supreme Court Denounces Third Degree," *New York Times*, July 20, 1902.

"The Passing of No. 300 Mulberry Street . . . Associations of Famous Criminals and Detectors of Crime," *New York Times*, September 21, 1902.

"Third Degree, a Myth," *New York Times*, August 7, 1907.

"Third Degree," *New York Times*, April 17, 1910 (Editorial).

"Ex-Chief Byrnes Dies of Cancer," *New York Times*, May 8, 1910.

"Inspector Byrnes," *New York Times*, May 9, 1910 (Editorial).

"New Police Methods Supersede the Old . . . The Work Inaugurated by the Late Inspector Thomas Byrnes," *New York Times*, May 15, 1910.

CHAPTER 9: THE CASE OF THE MURDERED WINE MERCHANT

Notes on the Louis Hanier murder case and the apprehension and conviction of Michael McGloin.

Books:

Burrows, G. Edwin and Mike Wallace. *Gotham: A History of New York City to 1898.* New York: Oxford University Press, 2000.

Byrnes, Thomas. *Professional Criminals of America.* New York: Cassell & Company, 1886.

Costello, Augustine E. *Our Police Protectors: History of the New York Police from the Earliest Period to the Present Time.* New York: C. F. Roper & Company, 1885.

Hawthorne, Julian. *A Tragic Mystery: From the Diary of Inspector Byrnes.* New York: Cassell, 1887.

Riis, Jacob. *The Making of an American.* New York: Macmillan, 1901.

Walling, George Washington. *Recollections of a New York Chief of Police.* New York: Caxton Book Concern, 1887.

Newspapers:

"Murdered by Burglars," *New York Times*, December 31, 1881.

"The Hanier Murder Case," *New York Times*, January 12, 1882.

"Hanier's Murderer Found . . . The Assassin and His Accomplices Run Down and Arrested," *New York Times*, February 2, 1882.

"The Hanier Murder Case," *New York Times*, February 3, 1882.

"Aid for Hanier's Family," *New York Times*, February 7, 1882.

"The Hanier Murder Case," *New York Times*, February 10, 1882.

"The Murder of Louis Hanier . . . Beginning the Trial of Michael M'Gloin," *New York Times*, March 2, 1882.

"M'Gloin Trial for the Murder of Louis Hanier," *New York Times*, March 3, 1882.

"M'Gloin Convicted . . . The Jury Quickly Find Him Guilty of Murder in the First Degree," *New York Times*, March 4, 1882.

"Young M'Gloin Sentenced to be Hanged," *New York Times*, March 7, 1882.

"The Last of the M'Gloin Gang," *New York Times*, June 19, 1882.

"The Murder of Louis Hanier," *New York Times*, October 28, 1882.

"Resentenced to Death," *New York Times*, November 11, 1882.

"Trying to Save M'Gloin," *New York Times*, December 10, 1882.

"M'Gloin Resentenced . . . to Be Hanged on March 9," *New York Times*, February 3, 1883.

"An Appeal for M'Gloin," *New York Times*, March 3, 1883.

"Two Murderers to Die . . . A Reprieve Refused by the Governor in M'Gloin's Case," *New York Times*, March 6, 1883.

"Their Last Night on Earth . . . M'Gloin and Majone Receive Their Friends in the Tombs," *New York Times*, March 9, 1883.

"A Hangman's Work Done . . . M'Gloin and Majone Suffer Death for Their Crimes," *New York Times*, March 10, 1883.

"M'Gloin Carried to His Grave," *New York Times*, March 12, 1883.

CHAPTER 10: AN UNSPEAKABLE ROTTENNESS

Notes on the Reverend Dr. Charles Parkhurst, his investigation into vice, the Lexow Committee and its investigation into New York City police corruption, the disputes between Parkhurst and Byrnes, and Byrnes's retirement and death.

Books:

Blake, E. Vale. *History of the Tammany Society*. New York: Souvenir Publishing Company, 1901.

Burrows, G. Edwin, and Mike Wallace. *Gotham: A History of New York City to 1898*. New York: Oxford University Press, 2000.

Dash, Mike. *Satan's Circus: Murder, Vice, Police Corruption, and New York's Trial of the Century*. New York: Three Rivers Press, 2007.

Franklin, Allan, and Thomas Nast (illustrator). *The Trail of the Tiger, Being an Account of Tammany from 1789; The Organization and Sway of the Bosses*. New York: Allan Franklin, 1928.

Howe, William F., and Abraham Hummel. *Danger: A True History of a Great City's Wiles and Temptations*. New York: Courier, 1886.

Lynch, Denis Tilden. *Boss Tweed: The Story of a Grim Generation*. New York: Transaction Publishers, 2002.

Mandelbaum, Seymour. *Boss Tweed's New York*. New York: Wiley, 1965.

Maurice, Arthur B. *Fifth Avenue*. New York: Dodd, Mead & Company, 1918.

Mayer, Grace M. *Once Upon a City*. New York: Macmillan, 1958.

Mohl, Raymond A. *The Making of Urban America*. Lanham, MD: SR Books, 1997.

Morton, James. *Gangland: The Early Years*. New York: Time Warner Paperbacks, 2004.

Nevins, Allan, and Thomas Milton Halsey. *The Diary of George Templeton Strong* (4 vols.). New York: Macmillan, 1952.

Newton, Michael. *The Encyclopedia of Robberies, Heists, and Capers*. New York: Facts on File, 2002.

O'Connor, Richard. *Hell's Kitchen*. New York: J.B. Lippincott Company, 1958.

Palmiotto, Michael. *Criminal Investigation*. Lanham, MD. University Press of America, 2004.

Panek, LeRoy. *The Origins of the American Detective Story*. Jefferson, NC: McFarland & Company, 2006.

Parkhurst, Charles. *My Forty Years in New York*. New York: Macmillan, 1923.

Parkhurst, Charles. *Our Fight with Tammany*. New York: Charles Scribner's Sons, 1895.

Patton, Clifford W. *The Battle for Municipal Reform: Mobilization and Attack, 1875–1900*. New York: American Council on Public Affairs, 1940.

Richmond, Rev. J. F. *New York and Its Institutions, 1609–1873*. New York: E. B. Treat, 1873.

Riis, Jacob. *The Making of an American*. New York: Macmillan, 1901.

Rovere, Richard. *Howe and Hummel*. New York: Michael Joseph, 1947.

Sloat, Warren. *Battle for the Soul of New York: Tammany Hall, Police Corruption, Vice, and Reverend Charles Parkhurst's Crusade against Them, 1892–1895*. New York: Cooper Square Press, 2002.

Steffens, Lincoln. *Shame of the Cities*. New York: McClure, Phillips & Company, 1905.

Newspapers:

"Dr. Parkhurst and the Grand Jury," *New York Times*, March 2, 1892 (Editorial).

"Dr. Parkhurst Is Rebuked," *New York Times*, March 2, 1892.

"Dr. Parkhurst Speaks Out," *New York Times*, March 14, 1892.

"Police Captains Testify," *New York Times*, March 26, 1892.

"Dr. Parkhurst Pleased," *New York Times*, April 2, 1892.

"Angry at the Jury . . . Police Authorities Do Not Like Its Presentments," *New York Times*, April 3, 1892.

"Dr. Parkhurst a Witness," *New York Times*, April 7, 1892.

"Dr. Parkhurst's Testimony," *New York Times*, April 9, 1892 (Letter).

"A Short Lived Rumor . . . Unfounded Statement Concerning Dr. Parkhurst," *New York Times*, April 11, 1892.

"Dr. Rylance's Advice to Social Reformers," *New York Times*, April 11, 1892.

"Supt. Murray Drops Out," *New York Times*, April 13, 1892.

"Dr. Parkhurst . . . An Explanation to Citizens," *New York Times*, April 14, 1892.

". . . Dr. Parkhurst Denounces the Police of New York," *New York Times*, May 13, 1892.

"Dr. Parkhurst's Plans," *New York Times*, May 16, 1892.

"Dr. Parkhurst Praised . . . His Work Endorsed by Several Prominent Clergymen," *New York Times*, May 18, 1892.

". . . Dr. Parkhurst's Society Believes He Should Be Removed," *New York Times*, May 23, 1892.

"Dr. Parkhurst's Methods," *New York Times*, May 23, 1892 (Editorial).

"Praise for Dr. Parkhurst," *New York Times*, May 27, 1892.

"Dr. Parkhurst Rubs It In," *New York Times*, May 29, 1892.

"They Are Stirred Up . . . Some Questions for Mr. Byrnes," *New York Times*, June 9, 1892 (Letter).

"Dr. Parkhurst and the Police . . . He Thinks Supt. Byrnes Is Determined to Antagonize Him," *New York Times*, December 2, 1892.

". . . Dr. Parkhurst's Detective, Gardner, Under Arrest," *New York Times*, December 6, 1892.

"Dr. Parkhurst Hits Back . . . His Prompt Rejoinder to the Police Superintendent Mr. Byrnes," *New York Times*, December 8, 1892.

". . . Mr. Byrnes Replies to Dr. Parkhurst," *New York Times*, December 9, 1892.

"What Byrnes Doesn't Do," *New York Times*, December 10, 1892.

"Dr. Parkhurst and the Police," *New York Times*, December 10, 1892 (Editorial).

". . . Two Sermons About Dr. Parkhurst and Inspector Byrnes," *New York Times*, December 12, 1892.

"To Investigate the Police . . . A Triumph for Dr. Parkhurst in the State Senate," *New York Times*, January 1, 1894 (Editorial).

"Dr. Parkhurst's Side of It," *New York Times*, January 5, 1894.

"Nicoll Answers Parkhurst . . . Denies Having Influenced the Special Grand Jury," *New York Times*, January 6, 1894.

"Capt. Slevin Exonerated . . . Charges of Dr. Parkhurst Are Not Sustained," *New York Times*, January 6, 1894.

"Dr. Parkhurst's Sarcasm," *New York Times*, January 18, 1894.

"Said He Was Parkhurst Agent . . . Arrested on Charges of Blackmail," *New York Times*, January 20, 1894.

". . . Hard to Find a Suitable Lawyer to Serve . . . Dr. Parkhurst's Views," *New York Times*, January 24, 1894.

"Supt. Byrnes Wins His Point," *New York Times*, February 3, 1894.

"Parkhurst to the Senators . . . Police Investigation, He Says, Should Be Secret," *New York Times,* February 3, 1894.

"Parkhurst Agents Cause Four Arrests in Accused Captain's Precinct," *New York Times*, February 10, 1894.

"More Evidence for the Grand Jury," *New York Times*, February 14, 1894.

"Ex-Parkhurst Agent Disappeared," *New York Times*, February 17, 1894.

"Political Influence at Work," *New York Times*, February 21, 1894.

"Results of Dr. Parkhurst's Activity," *New York Times*, March 16, 1894.

"Supt. Byrnes's Testimony," *New York Times*, April 7, 1894.

"Protectors of Criminals . . . Dr. Parkhurst's Opinion of the Police of the City," *New York Times*, April 11, 1894.

"Money for Police Captains," *New York Times*, June 2, 1894.

"Appeal to the Patrolmen . . . Dr. Parkhurst Asks Them to Come Forward and Give Testimony," *New York Times*, June 5, 1894.

"Money for a Commissioner . . . Miller Tells the Lexow Committee How He Deposited $350," *New York Times*, June 29, 1894.

"Four Sergeants Dismissed . . . Police Board Found Them Guilty of Bribe Taking," *New York Times*, August 16, 1894.

"More Trouble for Police . . . Lexow Committee to Resume Investigation," *New York Times*, September 10, 1894.

"Byrnes's Men Not Afraid," *New York Times*, September 24, 1894.

"Mr. Byrnes and the Police," *New York Times*, September 26, 1894 (Editorial).

"Mr. Byrnes's Defiance," *New York Times*, September 27, 1894 (Editorial).

"Dr. Parkhurst Honored," *New York Times*, November 28, 1894.

"Praised in His Own Pulpit . . . Tribute to Dr. Parkhurst in Madison Square Church," *New York Times*, November 30, 1894.

"Creeden's Captaincy Cost Him $15,000," *New York Times*, December 15, 1894.

"Dr. Parkhurst Suggests a Deal . . . Mr. Byrnes Says He Is Not Answering Insinuations," *New York Times*, December 26, 1894.

"Byrnes and His Money," *New York Times*, December 30, 1894.

"Parkhurst Finds Fault . . . He Says the Lexow Committee Flinched at the Crisis," *New York Times*, January 1, 1895.

"Mr. Byrnes's Ability," *New York Tribune*, January 1, 1895.

"Byrnes and Parkhurst," *New York Times*, January 1, 1895 (Editorial).

"Lexow's Tribute to Byrnes," *New York Times*, January 2, 1895.

"Failed to Face Byrnes . . . Dr. Parkhurst Had Been Subpoenaed as a Lexow Witness," *New York Times*, January 5, 1895.

"Superintendent Byrnes Will Reorganize the Force," *New York Times*, January 9, 1895.

"A Chance for Mr. Byrnes," *New York Times*, January 10, 1895.

"Byrnes Asked to Remain . . . Police Superintendent's Request for Retirement Returned by Mayor," *New York Times*, January 16, 1895.

"The Lexow Report Ready," *New York Times*, January 17, 1895.

"Does Not Suit Dr. Parkhurst," *New York Times*, January 19, 1895.

"Farewell to Williams . . . Retired from the Police Force at His Own Request," *New York Times*, May 25, 1895.

"Byrnes May Soon Retire," *New York Times*, May 26, 1895.

"Chief Byrnes Retired . . . Had Served 32 Years on the New York Police Force," *New York Times*, May 28, 1895.

"The Retirement of Chief Byrnes," *New York Times*, May 28, 1895 (Editorial).

"Mr. Roosevelt's Threat . . . They Depend on What Mr. Byrnes Is Reported to Have Said," *New York Times*, January 10, 1896.

"Ex-Chief Byrnes Dies of Cancer," *New York Times*, May 8, 1910.

"Inspector Byrnes," *New York Times*, May 9, 1910 (Editorial).

"Notables at Byrnes's Funeral," *New York Times*, May 11, 1910.

"New Police Methods Supersede the Old . . . The Work Inaugurated by the Late Inspector Thomas Byrnes," *New York Times*, May 15, 1910.

INDEX

ABOUT THE AUTHOR

J. North Conway is the author of a dozen books, including *King of Heists, The Cape Cod Canal: Breaking Through the Bared and Bended Arm, American Literacy,* and the novels *The Road to Ruin* and *Zig Zag Man.* He is an accomplished poet with poems appearing in *Poetry, The Antioch Review, The Columbia Review,* and the *Norton Book of Light Verse,* among many others. He teaches English at Bristol Community College in Fall River where he oversees the Writing Center, the college newspaper, and the literary magazine. He also teaches writing at the University of Massachusetts in Dartmouth.